1000
BIRDS

1000
BIRDS

A unique collection of 1000 species in exquisitely detailed paintings

Edited by Sarah Hoggett

CHARTWELL
BOOKS

Contents

FLIGHTLESS BIRDS   12

(ORDERS: Struthioniformes, Rheiformes, Casuariiformes, Apterygiformes, and Tinamiformes)

The first four orders listed here are often collectively referred to as the Ratites (from the Latin rata, a raft), a reference to their large, flat sternum, which lacks a keel, an important area of attachment for the major flight muscles. Since, in flightless birds, the flight muscles are not needed, so too the keel has disappeared. The remaining order in this grouping, Tinamiformes, can fly clumsily for short distances.

PENGUINS   15

(ORDER: Sphenisciformes)

All 18 species of southern-hemisphere Penguins are classified in a single order: Sphenisciformes. Medium-to-large flightless marine birds, penguins' wings are modified into powerful flippers, which help to propel them through water.

DIVERS AND GREBES   19

(ORDERS: Gaviiformes and Podicipediformes)

Both Gaviiformes (divers) and Podicipediformes (grebes) have distinctive breeding plumages. Divers occur at high latitudes in the northern hemisphere; their breeding plumage is white below, with a variable top color that always has vertical white stripes on the neck, making the birds easily identifiable. Similarly, the grebe's head, throat, and neck are often brightly colored in the breeding season.

OPEN OCEAN   21

(ORDER: Procellariiformes)

This large group of seabirds includes albatrosses; fulmars, shearwaters, and petrels; storm-petrels; and diving petrels. They have a very long upper arm (humerus); the resulting long wings give the albatrosses and shearwaters their characteristic gliding ability.

SEABIRDS AND FRESHWATER FISH EATERS   25

(ORDER: Pelecaniformes)

Probably the most popularly known of these species are the pelicans, with their long, straight bills and extensible throat pouches. Other families within the order include tropicbirds, gannets and boobies, cormorants and shags, darters, and frigatebirds. All are fish-eating birds, mostly marine. A distinguishing feature is that all species in this order are totipalmate—they have three webs linking the four toes.

WADING BIRDS   33

(ORDER: Ciconiiformes)

A big order of large, long-legged wading birds that prey mainly on fish and amphibians, but also on large insects such as locusts. This order includes three major families: herons and bitterns; storks; and ibises and spoonbills. It also includes two single-species families (the Hammerkop and Whale-headed Stork) and the small family of flamingoes.

WATER BIRDS   39

(ORDER: Anseriformes)

This large group include the swans, geese, and ducks of the Anatidae family, and the screamers of the Anhimidae family.

BIRDS OF PREY   49

(ORDER: Falconiformes)

The Falconiformes order is a large group of five families containing all the familiar birds of prey that hunt by day, including falcons, hawks, eagles, and vultures. It also contains the few species of caracara, which, unusually for birds of prey, eat some fruit seeds or other plant material. Two unusual families contain only one species each: the Osprey and the Secretary Bird.

A MARSHALL EDITIONS BOOK

This edition published in 2015 by
CHARTWELL BOOKS
an imprint of Book Sales
a division of Quarto Publishing Group USA Inc.
142 West 36th Street, 4th Floor
New York, New York 10018
USA

Copyright © 2015 Marshall Editions Plc.

ISBN: 978-0-7858-3274-4
QUAR.MTBRD

Conceived, designed,
and produced by
Marshall Editions
Part of the Quarto Group
The Old Brewery
6 Blundell Street
London N7 9BH

Printed in China by
Shanghai Offset Printing
Products Ltd.

10 9 8 7 6 5 4 3 2 1

The material in this book was
originally published in
The Illustrated Encyclopedia of Birds

Introduction

The world is inhabited by nearly 10,000 species of bird, and no group of animals—even the mammals such as ourselves—arouses our interest so much. Their colors, songs, and conspicuousness combine to make birds the ideal objects for study and aesthetic appreciation, and the way in which many of them come to feeding tables put out for them in winter makes it easy for us to observe their antics. But their attractive nature does not merely make them fun to watch: professional zoologists have also turned to them for study, and this study has, in turn, led the way to our understanding of many aspects of the natural world, including taxonomy, behavior, and ecology.

Sadly, with the increasing changes that humans are bringing to our environment, some of these studies have taken on a new urgency. Pollution, the introduction of pests, overhunting and, above all, habitat destruction, have had a serious effect on the populations of many bird species. Currently, worldwide almost 1,400— roughly one in eight of the world's bird species—are considered by the International Union for Conservation of Nature (IUCN) to be threatened, with almost 200 more being classed as critically endangered; some of these species have not been sighted for many years and may already have succumbed. The IUCN "Red List" sets out the current status of the world's birds.

It is probably that more than 150 bird species have been exterminated since the year 1500. And there is growing evidence

to suggest that the spread of peoples around the world even earlier than this, especially the spread through the Pacific islands, may have wiped out many more before written records were kept. The ancestors of the Maoris, for example, exterminated all the moas in New Zealand—at least 12 species.

We urgently need to know more about birds and their habitat requirements in order to be able to afford them the protection they need. Habitat protection is particularly imperative, because many species have very special requirements as far as their living conditions are concerned. If we can protect the habitats essential to the survival of these birds, not only may we save for future generations many of the currently threatened species, but we will also save countless thousands of other animals and plants that live in and comprise these same habitats.

We hope that this book will increase our understanding of this irreplaceable part of our natural heritage. It is not possible, of course, to describe and illustrate every one of the 9,300 species, but over 170 families of living birds are represented and we have endeavored to describe a variety of species from each. Birds have been selected to provide typical examples from throughout each family's range and to cover some of the more unusual or endangered species. If this book's publication contributes in any way to the growing awareness of the need for greater environmental responsibility on the part of humans, then all concerned will feel that their efforts have been worthwhile.

About This Book

More than 40 experts and 15 artists contributed to this book, which, through the excellence of its illustrations and text, reveals the rich and beautiful diversity of the world's bird kingdom.

Classification

Currently, the classification of birds is in a state of flux: new scientific techniques, especially those examining the similarity of the DNA between different families and even species of birds, are indicating that important changes to the traditional classification may be necessary. As yet, many of these exciting issues are not fully resolved, so in this book we have erred on the side of tradition and caution.

It is not always possible to be certain whether two groups of birds—for example, ones living on different islands—belong to the same species or to two different ones. In the same way, there is no final, objective measure of whether certain groups of species should all belong to one family or order or be divided into two. One can aim for consistency, but in the end it is a matter of opinion. As a result, no two books on the subject of birds of the world will necessarily contain the same number of species or families or even orders.

Birds form the Class Aves of the Phylum Chordata (animals with a spinal cord). Within this class, birds have been divided into two subclasses—the Archaeomithes, containing only *Archaeopteryx* and the fossil toothed birds such as *Hesperomis*, and the Neomithes, containing all other birds. The latter group has been subdivided into two superorders, the Palaeognathae and the Neognathae. The former contains the large flightless birds such as the Ostrich and Emu and some primitive flying birds, while the latter contains all the other birds that are alive today. This main subdivision of the birds is made primarily on the basis of their palate structure.

There are nearly 10,000 species of birds alive in the world today. These are organized into 28–30 orders of birds, most of which are represented in this book. Within the superorder Neognathae, there is a major division. A single order, the Passeriformes, contains well over half of all the species of living birds. This order contains many of the common small birds such as thrushes and tits. In this book, this great group of birds is referred to as the perching birds.

The pages that follow contain full-color illustrations of 1,000 species of bird. Selected species are arranged with descriptions on every page.

To give an idea of the variation that can exist between birds of the same species, illustrations may show significant differences between male ♂ and female ♀, juvenile (juv), and immature (imm) birds, and between breeding and non-breeding plumage. Except where otherwise indicated, adult breeding plumage is assumed. A selection of distinctive races (subspecies) has also been illustrated.

Except in a few cases where the arrangement of birds necessitated a departure from this sequence, the birds are arranged taxonomically by order and family.

Group heading

Heading identifies where a new group of birds that share certain characteristics begins.

Map

Occasionally, maps show the bird's range.

Male/female subjects

Illustrations often include a male and female subject for purposes of comparison.

Description

Description accompanies each bird and paints a portrait of its characteristic behavior.

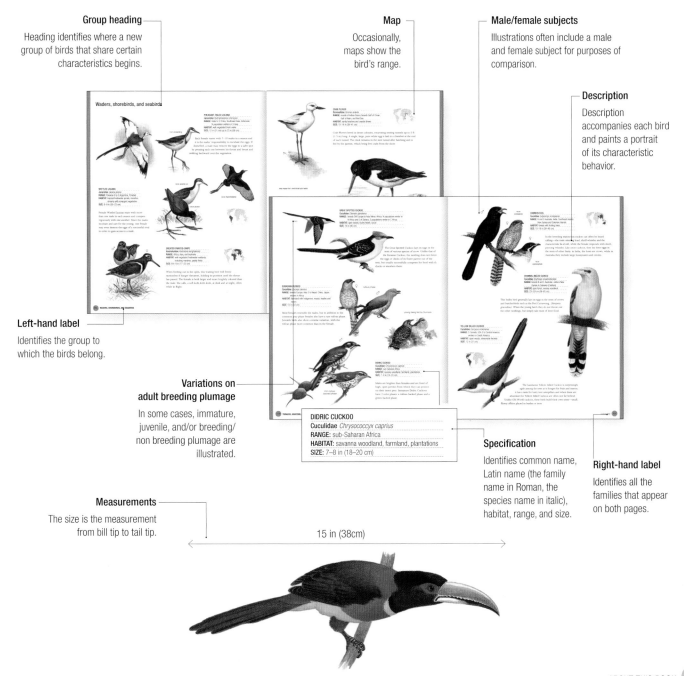

Left-hand label

Identifies the group to which the birds belong.

Variations on adult breeding plumage

In some cases, immature, juvenile, and/or breeding/non breeding plumage are illustrated.

DIDRIC CUCKOO
Cuculidae *Chrysococcyx caprius*
RANGE: sub-Saharan Africa
HABITAT: savanna woodland, farmland, plantations
SIZE: 7–8 in (18–20 cm)

Specification

Identifies common name, Latin name (the family name in Roman, the species name in italic), habitat, range, and size.

Right-hand label

Identifies all the families that appear on both pages.

Measurements

The size is the measurement from bill tip to tail tip.

15 in (38cm)

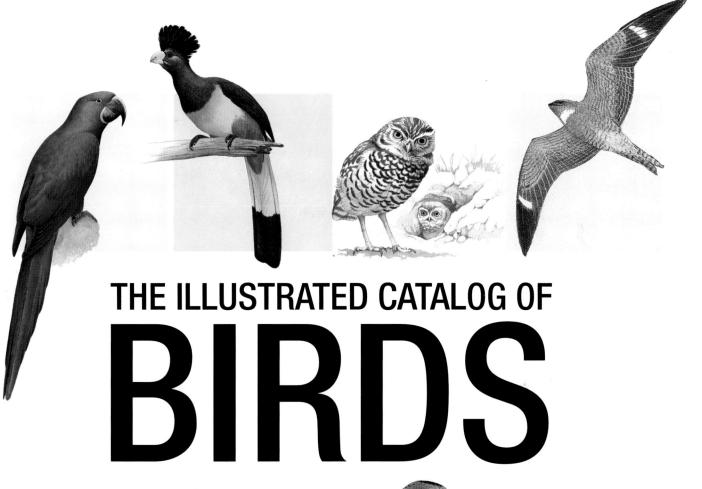

THE ILLUSTRATED CATALOG OF
BIRDS

Flightless birds

OSTRICH
Struthionidae *Struthio camelus*
RANGE: Africa: formerly widespread throughout and into Middle East; now fragmented, with main populations in W and E Africa and South Africa
HABITAT: dry savanna
SIZE: 79–98½ in (200–250 cm) high to top of head

Adapted to survive in dry conditions, the Ostrich can run swiftly over open terrain, compensating for its inability to fly. The male chooses a breeding site and 3 or more females may mate with him, each laying a clutch of 2−11 creamy white eggs.

race *massaicus* "Masai Ostrich"

race *molybdophanes* "Somali Ostrich"

juv

race *massaicus* with eggs and chick

GREATER RHEA
Rheidae *Rhea americana*
RANGE: S Brazil to Patagonia
HABITAT: grassland
SIZE: 51 in (130 cm) high to top of head

In spring, the males become solitary and aggressive, fighting to win harems of 2−15 females. Each successful male constructs a nest scrape about 3 ft (1 m) in diameter, in which the females lay their eggs. The male assumes responsibility for incubation.

EMU
Dromaiidae *Dromaius novaehollandiae*
RANGE: Australia
HABITAT: open and semi-arid bush
SIZE: 71 in (180 cm) high to top of head

The Emu is a nomadic species, some individuals ranging as far as 620 miles (1,000 km) in a single year as they follow the pattern of rainfall. Each male mates with 1−3 females, and a total of 8−20 blue-green eggs are laid in the nest depression.

turning eggs

DOUBLE-WATTLED CASSOWARY
Casuariidae *Casuarius casuarius*
RANGE: New Guinea, N Australia
HABITAT: moist forest
SIZE: 63 in (160 cm) high to top of head

DWARF CASSOWARY
Casuariidae *Casuarius bennetti*
RANGE: New Guinea, New Britain
HABITAT: forest up to 10,000 ft (3,000 m)
SIZE: 43 in (110 cm) high to top of head

Solitary for much of the year, apart from the breeding season. Courtship is initiated by the male; after laying her eggs, the female will wander through the territories of several males, mating with each one and laying eggs in each of their nests. The males incubate the eggs and care for the young.

The Dwarf Cassowary, or Moruk, is widely regarded as the world's most dangerous bird; prior to nesting, the females may become exceedingly aggressive. This species ranges higher than the other cassowaries. The horny head casque may be used to turn over leaf litter for food.

BROWN KIWI
Apterygidae *Apteryx australis*
RANGE: New Zealand
HABITAT: native forest, pine plantations
SIZE: 27½ in (70 cm)

Flightless and nocturnal, the Brown Kiwi's coarse body feathers protect it when moving through dense thickets. Its diet includes beetles, grubs, pond-life, and fallen berries. It can detect items of food under the soil, using the nostrils at the tip of the long bill.

LITTLE SPOTTED KIWI
Apterygidae *Apteryx owenii*
RANGE: South Island of New Zealand
HABITAT: dry, open forest, woodland, meadows
SIZE: 19½ in (50 cm)

Relative to its body size, the Little Spotted Kiwi lays the largest egg of any bird. The egg is 4–5 times heavier than those of similar-sized birds.

GREAT TINAMOU
Tinamidae *Tinamus major*
RANGE: SE Mexico to E Bolivia and Brazil
HABITAT: tropical and subtropical rain forest
SIZE: 18 in (45 cm)

Heard more often than it is seen, like all tinamous the Great Tinamou spends most of its time on the ground.

LITTLE TINAMOU
Tinamidae *Crypturellus soui*
RANGE: S Mexico to E Bolivia and SC Brazil
HABITAT: scrubby forest edge, secondary forest, overgrown clearings
SIZE: 9½ in (24 cm)

The Little Tinamou lays 2 eggs the color of terracotta clay, which are incubated by the male alone. Outside the breeding season, the birds often gather in foraging parties.

ANDEAN TINAMOU
Tinamidae *Nothoprocta pentlandii*
RANGE: Andes from S Ecuador to N Chile and N Argentina
HABITAT: puna meadows above 10,000 ft (3,000 m)
SIZE: 11 in (28 cm)

With its cryptic coloration, the Andean Tinamou is extremely difficult to spot. When disturbed, it will fly off strongly with intermittent wing beats, rather like a partridge.

THICKET TINAMOU
Tinamidae *Crypturellus cinamomeus*
RANGE: Mexico, Costa Rica, Colombia, Venezuela
HABITAT: semi-arid regions in scrubby woodland and forest edge
SIZE: 12 in (30 cm)

The Thicket Tinamou feeds on insects, berries, and other vegetation that it finds on the ground. The song consists of a mournful trio of fluty whistles.

ELEGANT CRESTED TINAMOU
Tinamidae *Eudromia elegans*
RANGE: Argentina, Paraguay, Bolivia, N Chile
HABITAT: arid and semi-arid steppe, scrub and woodland
SIZE: 16 in (40 cm)

The Elegant Crested Tinamou has only 3 toes on each foot, lacking the backward-pointing fourth toe, which may allow it to run more efficiently.

Penguins

KING PENGUIN
Spheniscidae *Aptenodytes patagonicus*
RANGE: subantarctic, Falkland Islands
HABITAT: oceanic; breeds on coasts
SIZE: 37½ in (95 cm)

Each pair raises only 2 chicks every 3 years. A single egg is laid in November (early summer). The parents virtually stop feeding the chick in winter. Regular feeding starts again in September and the chick fledges 2–3 months later. The parents cannot lay again until February (late summer). By winter the chicks are still very small and many die during the next few months.

fully grown chick

GENTOO PENGUIN
Spheniscidae *Pygoscelis papua*
RANGE: Antarctic, subantarctic, S South America
HABITAT: oceanic; breeds on coasts
SIZE: 32 in (81 cm)

Breeding starts as the snow clears in spring: the 2 eggs are laid in a saucer of vegetation and pebbles and incubated by both parents. About a month after hatching, the chicks gather into creches, while the parents make short daily trips to gather food.

EMPEROR PENGUIN
Spheniscidae *Aptenodytes forsteri*
RANGE: Antarctic
HABITAT: oceanic; breeds on pack ice
SIZE: 45 in (115 cm)

The largest of the penguins, each pair produces an egg in May/June (early winter). While the female goes to sea to feed, the male incubates the egg for 60 days, losing 45 percent of his body weight. The female returns around the time of hatching and feeds the chick, freeing the male to feed in open water.

well-grown chick

ADÉLIE PENGUIN
Spheniscidae *Pygoscelis adeliae*
RANGE: Antarctic
HABITAT: oceanic; breeds on rocky coasts
SIZE: 28 in (71 cm)

Suitable breeding sites are limited: the adults must have access to ice-free open water to provide food for their chicks. Laid in late November, the eggs are incubated first by the male and then by the female. After 3–4 weeks in the nest, the chicks band together in creches while the adults gather food.

ROCKHOPPER PENGUIN

Spheniscidae *Eudyptes chrysocome*
RANGE: subantarctic islands, S South America
HABITAT: oceanic; breeds on island cliffs
SIZE: 21½ in (55 cm)

Instead of waddling along like most penguins, the Rockhopper hops from boulder to boulder with its feet together, head thrust forward and flippers held back—hence the name. The birds generally come ashore at a particular landing place, then ascend to the colony along customary, well-worn paths.

CHINSTRAP PENGUIN

Spheniscidae *Pygoscelis antarctica*
RANGE: Antarctic
HABITAT: oceanic; breeds on rocky coasts
SIZE: 27 in (68 cm)

Where Chinstraps breed alongside Gentoos or Adelies, the males may attack their larger neighbors and oust them from their nests. Generally, though, they prefer better-drained sites, nesting on sloping, rocky ground that the other 2 species avoid. They lay later than the others and the female takes the first shift of incubation.

FJORDLAND CRESTED PENGUIN

Spheniscidae *Eudyptes pachyrhynchus*
RANGE: New Zealand, on SW of South Island (Fjordland), and Stewart Island
HABITAT: rocky shores; breeds in coastal forest or small caves
SIZE: 28 in (71 cm)

Also known as the Victoria Penguin, the Fjordland Crested Penguin nests in small groups. The female lays 2 eggs, the second considerably larger than the first. Both eggs hatch, but only one chick is reared—usually from the second egg.

ROYAL PENGUIN

Spheniscidae *Eudyptes schlegeli*
RANGE: Macquarie Island, S of New Zealand
HABITAT: oceanic; breeds on coasts
SIZE: 30 in (76 cm)

The Royal Penguin may be only a race or color phase of the Macaroni Penguin, but it differs from the latter in its larger size, stouter bill, and the gray and white sides to its face, chin, and throat.

MACARONI PENGUIN

Spheniscidae *Eudyptes chrysolophus*
RANGE: subantarctic, South America
HABITAT: oceanic; breeds on coasts
SIZE: 27½ in (70 cm)

Like the Rockhopper, the Macaroni Penguin lays 2 eggs, the first much smaller than the second and either failing to hatch or producing a weak chick that soon dies. Incubation is carried out in 2 long shifts, 1 by each parent, during which each loses up to 30 percent of its body weight.

YELLOW-EYED PENGUIN

Spheniscidae *Megadyptes antipodes*
RANGE: New Zealand, on SE South Island, Stewart, Auckland, and Campbell islands
HABITAT: inshore waters; breeds in scrub or low forest
SIZE: 30 in (76 cm)

One of the rarest of all penguins, Yellow-eyed Penguins feed mainly on fish and squid, coming ashore every night to roost on sandy beaches. Each bird is a resident of a particular area and they form strong, long-lasting pair-bonds.

LITTLE PENGUIN

Spheniscidae *Eudyptula minor*
RANGE: New Zealand, Chatham Island, S Australia, Tasmania
HABITAT: inshore; roosts and breeds on coast
SIZE: 16 in (40 cm)

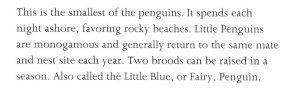

This is the smallest of the penguins. It spends each night ashore, favoring rocky beaches. Little Penguins are monogamous and generally return to the same mate and nest site each year. Two broods can be raised in a season. Also called the Little Blue, or Fairy, Penguin.

JACKASS PENGUIN
Spheniscidae *Spheniscus demersus*
RANGE: coasts of S Africa
HABITAT: cool coastal seas; breeds on coast
SIZE: 27½ in (70 cm)

Although it feeds in the cool Benguela Current, the Jackass Penguin breeds on dry land under the hot African sun. It avoids overheating by nesting in burrows or under rocks, and by being active on land only at night.

HUMBOLDT PENGUIN
Spheniscidae *Spheniscus humboldti*
RANGE: coastal Peru and Chile to 40° S
HABITAT: shores, offshore islands and offshore waters
SIZE: 27 in (68 cm)

The Humboldt, or Peruvian, Penguin feeds largely on fish such as anchovies, co-operating to herd them into compact shoals that can be preyed on at will. They nest at any time of year and new eggs, hatchlings, and large chicks may appear side by side.

juv

juv

GALAPAGOS PENGUIN
Spheniscidae *Spheniscus mendiclus*
RANGE: Galapagos Islands
HABITAT: coasts and offshore waters
SIZE: 19½ in (50 cm)

Galapagos Penguins generally nest in small groups on sheltered coasts and, since soft soil for burrowing is rare on the Galapagos Islands, the 2 eggs are generally laid in caves or holes in the volcanic rock.

MAGELLANIC PENGUIN
Spheniscidae *Spheniscus magellanicus*
RANGE: S coast of South America from Chile to Brazil
HABITAT: coasts and offshore islands
SIZE: 27½ in (70 cm)

Magellanic Penguins use their feet to dig holes big enough to accommodate both adults in grassy slopes or beneath forest trees, often high above the water. The adults prey mainly on fish and cuttlefish, returning to their burrows and feeding their brood by regurgitation.

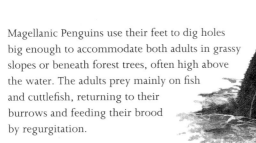

chick in nesting burrow

Divers and Grebes

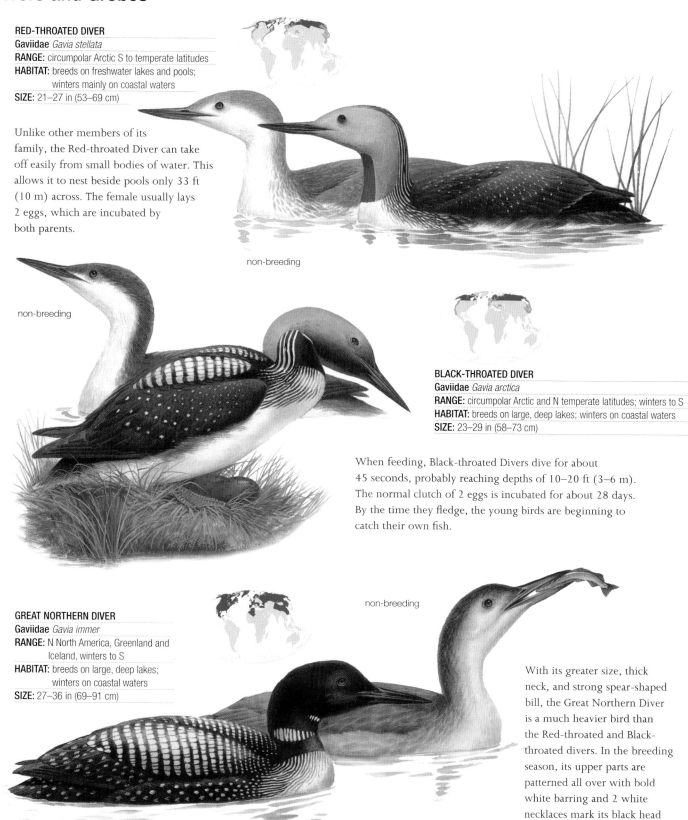

RED-THROATED DIVER
Gaviidae *Gavia stellata*
RANGE: circumpolar Arctic S to temperate latitudes
HABITAT: breeds on freshwater lakes and pools;
winters mainly on coastal waters
SIZE: 21–27 in (53–69 cm)

Unlike other members of its
family, the Red-throated Diver can take
off easily from small bodies of water. This
allows it to nest beside pools only 33 ft
(10 m) across. The female usually lays
2 eggs, which are incubated by
both parents.

non-breeding

non-breeding

BLACK-THROATED DIVER
Gaviidae *Gavia arctica*
RANGE: circumpolar Arctic and N temperate latitudes; winters to S
HABITAT: breeds on large, deep lakes; winters on coastal waters
SIZE: 23–29 in (58–73 cm)

When feeding, Black-throated Divers dive for about
45 seconds, probably reaching depths of 10–20 ft (3–6 m).
The normal clutch of 2 eggs is incubated for about 28 days.
By the time they fledge, the young birds are beginning to
catch their own fish.

non-breeding

GREAT NORTHERN DIVER
Gaviidae *Gavia immer*
RANGE: N North America, Greenland and
Iceland, winters to S
HABITAT: breeds on large, deep lakes;
winters on coastal waters
SIZE: 27–36 in (69–91 cm)

With its greater size, thick
neck, and strong spear-shaped
bill, the Great Northern Diver
is a much heavier bird than
the Red-throated and Black-
throated divers. In the breeding
season, its upper parts are
patterned all over with bold
white barring and 2 white
necklaces mark its black head
and neck.

non-breeding

PIED-BILLED GREBE
Podicipedidae *Podilymbus podiceps*
RANGE: S South America N to S Canada
HABITAT: shallow standing or slow-moving fresh water
SIZE: 12–15 in (31–38 cm)

Many Pied-billed Grebes are sedentary, spending summer and winter on the same stretch of water. They sometimes form loose flocks in winter but break up into breeding pairs and establish territories in the spring.

non-breeding

GREAT CRESTED GREBE
Podicipedidae *Podiceps cristatus*
RANGE: temperate Eurasia, E and South Africa, Australia, and New Zealand
HABITAT: shallow, standing, or slow-moving fresh water with emergent vegetation; moves to estuaries and coastal lagoons in winter
SIZE: 18–20 in (46–51 cm)

Both sexes have a double black head crest and chestnut and black tippets (ear ruffs) and, during courtship, erect these feathers. The pair indulge in a "weed-dance," during which pieces of waterweed are held in the bill as the 2 birds come together and rear up out of the water, swinging their heads from side to side.

SLAVONIAN GREBE
Podicipedidae *Podiceps auritus*
RANGE: circumpolar N North America and Eurasia
HABITAT: breeds on both small and large waters; winters on large lakes and sheltered coasts
SIZE: 12–15 in (31–38 cm)

non-breeding

The courtship behavior of the Slavonian Grebe is dramatic. In one ritual, the display feathers are smoothed down as one bird rears up out of the water and bends its head and neck downward. As it does so, it bears a striking resemblance to a penguin and this display has been called the "ghostly penguin dance."

WESTERN GREBE, CLARK'S GREBE
Podicipedidae *Aechmophorus occidentalis, A. clarkii*
RANGE: W North America, from S Canada to Mexico
HABITAT: breeds on freshwater lakes; winters mainly on the sea
SIZE: 22–29 in (56–74 cm)

Clark's Grebe

Western Grebes perform a series of elaborate courtship rituals. During their "rushing" ceremony, for example, male and female rise up out of the water together. Holding themselves erect, with only their legs under the surface, they rush along side by side for about 22–33 yd (20–30 m) before sinking back into the water.

Western Grebe

Open ocean

juv

WANDERING ALBATROSS
Diomedeidae *Diomedea exulans*
RANGE: S oceans, N of 60° S; breeds on several
islands across S oceans
HABITAT: oceanic
SIZE: 42–53 in (107–135 cm)

Along with the Royal Albatross *D. epomophora* and the Amsterdam Island
Albatross *D. amsterdamensis*, these 3 species have the greatest wingspans of any
bird, with a spread of 8–11 ft (2.5–3.3 m). The birds spend most of their time
out over the open ocean, sometimes covering up to 300 miles (500 km) a day.
Wandering Albertrosses come to land on subantarctic islands only to nest and rear
its young. They are slow-breeding but long-lived, with an average lifespan of 30
years. Breeding is possible only in alternate years.

adult and egg at nest

WAVED ALBATROSS
Diomedeidae *Diomedea irrorata*
RANGE: SE Pacific Ocean; breeds on Hood Island, (Galapagos)
and Isla de la Plata (W of Ecuador)
HABITAT: waters of Humboldt Current
SIZE: 33–37 in (84–94 cm)

This exclusively tropical albatross feeds on fish, squid, and other invertebrates.
Its long, narrow wings make it an efficient glider but give it poor braking
power and a high stalling speed, making land arrivals and departures difficult,
especially on its nesting islands, which are strewn with boulders and cacti.

adult feeding
chick at nest

BLACK-BROWED ALBATROSS
Diomedeidae *Diomedea melanophris*
RANGE: S oceans, from 65° to 10° S; breeds on several
islands across S oceans
HABITAT: oceanic
SIZE: 32½ –36½ in (83–93 cm)

This species nests alongside the similar Gray-headed
Albatross *D. chrysostoma*, often gathering in great
colonies. The male arrives at the colony a week before the
female, who stays for 1 day for mating, goes to sea for
another 10 days, and finally returns 2 days before laying.

SOOTY ALBATROSS

Diomedeidae *Phoebetria fusca*
RANGE: Atlantic and Indian oceans; breeds on several
                islands in this region
HABITAT: oceanic
SIZE: 33–35 in (84–89 cm)

The Sooty Albatross breeds on cliffs or at sites inland where there is
sufficient slope in front of the nests to enable it to take off easily. The birds
start breeding when they are 11–13 years old, after a 3–4-year courtship,
and young are reared only in alternate years.

juv

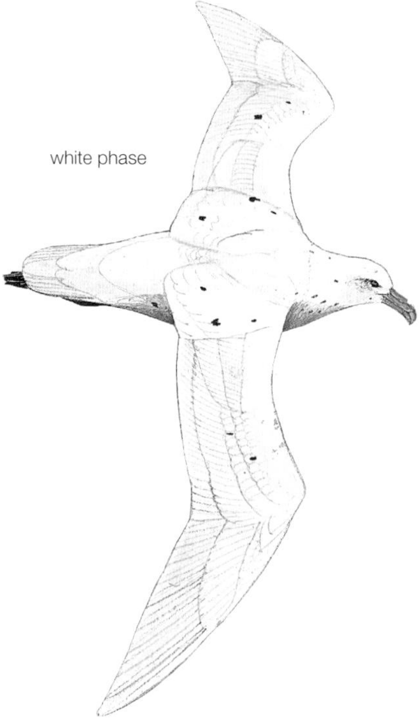

white phase

SOUTHERN GIANT PETREL

Procellariidae *Macronectes giganteus*
RANGE: S oceans, N to 10° S; breeds on various
                islands and on Antarctic coasts
HABITAT: oceanic
SIZE: 34–39 in (86–99 cm)

Rivalling some of the albatrosses in size,
these birds use their massive bills to rip into
the flesh of dead animals such as seals and
whales. The nest is a low saucer of pebbles
or soil and vegetation. Both sitting adults
and nestlings defend themselves with the
common petrel habit of spitting oil.

imm

PINTADO PETREL
Procellariidae *Daption capense*
RANGE: S oceans and W coast of
South America; breeds on
islands in S oceans
HABITAT: oceanic
SIZE: 15–16 in (38–40 cm)

Pintado Petrels breed in colonies
on cliff faces, making pebble nests
on open ledges.

NORTHERN FULMAR
Procellariidae *Fulmarus glacialis*
RANGE: North Pacific and Atlantic oceans
HABITAT: oceanic; breeds on coasts
SIZE: 18–19½ in (45–50 cm)

Nests are sited on sea cliffs, but sometimes
farther inland on cliffs, walls, and buildings.
The birds visit the sites for most of the year,
performing soaring displays and uttering
cackling calls.

CAHOW/BERMUDA PETREL
Procellariidae *Pterodroma cahow*
RANGE: non-breeding range unknown; breeds on 5 small islets
off E Bermuda
HABITAT: open seas; breeds on rocky islets
SIZE: 16 in (41 cm)

The Cahow takes its name from its eerie mating call, heard
in late fall. The birds lay their single egg in a rocky burrow
formed by water erosion.

at nest burrow

BROAD-BILLED PRION
Procellariidae *Pachyptila vittata*
RANGE: S oceans; breeds on various islands in S oceans, also on
coasts of South Island (New Zealand)
HABITAT: oceanic
SIZE: 10–12 in (25–30 cm)

The edges of the Broad-billed Prion's bill are fringed
with comblike plates that act as filters: the bird scoops a
mouthful of water and squeezes it back out through the
plates, leaving the prey behind.

CORY'S SHEARWATER
Procellariidae *Calonectris diomedea*
RANGE: breeds Mediterranean and Atlantic islands; winters E coast
North America, S to Uruguay, and into W Indian Ocean
HABITAT: warm seas
SIZE: 18–21 in (46–53 cm)

Cory's Shearwaters take most of their food from the water's surface,
eating fish and crustaceans. They sometimes gather in such huge
concentrations on the sea that they have been mistaken for land.

SHORT-TAILED SHEARWATER
Procellariidae *Puffinus tenuirostris*
RANGE: breeds S Australia, Tasmania; migrates to
N Pacific after breeding
HABITAT: coasts and offshore waters in breeding
season; open ocean otherwise
SIZE: 16–17 in (41–43 cm)

This species lives in flocks, diving from the ocean surface or from the air 1 yd (1 m) or more beneath the waves to catch krill, small squid, and fish. They nest in burrows under tussocks.

MANX SHEARWATER
Procellariidae *Puffinus puffinus*
RANGE: breeds N Atlantic and Mediterranean
islands; migrates S as far as South
America after breeding
HABITAT: offshore seas above continental shelf
SIZE: 12–15 in (30–38 cm)

Manx Shearwaters nest in colonies, usually on isolated islands arriving at the colonies as early as February.

race *mauretanicus*
"Balearic Shearwater"

LITTLE SHEARWATER
Procellariidae *Puffinus assimilis*
RANGE: N and S Atlantic, S Pacific,
and Indian oceans; breeds
on Atlantic islands and the
Antipodes Islands
HABITAT: coastal waters
SIZE: 10–12 in (25–30 cm)

Unlike most shearwaters, Little Shearwaters are solitary. These birds occupy the nest area for up to 4 months before the eggs are laid, defending the site against other shearwaters.

COMMON DIVING-PETREL
Pelecanoididae *Pelecanoides urinatrix*
RANGE: breeds on many S ocean islands, coasts of S Australia, Tasmania,
New Zealand
HABITAT: oceanic
SIZE: 8–10 in (20–25 cm)

The Common, or Subantarctic, Diving-Petrel is known in New Zealand by the Maori name of "Kuaka," which describes its call. It is especially vocal at night, when it moves to and from its nest burrows under the cover of darkness.

WILSON'S STORM-PETREL
Hydrobatidae *Oceanites oceanicus*
RANGE: breeds from Tierra del Fuego and the Falkland
Islands to the coasts of Antarctica; migrates
to N Indian Ocean and N Atlantic Ocean after
breeding season
HABITAT: oceanic
SIZE: 6–7½ in (15–19 cm)

Wilson's Storm-Petrel regularly gathers in large flocks to feed and follows in the wake of ships. The egg, laid in a burrow, is one-quarter of the adult's weight.

LEACH'S STORM-PETREL
Hydrobatidae *Oceanodroma leucorhoa*
RANGE: breeds from Japan NE to Alaska, then S to
Mexico; winters S to C Pacific and S Atlantic
HABITAT: oceanic
SIZE: 7½–8½ in (19–22 cm)

Generally solitary at sea, this bird breeds in colonies under banks and boulders, excavating nest-burrows up to 6 ft (1.8 m) long with its bill and feet.

Seabirds and freshwater fish eaters

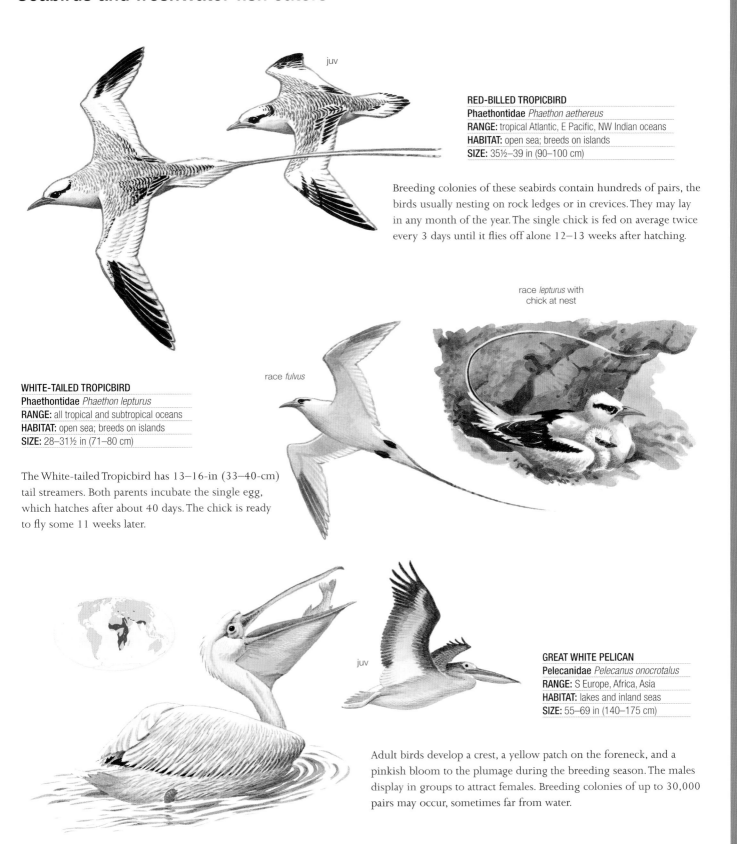

juv

RED-BILLED TROPICBIRD
Phaethontidae *Phaethon aethereus*
RANGE: tropical Atlantic, E Pacific, NW Indian oceans
HABITAT: open sea; breeds on islands
SIZE: 35½–39 in (90–100 cm)

Breeding colonies of these seabirds contain hundreds of pairs, the birds usually nesting on rock ledges or in crevices. They may lay in any month of the year. The single chick is fed on average twice every 3 days until it flies off alone 12–13 weeks after hatching.

race *lepturus* with chick at nest

race *fulvus*

WHITE-TAILED TROPICBIRD
Phaethontidae *Phaethon lepturus*
RANGE: all tropical and subtropical oceans
HABITAT: open sea; breeds on islands
SIZE: 28–31½ in (71–80 cm)

The White-tailed Tropicbird has 13–16-in (33–40-cm) tail streamers. Both parents incubate the single egg, which hatches after about 40 days. The chick is ready to fly some 11 weeks later.

juv

GREAT WHITE PELICAN
Pelecanidae *Pelecanus onocrotalus*
RANGE: S Europe, Africa, Asia
HABITAT: lakes and inland seas
SIZE: 55–69 in (140–175 cm)

Adult birds develop a crest, a yellow patch on the foreneck, and a pinkish bloom to the plumage during the breeding season. The males display in groups to attract females. Breeding colonies of up to 30,000 pairs may occur, sometimes far from water.

AUSTRALIAN PELICAN
Pelecanidae *Pelecanus conspicilliatus*
RANGE: Australia and Tasmania
HABITAT: shallow marine and inland waters
SIZE: 59–71 in (150–180 cm)

The Australian Pelican feeds, roosts, and nests in large flocks. They breed on small islands and may lay their eggs at any time of the year. Two weeks after hatching, the young may climb into the adult's pouch to feed on regurgitated food.

non-breeding

AMERICAN WHITE PELICAN
Pelecanidae *Pelecanus erythrorhynchos*
RANGE: North America
HABITAT: freshwater lakes and shallow coastal waters
SIZE: 50–70 in (127–178 cm)

The American White Pelican occurs in flocks at all times. They avoid perching on trees, preferring to rest on the ground, often on islands and sand-spits; they roost near the water's edge.

BROWN PELICAN
Pelecanidae *Pelecanus occidentalis*
RANGE: Pacific and Atlantic coasts of North and South
America; Galapagos Islands
HABITAT: shallow coastal waters and islands
SIZE: 43–54 in (110–137 cm)

Unlike the other pelicans, this species feeds by diving for fish, making spectacular plunges into the water from heights of 10–33 ft (3–10 m) above the surface. As it enters the water, it opens its bill and traps the prey in its expanded pouch.

non-breeding

NORTHERN GANNET
Sulidae *Sula bassana*
RANGE: E and W coasts of North Atlantic
HABITAT: marine offshore
SIZE: 35½ in (90 cm)

Renowned for its spectacular plunging dives from heights of up to 100 ft (30 m) with its wings half-folded and its body dropping vertically into the water. Northern Gannets nest in huge colonies and egg-laying takes place on a consistently similar date every year.

PERUVIAN BOOBY
Sulidae *Sula variegata*
RANGE: coastal Peru and N Chile
HABITAT: offshore waters
SIZE: 29 in (74 cm)

One of the 3 abundant seabirds of the famous guano islands of Peru (together with the Guanay Cormorant and the Chilean Pelican), the Peruvian Booby relies on the shoals of anchovettas in the cold Humboldt Current to sustain its immense local concentrations.

ABBOTT'S BOOBY
Sulidae *Sula abbotti*
RANGE: E Indian Ocean
HABITAT: open sea
SIZE: 31 in (79 cm)

Abbott's Booby nests only on Christmas Island. The species' breeding cycle takes 15–18 months, so successful pairs nest once every two years while unsuccessful pairs may breed in successive years or take "rest years." The juvenile birds' plumage closely resembles that of the adult males.

♀ with chick at nest

juv

MASKED BOOBY
Sulidae *Sula dactylatra*
RANGE: all tropical oceans
HABITAT: open sea
SIZE: 30–33 in (76–84 cm)

Also known as the Blue-faced Booby, this bird's breeding colonies may contain thousands of pairs. The usual clutch is 2 eggs, although the first-hatched chick invariably kills its sibling early in life. The laying of a second egg is an insurance policy against breeding failure.

white-tailed brown phase

brown phase

RED-FOOTED BOOBY
Sulidae *Sula sula*
RANGE: all tropical oceans
HABITAT: open sea
SIZE: 28–31 in (71–79 cm)

The Red-footed Booby nests in trees, which may have partly protected it from human disturbance. The birds breed opportunistically, waiting for an ample food supply. Juveniles can be distinguished from the adults by their blackish-brown bills, purplish facial skin, and yellowish legs.

white-tailed
and white-headed
brown phase

♂
race *brewsteri*

BROWN BOOBY
Sulidae *Sula leucogaster*
RANGE: all tropical oceans
HABITAT: open sea
SIZE: 29½–31½ in (75–80 cm)

race *plotus*

The Brown Booby breeds mainly on islands, often on cliffs or steep slopes. On well-vegetated slopes, the birds will perch freely in trees. The birds spend much time in the air and perform some of their courtship rituals in flight. Breeding colonies tend to be smaller and more scattered than those of the Red-footed and Masked Boobies.

DOUBLE-CRESTED CORMORANT
Phalacrocoracidae *Phalacrocorax auritus*
RANGE: North America
HABITAT: marine and inland waters
SIZE: 29–36 in (74–91 cm)

This medium-sized, gregarious cormorant breeds in colonies containing up to 3,000 pairs, both on the coast and inland close to dependable supplies of food. The birds lose the double crest on the crown after pairing.

non-breeding

CAPE CORMORANT
Phalacrocoracidae *Phalacrocorax capensis*
RANGE: South Africa, Namibia
HABITAT: Coasts
SIZE: 24–25 in (61–64 cm)

The Cape Cormorant's huge breeding colonies may contain 100,000 birds, the nests placed on cliffs, on the ground, or in bushes. The female usually lays 2–3 eggs and breeding is timed to coincide with periods when pilchards are especially abundant.

race *lucidus* "White-breasted Cormorant"

race *sinensis*

race *carbo*

GREAT CORMORANT
Phalacrocoracidae *Phalacrocorax carbo*
RANGE: N Atlantic, Africa, Eurasia, Australasia
HABITAT: coastal and fresh water
SIZE: 32–39 in (80–100 cm)

There are several races of the Great Cormorant, showing varying amounts of white in the plumage. Its daily intake of food averages 14–25 oz (400–700 g), equivalent to some 15 percent of its body weight. The birds catch their prey during underwater dives that may last for over a minute.

non-breeding

SHAG
Phalacrocoracidae *Phalacrocorax aristotelis*
RANGE: coastal W and S Europe and N Africa
HABITAT: marine coasts
SIZE: 25½–32 in (65–80 cm)

The Shag has a sonorous grunting call, often accompanied by throat-clicking. It prefers clear, cold seas, avoiding estuaries and inland waters, and will travel up to 7 miles (11 km) from its colony in order to feed. After breeding, the birds tend to disperse along the coast.

GUANAY CORMORANT
Phalacrocoracidae *Phalacrocorax bougainvillei*
RANGE: coastal Peru and Chile
HABITAT: marine coasts
SIZE: 30 in (76 cm)

non-breeding

feeding chicks at nest

The Guanay Cormorant used to breed in colonies of hundreds of thousands, or even millions per island, on islands off Peru. The birds still breed at densities of about 3 nests per yard (metre). Overfishing and the effects of El Niño are contributing to its decline.

race *hypoleuces*

PIED CORMORANT
Phalacrocoracidae *Phalacrocorax varius*
RANGE: Australia and New Zealand
HABITAT: coasts; also estuaries and inland waters
SIZE: 26–33 in (66–84 cm)

This striking cormorant, although patchily distributed, sometimes congregates in groups of many thousands. Throwing back the head is a typical part of cormorant courtship ritual, and in the Pied Cormorant the display is greatly enhanced by the bird's bright facial pattern.

RED-LEGGED CORMORANT
Phalacrocoracidae *Phalacrocorax gaimardi*
RANGE: SW South America
HABITAT: marine coasts
SIZE: 28–30 in (71–76 cm)

This bird is unusual among the cormorants for its relatively solitary habits, unexpectedly chirpy voice, and restricted distribution. Only occasionally do the birds cluster densely enough to be termed colonial. Similarly, when foraging, the Red-legged Cormorant often flies singly for long distances and hunts alone or in pairs.

non-breeding

race *atriceps*
"Blue-eyed
Cormorant"

race *albiventor*
"Falkland
Islands Shag"

IMPERIAL SHAG
Phalacrocoracidae *Phalacrocorax atriceps*
RANGE: S South America, subantarctic islands,
Antarctic peninsula
HABITAT: marine coasts
SIZE: 28 in (72 cm)

Several races of the Imperial Shag are recognized. They have varying amounts of white in their plumage and differently colored caruncles (swollen outgrowths at the base of the upper mandible of the bill), but all have distinctive blue rings around the eyes throughout the year and a forward-curving, wispy crest in the breeding season.

PYGMY CORMORANT
Phalacrocoracidae *Phalacrocorax pygmeus*
RANGE: Eurasia
HABITAT: inland waters
SIZE: 18–21½ in (45–55 cm)

The smallest of the cormorants, the Pygmy Cormorant prefers densely vegetated lowland freshwater habitats in warm latitudes. It nests in trees or among reeds, most colonies numbering tens or hundreds of birds. Young birds leave the nest before they can fly; they fledge after about 10 weeks.

non-breeding

FLIGHTLESS CORMORANT
Phalacrocoracidae *Nannopterum harrisi*
RANGE: Galapagos Islands
HABITAT: marine, close to breeding islands
SIZE: 35 in (89 cm)

The Flightless Cormorant occurs only on the islands of Femandina and Isabela in the Galapagos archipelago. It is highly sedentary and has only vestigial wings. It feeds by diving into the sea from the shore; octopuses form a large part of its diet.

AMERICAN DARTER
Anhingidae *Anhinga anhinga*
RANGE: SE USA to N South America
HABITAT: inland and brackish waters; can occur on coasts
SIZE: 34 in (86 cm)

The American Darter often swims with only the head and neck above the surface, the neck held in a sinuous S-shape. Like other darters, it has a hinge mechanism in its neck, enabling it to snap its head forward suddenly to seize prey. Darters are gregarious birds, sometimes breeding in groups of several hundred.

chick at nest

CHRISTMAS ISLAND FRIGATEBIRD
Fregatidae *Fregata andrewsi*
RANGE: Christmas Island and surrounding seas
HABITAT: oceanic
SIZE: 35–40 in (89–102 cm)

This species breeds only on Christmas Island in the eastern Indian Ocean. The males display in small groups to passing females by presenting their inflated scarlet throat pouch, trembling their outspread wings, and producing a distinctive warbling call. If a female is attracted, she descends alongside him. After mating, the pair build a flimsy nest of twigs on the display site.

juv

GREAT FRIGATEBIRD
Fregatidae *Fregata minor*
RANGE: tropical and subtropical Indian and Pacific oceans, and off Brazil
HABITAT: open sea
SIZE: 34–39 in (86–100 cm)

The Great Frigatebird's breeding cycle is one of the longest in the seabird world, with the single young requiring 6 months to fledge and at least a further 6 months of support from its parents. Adults can therefore breed only once in 2 years.

Wading birds

juv

GRAY HERON
Ardeidae *Ardea cinerea*
RANGE: widespread in Eurasia and Africa
HABITAT: shallow freshwaters of all types; also
coasts, especially in winter
SIZE: 35½–38½ in (90–98 cm)

This species haunts a variety of waterside habitats.
Gray Herons usually build their nests in tall trees
up to 80 ft (25 m) above the ground. Colony size is
variable, with about 200 being the maximum in most
areas. A pair readily lays another clutch of eggs if their
first is destroyed; they can repeat this 2–3 times.

GREAT BLUE HERON
Ardeidae *Ardea herodias*
RANGE: S Canada to Central America, Caribbean, Galapagos
Islands; winters S USA to N South America
HABITAT: river edges, marshes, swamps, mudflats
SIZE: 40–50 in (102–107 cm)

Great Blue Herons forage largely in water,
walking slowly or waiting for prey to draw near.
Breeding adults have plumes on their backs and
perform elaborate courtship displays. They nest in
colonies, with nests in trees up to 130 ft (40 m)
above the ground.

GOLIATH HERON
Ardeidae *Ardea goliath*
RANGE: S and E Africa, Madagascar, S Iraq
HABITAT: coastal and inland wetlands with extensive shallows
SIZE: 53–59 in (135–150 cm)

This huge bird feeds chiefly on fish, including
specimens up to 4½–6½ lb (2–3 kg) in weight. The
nest is up to 3 ft (1 m) across. The 2–3 pale blue
eggs are incubated by both parents for about 4 weeks
and the young take a further 6 weeks to fledge.

juv

PURPLE HERON
Ardeidae *Ardea purpurea*
RANGE: S Eurasia, Africa
HABITAT: freshwater wetlands with extensive
emergent vegetation
SIZE: 31–35½ in (78–90 cm)

The Purple Heron nests in colonies of up to 20 pairs. The nest is a platform of reeds or twigs; extra platforms are often constructed nearby and used by the non-incubating bird and, later, by the developing young.

LITTLE EGRET
Ardeidae *Egretta garzetta*
RANGE: S Eurasia, Africa, and Australasia
HABITAT: shallow fresh and brackish water,
also estuaries and coasts
SIZE: 21½ –25½ in (55–65 cm)

Little Egret colonies can contain many hundreds or even thousands of pairs. They are remarkably agile when climbing over thin twigs and build their nests in trees. The young leave the nest before fledging to perch on nearby branches.

winter

CATTLE EGRET
Ardeidae *Bubulcus ibis*
RANGE: S Eurasia, Africa, Australasia, S USA, and
northern S America
HABITAT: freshwater wetlands, farmland, and open
country
SIZE: 19–21 in (48–53 cm)

winter

Cattle Egrets commonly feed around grazing cattle and wild game herds, which flush prey such as grasshoppers, beetles, and lizards from cover as they move. They nest in dense colonies, often in company with other species, with as many as 100 nests in a single tree.

juv

SQUACCO HERON
Ardeidae *Ardeola ralloides*
RANGE: S Europe, SW Asia, Africa
HABITAT: freshwater marshes, swamps, and lakes
SIZE: 17–18½ in (44–47 cm)

The Squacco Heron gains an elegant crest and ornamental back plumes for the breeding season, and its bill and legs, which are yellowish-green in winter, change to blue and pink respectively. Each clutch contains 3–6 eggs laid on a platform of twigs or reeds.

race virescens

race sundevalli

race rogersi

GREEN-BACKED HERON
Ardeidae *Butondes striatus*
RANGE: worldwide tropics and subtropics
HABITAT: freshwater and coastal wetlands
SIZE: 16–19 in (40–48 cm)

The Green-backed, or Striated, Heron is usually a secretive species, feeding mainly at night. Most nests are solitary and placed in low bushes or trees, often overhanging water. The nest itself is built of twigs, but is so flimsy that the 1–4 eggs may be visible from below.

juv

BLACK-CROWNED NIGHT HERON
Ardeidae *nycticorax*
RANGE: worldwide except N temperate regions and Australia
HABITAT: salt, brackish and freshwater wetlands
SIZE: 23–25½ in (58–65 cm)

The Black-crowned Night Heron is active mainly in the evening and through the night, hunting for frogs and toads, small fish, and crustaceans. Breeding takes place in colonies in trees, with up to 30 nests crowded into a single tree.

AMERICAN BITTERN
Ardeidae *Botaurus lentiginosus*
RANGE: C Canada to C USA; winters S USA, Caribbean, Mexico, Central America
HABITAT: fresh and saltwater marshes, swamps and bogs
SIZE: 25 in (64 cm)

The American Bittern is a stocky brown heron with a black and brown wing pattern in flight. Juvenile birds have more streaking on the back and breast, but closely resemble adults. The male American Bittern's 3-syllable pumping or booming call probably serves to advertise territory as well as to attract females.

HAMMERKOP
Scopidae *Scopus umbretta*
RANGE: S and C Africa, Madagascar
HABITAT: shallow fresh water
SIZE: 19½ in (50 cm)

Hammerkops build huge, domed nests up to 6 ft (2 m) high and across from sticks, reeds, grass and dead plant stems. The entrance hole is reduced in size with mud and the nest itself is lined with waterweed and dry grass. The whole structure may take 6 weeks to build.

juv

WHALE-HEADED STORK

Balaenicipitidae *Balaeniceps rex*
RANGE: Sudan, Uganda, Democratic Republic of the Congo to the Republic of Zambia
HABITAT: swamps
SIZE: 39–47 in (100–120 cm)

This species takes its name (and its alternative name of Shoebill) from its huge, clog-shaped bill, which is probably an adaptation for catching and holding the large, slippery lungfish that form one of its main sources of food. Its eyes are also exceptionally large and set forward, giving it binocular vision.

WOOD STORK

Ciconidae *Mycteria americana*
RANGE: SE USA, Mexico, Central America, W South America to N Argentina
HABITAT: ponds, marshes, swamps, lagoons
SIZE: 34–40 in (86–102 cm)

Wood Storks are gregarious birds—sometimes flocks of 100 or more soar high above the ground on thermals. They forage in water up to their bellies, moving their open bill from side to side. They nest colonially, with up to 25 nests per tree placed up to 100 ft (20 m) above the ground.

AFRICAN OPEN-BILL STORK

Ciconidae *Anastomus lamelligerus*
RANGE: sub-Saharan Africa, Madagascar
HABITAT: swamps, marshes, flooded areas and margins
of large rivers
SIZE: 35½ in (90 cm)

When this species closes its bill, the 2 halves curve away from each other to leave a wide gap —hence the common name. The bird's principal food is large water snails: by inserting the tip of its bill into the snail, the stork can snip through the muscle and withdraw the snail from its shell.

juv

BLACK STORK

Ciconidae *Ciconia nigra*
RANGE: temperate and S Eurasia, S Africa
HABITAT: forest swamps; also open, drier country
SIZE: 37½–39 in (95–100 cm)

at nest

Some Black Storks inhabit wet places, particularly well-wooded areas, where the birds breed in large trees. The other habitat type is much drier, more open country, where the birds nest on cliff ledges or even in caves, at altitudes of up to 6,500 ft (2,000 m).

WHITE STORK
Ciconidae *Ciconia ciconia*
RANGE: temperate and S Europe, N Africa, S and E Asia; winters in Africa, India and S Asia
HABITAT: open, moist lowlands and wetlands, generally close to human habitation
SIZE: 39–45 in (100–115 cm)

The main display of the White Stork involves bill-clapping, in which the mandibles are clapped rapidly together. This persists as a form of greeting between the pair throughout the nesting period.

MARABOU STORK
Ciconidae *Leptoptilos crumeniferus*
RANGE: tropical and subtropical Africa
HABITAT: large wetlands and open country
SIZE: 59 in (150 cm)

An adult Marabou Stork has a large throat pouch that hangs down in front of its neck, containing a system of air sacs that can be inflated and deflated. This is not a food-storing crop, but may have a role in courtship display. Marabou Storks obtain much of their food from scavenging.

SACRED IBIS
Threskiornithidae *Threskiornis aethiopica*
RANGE: sub-Saharan Africa, Madagascar, Iraq
HABITAT: inland and coastal shallow wetlands
SIZE: 25½–29½ in (65–75 cm)

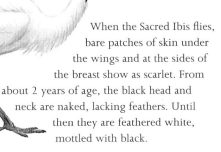

When the Sacred Ibis flies, bare patches of skin under the wings and at the sides of the breast show as scarlet. From about 2 years of age, the black head and neck are naked, lacking feathers. Until then they are feathered white, mottled with black.

HERMIT IBIS
Threskiornithidae *Geronticus eremita*
RANGE: NW Africa and Turkey
HABITAT: mountainous and semi-arid deserts; also upland wetlands, farmland
SIZE: 28–31 in (71–79 cm)

Critically endangered, the few remaining colonies of the Hermit Ibis (also known as the Northern Bald Ibis or Waldrapp) are on cliffs in steep valleys. Here, nests of twigs, grass, and straw are built, often decorated with bits of paper.

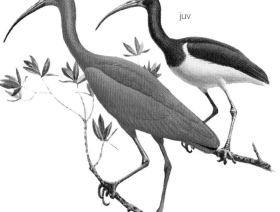

juv

SCARLET IBIS
Threskiornithidae *Eudocimus ruber*
RANGE: Venezuela, Colombia, coastal Guianas and Brazil; Trinidad
HABITAT: coastal swamps, mangroves, lagoons, estuaries, mudflats
SIZE: 24 in (61 cm)

Scarlet Ibises feed mainly on crabs, molluscs, and other invertebrates, probing for them on mudflats with their curved bills. They will also take fish, frogs, and insects. They breed colonially, constructing nests of twigs and sticks.

GLOSSY IBIS
Threskiornithidae *Plegadis falcinellus*
RANGE: widespread but scattered in Central America, Africa, S Eurasia, and Australasia
HABITAT: shallow freshwater and coastal wetlands
SIZE: 22–26 in (56–66 cm)

The overall dark chestnut and black plumage of this bird is shot with a purple and green iridescence that gives the species its name. Glossy Ibises breed in colonies, sometimes of thousands of pairs. Outside the breeding season, flocks feed in shallow wetlands and open fields.

winter

WHITE SPOONBILL
Threskiornithidae *Platalea leucorodia*
RANGE: temperate and S Eurasia, India, tropical W and NE Africa
HABITAT: shallow fresh, brackish, and saltwater wetlands
SIZE: 31–35 in (79–89 cm)

juv

This bird feeds with the mandibles of its bill held slightly open and the tip immersed in shallow water. As the bird swings its head from side to side, the bill makes scything movements below the surface in search of shrimps and other aquatic life.

ROSEATE SPOONBILL
Threskiornithidae *Ajaia ajaja*
RANGE: SE USA, Central America, Colombia, Ecuador, E Peru, Bolivia, N Argentina
HABITAT: marshes, lagoons, mangroves, mudflats
SIZE: 32 in (81 cm)

Roseate Spoonbills are monogamous and have elaborate courtship behavior that includes the presentation of twigs, flight displays, and bill-clapping. They sweep their bills through shallow water to catch small fish, crustaceans, and other aquatic invertebrates, and also eat some plant material.

juv

GREATER FLAMINGO
Phoenicopteridae *Phoenicopterus ruber*
RANGE: S Europe, SW Asia, E, W and N Africa, West Indies, Central America, Galapagos Islands
HABITAT: saline or alkaline lakes, lagoons, and deltas
SIZE: 49–57 in (125–145 cm)

The bill is an adaptation for feeding: small crustaceans are sifted from the bottom mud by a pumping action of the tongue, which forces mud and water through the lamellae (platelike structures) on either side of the bill. The long legs and neck allow the birds to feed in deeper water than other species.

race *roseus*

ANDEAN FLAMINGO
Phoenicopteridae *Phoenicoparrus andinus*
RANGE: Andes of Peru, Bolivia, Chile, Argentina above 8,000 ft (2,500 m)
HABITAT: salt lakes
SIZE: 40 in (102 cm)

feeding chick on nest

The downy white chicks have straight bills at first and are fed liquid secretions containing fat, protein, carbohydrates, and blood cells until their bills are fully developed. This avian "milk" is rich in red pigment, giving the feathers their coloring.

Water birds

CRESTED SCREAMER
Anhimidae *Chauna torquata*
RANGE: S Brazil, Uruguay, and N Argentina
HABITAT: marshes in open grassland and woodland
SIZE: 33½–37½ in (85–95 cm)

Screamers take their name from their loud, far-carrying calls. Two sharp, bony spurs project from the bend of each wing. The spurs are used in fighting, either between rival screamers or to drive off enemies, including hunting dogs and other predators.

MAGPIE GOOSE
Anatidae *Anseranas semipalmata*
RANGE: N Australia and S New Guinea
HABITAT: overgrown swamps and lagoons and adjacent farmland
SIZE: 29½–33½ in (75–85 cm)

♀ feeding chick

The natural food of the Magpie Goose includes aquatic plants and seeds. The nest is a large platform of vegetation, plucked off and trampled in shallow water, before being built up into a mound. Uniquely among wildfowl, the parents feed their young bill to bill.

WHITE-FACED WHISTLING DUCK
Anatidae *Dendrocygna viduata*
RANGE: tropical South America, sub-Saharan Africa, Madagascar and the Comoro Islands
HABITAT: rivers, lakes, swamps, marshes
SIZE: 17–19 in (43–48 cm)

MUTE SWAN
Anatidae *Cygnus olor*
RANGE: temperate Eurasia; introduced to parts of North America, South Africa, and Australia
HABITAT: lowland freshwater lakes and marshes; coastal lagoons and estuaries
SIZE: 49–61 in (125–155 cm)

♀

♂

The species is misnamed, since it utters a variety of snoring, snorting, and hissing calls. Males (called cobs) have larger knobs on their bills than females (pens), especially in the breeding season. A pair will vigorously defend a territory around their nest.

juv

A pair of White-faced Whistling Ducks will indulge in mutual preening, with the 2 birds facing one another and nibbling gently at each other's head and neck feathers; it is likely that this helps to reinforce the pair bond.

juv

BLACK SWAN
Anatidae *Cygnus atratus*
RANGE: Australia; introduced into New Zealand
HABITAT: large freshwater and brackish marshes and
lagoons; also estuaries and coastal bays
SIZE: 45–55 in (115–140 cm)

The Black Swan occurs in enormous
flocks, up to 50,000 strong. Like
many Australian waterbirds, the
Black Swan can delay breeding in
times of drought but can quickly
take advantage of sudden rains
and flood conditions.

TUNDRA SWAN
Anatidae *Cygnus columbianus*
RANGE: breeds Arctic North America and Eurasia; winters
S to temperate latitudes
HABITAT: breeds on marshy tundra; winters on freshwater
marshes and estuaries
SIZE: 47–59 in (120–150 cm)

race *columbianus*
"Whisting Swan"

race *bewicki*
"Bewick's Swan"
variations in
bill pattern

The three races of the all-white Tundra
Swan include the Whistling Swan
C. c. columbianus of North America
and the Bewick's Swan *C. c. bewickii*
of Eurasia, both illustrated. The
amount of yellow on the Bewick's
Swan's bill is extremely variable and
can be used to identify
individual birds.

race *bewickii*
"Bewick's Swan"

WHITE-FRONTED GOOSE
Anatidae *Anser albifrons*
RANGE: circumpolar Arctic; winters S to temperate latitudes
HABITAT: breeds in tundra; winters on open marshes and on
agricultural land
SIZE: 26-34 in (66–86 cm)

race *flavirostris*

race *albifrons*
juv

race *albifrons*

White-fronted Geese have a high-pitched, laughing call
and are actually named "laughing geese" in more than
one European language. There are 4 or 5 races,
distinguished by bill color and plumage.

race *anser*   race *rubrirostris*

GREYLAG GOOSE
Anatidae *Anser anser*
RANGE: mainly temperate latitudes of Eurasia
HABITAT: freshwater marshes and open water;
often winters on farmland
SIZE: 29½–35½ in (75–90 cm)

There are 2 races: *A. a. anser* breeds in Europe, while the
pink-billed *A. a. rubrirostris* breeds in Asia. The bill is
adapted for probing in marshy ground and pulling up
roots and stems; it is also ideal for grazing.

SNOW GOOSE
Anatidae *Anser caerulescens*
RANGE: Arctic North America; winters on both seaboards
and S to Gulf of Mexico
HABITAT: breeds on Arctic tundra; winters on freshwater
and salt marshes, farmland
SIZE: 25½–33 in (65–84 cm)

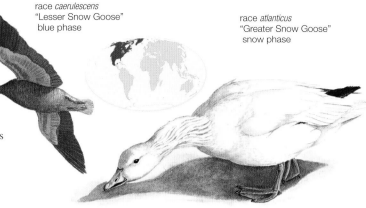

race *caerulescens*
"Lesser Snow Goose"
blue phase

race *atlanticus*
"Greater Snow Goose"
snow phase

The 2 races, the Greater and the Lesser, are distinguished
mainly by size. While the adult Greater Snow Goose is always
white, the Lesser Snow Goose shows both the white "snow"
phase and a dark gray "blue" phase.

HAWAIIAN GOOSE
Anatidae *Branta sandvicensis*
RANGE: confined to the Hawaiian Islands
HABITAT: sparsely vegetated slopes of volcanoes
SIZE: 22–28 in (56–71 cm)

The Hawaiian Goose has only partial
webbing on its feet, reflecting its
largely terrestrial habits. The nest is a
simple scrape in the ground, usually in the
shelter of a rock or a clump of vegetation.

CANADA GOOSE
Anatidae *Branta canadensis*
RANGE: Arctic and temperate North America;
introduced into Europe and New Zealand
HABITAT: lowland wetlands
SIZE: 21½–43 in (55–110 cm)

race *minima*

The Canada Goose has been divided into
10–12 races, based on distribution, size, and
coloring. The smallest races (such as *B. c. minima*
from west Alaska) breed in the Arctic; the
larger races (such as *B. c. canadensis* from
eastern Canada) breed farther south.

race *canadensis*

RED-BREASTED GOOSE
Anatidae *Branta ruficollis*
RANGE: breeds in the Siberian Arctic; winters close to
the Black, Caspian, and Aral seas
HABITAT: breeds on tundra; winters on open farmland
close to major wetlands
SIZE: 21–21½ in (53–55 cm)

A remarkable association exists between this scarce, strikingly plumaged goose and
various birds of prey. Red-breasted Geese nest on the Arctic tundra, concentrating
in small groups of up to 5 pairs around the nests of Peregrines, Rough-legged
Buzzards and, sometimes, large gulls. In defending their own nests against
predators, these aggressive birds keep intruders, such as gulls and Arctic foxes,
away from the nests of the surrounding geese.

winter

♂ ♂

FRECKLED DUCK
Anatidae *Stictonetta naevosa*
RANGE: Australia
HABITAT: open freshwater and brackish lakes and swamps
SIZE: 19½–21½ in (50–55 cm)

Prolonged drought in the areas where it is most numerous sends birds wandering over great distances. Where they find water, pairs quickly settle down to breed and rear young. Later, if conditions permit, there will be a return to their normal distribution until the next drought again disperses the birds.

MAGELLAN GOOSE
Anatidae *Chloephaga picta*
RANGE: S South America and the Falkland Islands
HABITAT: grassland and marshes
SIZE: 23½–25½ in (60–65 cm)

The white and gray male has a whistling call used in display, to which the rufous and gray-brown female responds with a lower cackling. The illustration shows the 2 races: the Lesser *C. p. picta*, with its white and barred phases, and the Greater *C. p. leucoptera*.

race *picta*
"Lesser Magellan Goose"
white phase

♂

♀

race *leucoptera*
"Great Magellan Goose"

♂

race *picta*
barred phase

EGYPTIAN GOOSE
Anatidae *Alopochen aegyptiacus*
RANGE: Nile valley and sub-Saharan Africa
HABITAT: tropical and subtropical wetlands
SIZE: 25–29 in (63–73 cm)

The Egyptian Goose has 2 color phases, one gray-brown on the upperparts, the other red-brown. The species is remarkable for the great variety of nest sites that it uses: some nest on the ground, others on cliffs or old buildings, and some in the abandoned nests of other birds, often high in the crowns of trees.

COMMON SHELDUCK
Anatidae *Tadorna tadorna*
RANGE: temperate Eurasia; winters S to N Africa, India, China, and Japan
HABITAT: estuaries, shallow seas
SIZE: 23–26 in (58–67 cm)

In early spring, the males court the females with melodious whistling calls, rearing up and throwing back their heads. The young of several broods often combine into large "creches" under the care of just a few of the parents. The rest of the adults depart for their molting grounds.

♀

juv

♂

♂

MAGELLANIC FLIGHTLESS STEAMER DUCK
Anatidae *Tachyeres pteneres*
RANGE: extreme S South America
HABITAT: marine, especially rocky or gravelly coasts
with offshore kelp beds
SIZE: 24–33 in (61–84 cm)

juv

Although incapable of flight, it can escape predators by furiously threshing over the water with its stubby wings. The males, in particular, also use their wings to strike one another in combat. The blows are reinforced by large bony knobs on the carpal joints at the bends of the wings.

MUSCOVY DUCK
Anatidae *Cairina moschata*
RANGE: Central and South America
HABITAT: freshwater marshes and pools in
wooded areas; brackish coastal lagoons
SIZE: 26–33 in (66–84 cm)

The Muscovy Duck has been widely introduced outside its native lands as a domestic fowl. In the wild, these shy birds roost in small groups in trees, safe from ground predators. Both wild and domestic Muscovy Ducks prefer to nest in holes in trees, and they take readily to nest-boxes.

race melanotos

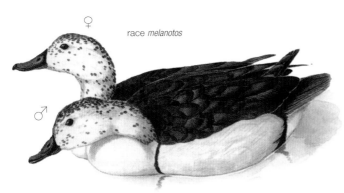

COMB DUCK
Anatidae *Sarkidiornis melanotos*
RANGE: sub-Saharan Africa, India, Southeast Asia,
and tropical South America
HABITAT: rivers, swamps, lakes
SIZE: 22–30 in (56–76 cm)

Outside the breeding season, flocks of Comb Ducks often consist entirely of males or of females. During the breeding season, each male may have 2 mates and several nesting "pairs" can form small breeding colonies.

WOOD DUCK
Anatidae *Aix sponsa*
RANGE: North America: E population breeds S Canada to Florida,
W population breeds British Columbia to California;
winters in S of breeding range
HABITAT: fresh waters in wooded areas; more open flooded
areas in winter
SIZE: 17–20 in (43–51 cm)

The remarkable coloration of the male Wood Duck greatly contrasts with the mottled gray-brown of the female. It was the drake's superb plumage that nearly led to the species' extinction: in the 19th century the feathers were in great demand for ornament and for fishing flies.

TORRENT DUCK
Anatidae *Merganetta armata*
RANGE: Andes
HABITAT: fast-flowing streams
SIZE: 17–18 in (43–46 cm)

race *armata*
"Chilean Torrent Duck"

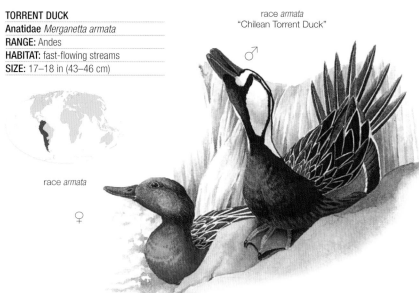

race *armata*

With its streamlined shape, powerful legs, a broad, stiff tail used for steering, and sharp claws to enable it to cling to slippery rocks, the Torrent Duck is perfectly adapted to life in fast-flowing water. The ducklings are able to tackle the most turbulent water as soon as they hatch.

AMERICAN WIGEON
Anatidae *Anas americana*
RANGE: breeds N and C North America; winters S to Gulf of Mexico
HABITAT: freshwater marshes, ponds; winters on marshes, coastal lagoons
SIZE: 18–22 in (45–56 cm)

Although classed as a dabbling duck, the American Wigeon obtains only some of its plant food by dabbling in shallow water. More often, tightly packed flocks of birds graze on marshes and pastures. The nest is a shallow cup of grasses in concealing vegetation near water.

race *crecca*

race *carolinensis*

race *crecca*

GREEN-WINGED TEAL
Anatidae *Anas crecca*
RANGE: breeds North America, N Eurasia; winters S USA, Central America, Caribbean, temperate Eurasia, tropical Asia
HABITAT: freshwater pools, marshes; in winter also on estuaries, coastal lagoons
SIZE: 13–15 in (34–38 cm)

This abundant small duck has 2 distinct races, the European *A.c. crecca*, with a horizontal white flank stripe, and the North American *A. c. carolinensis*, with a vertical white chest stripe. These are male characteristics; females are indistinguishable.

MALLARD
Anatidae *Anas platyrhynchos*
RANGE: N hemisphere, N of the tropics; introduced to Australia and New Zealand
HABITAT: wide range of fresh and coastal waters
SIZE: 20–25½ in (50–65 cm)

The success of the Mallard, ancestor of most domestic ducks, reflects its supreme adaptability. It can become completely tame in urban areas, relying on human handouts for food, although it is as wild as any wildfowl in other habitats.

AMERICAN BLACK DUCK
Anatidae *Anas rubripes*
RANGE: NE North America; winters S to Gulf of Mexico
HABITAT: freshwater marshes in woods; winters on estuaries, coastal marshes
SIZE: 21–24 in (53–61 cm)

As with some other close relatives of the Mallard but unlike nearly all other northern hemisphere dabbling ducks, the male lacks any bright nuptial plumage.

NORTHERN PINTAIL
Anatidae *Anas acuta*
RANGE: Eurasia and North America; winters S to Panama, C Africa, India, Philippines
HABITAT: open marshes; winters on estuaries and coastal lagoons
SIZE: male 25–29 in (63–74 cm) including 4-in (10-cm) central tail feathers; female 17–25 in (43–63 cm)

Apart from pecking at grain, Northern Pintails feed mainly in the water. They upend, using their long necks to reach deeper than other ducks sharing their range. They scour the bottom of pools and marshes for plant roots and leaves, as well as aquatic invertebrates.

NORTHERN SHOVELER
Anatidae *Anas clypeata*
RANGE: Eurasia and North America S of the Arctic Circle; winters S to the subtropics
HABITAT: freshwater pools and marshes; also on estuaries and coastal lagoons in winter
SIZE: 17–20 in (44–52 cm)

Groups of Northern Shovelers often circle slowly as they feed. Their combined paddling action brings food items —tiny seeds and floating animals—to the surface in deep water. Northern Shovelers will also dabble in shallows, selecting larger food items.

MARBLED TEAL
Anatidae *Marmaronetta angustirostris*
RANGE: Mediterranean region E to Pakistan and NW India
HABITAT: shallow freshwater and brackish lakes, lagoons and marshes
SIZE: 15–16½ in (39–42 cm)

Although it resembles the teals, which are dabbling ducks, this species is now generally regarded as more closely related to the pochards, or diving ducks, and is increasingly known as the Marbled Duck. In particular, its courtship displays and other behavior patterns are more similar to the diving ducks.

RED-CRESTED POCHARD
Anatidae *Netta rufina*
RANGE: E Europe and SC Asia
HABITAT: freshwater lakes, rivers, deltas and coastal lagoons
SIZE: 21–22½ in (53–57 cm)

The birds lay a clutch of up to 10 pale green or olive eggs in a well-concealed nest of aquatic vegetation, often built on a base of twigs. The female incubates alone, while the male moves away and joins other males for the annual molt.

CANVASBACK
Anatidae *Aythya valisineria*
RANGE: S Canada to Mexico
HABITAT: breeds on prairie marshes; winters on lakes, lagoons and estuaries
SIZE: 19–24 in (48–61 cm)

The Canvasback is the largest of the pochards, or diving ducks. Both male and female have a relatively long sloping forehead, high, peaked crown, long bill, and long neck, giving them a distinctive silhouette.

TUFTED DUCK
Anatidae *Aythya fuligula*
RANGE: Eurasia
HABITAT: lakes and ponds, sometimes in towns; winters on larger waters, estuaries, lagoons
SIZE: 16–18½ in (40–47 cm)

Tufted Ducks gather in large winter flocks and breed in loose colonies with their nests only a few yards (metres) apart. They are expert divers, able to reach depths of 16–20 ft (5–6 m) and remain underwater for 20–30 seconds.

COMMON EIDER
Anatidae *Somateria mollissima*
RANGE: Arctic and N temperate Eurasia and North America
HABITAT: coastal waters, estuaries
SIZE: 19½–28 in (50–71 cm)

The down feathers with which the female Common Eider lines the nest have long been valued by people for their insulating properties. She incubates her clutch of 4–6 olive-green eggs for 28 days; after hatching, the young from several broods may come together to form a "creche."

HARLEQUIN DUCK

Anatidae *Histrionicus histrionicus*
RANGE: Iceland, Greenland, Labrador, NW North America, NE Siberia, and Japan
HABITAT: fast-flowing rivers and streams and inshore coastal waters
SIZE: 13–18 in (34–45 cm)

Swimming with the current, the Harlequin Duck can shoot rapids and pass through turbulent water without difficulty. In flight, the Harlequin Duck passes fast and low over the water, precisely following each bend in a stream.

LONG-TAILED DUCK

Anatidae *Clangula hyemalis*
RANGE: Arctic Eurasia and North America; winters S to cool temperate regions
HABITAT: breeds on tundra pools and by the coast; winters in sea bays
SIZE: 14–18½ in (36–47 cm)

Long-tailed Ducks have 4 plumage changes a year: both sexes have distinct summer, fall, winter, and eclipse plumages. They are sea ducks, spending nearly all their time on salt water, and accomplished divers, remaining underwater for as long as a minute and reaching depths of 180 ft (55 m).

COMMON SCOTER

Anatidae *Melanitta nigra*
RANGE: Arctic and N temperate Eurasia and North America; winters to the S
HABITAT: breeds on freshwater lakes and marshes; winters in sea bays and estuaries
SIZE: 17–21 in (44–54 cm)

In the Eurasian race *M. n. nigra* the yellow patch on the bill covers only a small area halfway along the upper mandible, but in the North American race *M. n. americana* (sometimes regarded as a separate species), the yellow covers most of the upper mandible and a prominent knob at the base of the bill.

COMMON GOLDENEYE

Anatidae *Bucephala clangula*
RANGE: N Eurasia and North America; winters to S
HABITAT: breeds on lakes and pools in forests; winters on lakes, estuaries, sea bays
SIZE: 16½–19½ in (42–50 cm)

The Common Goldeneye's head is distinctively rounded and its steep forehead and short bill help in identification at long range. The bird's natural breeding site is a cavity in a tree or a dead stump.

HOODED MERGANSER

Anatidae *Mergus cucullatus*

RANGE: 2 populations. W population breeds S Alaska to NW USA; winters S Alaska to California. E population breeds S Canada, N and C USA; winters Florida, N Mexico

HABITAT: breeds and winters by rivers and lakes in forests; also winters on estuaries, coasts

SIZE: 16½–19½ in (42–50 cm)

The male Hooded Merganser has a pronounced black-and-white crest on his head that, when raised, forms a quarter-circle of white outlined in black. The Hooded Merganser places its nest in a hole in a tree up to 52 ft (16 m) above the ground. Here the female lays and incubates 6–12 white eggs.

RED-BREASTED MERGANSER

Anatidae *Mergus serrator*

RANGE: N Eurasia and North America; winters S to Mediterranean, E China, Gulf of Mexico

HABITAT: breeds by rivers, estuaries and coasts; winters on estuaries and coastal bays

SIZE: 20½–23 in (52–58 cm)

The Red-breasted Merganser is as much at home on the sea as on fresh water. It is a long-necked, long-bodied duck, whose bill is long and thin with a hooked tip. Serrations along the sides of the mandibles help the bird grasp fish.

race *jamaicensis*
♀

race *ferruginea*
"Peruvian Ruddy Duck"
♂

race *jamaicensis*
♂

RUDDY DUCK

Anatidae *Oxyura jamaicensis*

RANGE: North and South America; introduced into Britain

HABITAT: breeds and winters on well-vegetated lakes; also winters on coastal lagoons and bays

SIZE: 14–17 in (35–43 cm)

When displaying, the male Ruddy Duck rushes over the water, paddling furiously, with his tail and lower body submerged, chest lifted out of the water, shoulders hunched, head down, and bill pressed down onto his raised chest.

MUSK DUCK

Anatidae *Biziura lobata*

RANGE: : S Australia and Tasmania

HABITAT: breeds by freshwater and brackish lakes and marshes; winters on lakes, estuaries, and coastal bays

SIZE: male 24–29 in (61–73 cm); female 18½–23½ in (47–60 cm)

Both sexes of the Musk Duck have dark oily-looking plumage, but the male alone has a flat lobe of skin hanging down below the lower mandible. The male is also nearly one-third larger than the female—an unusual size difference in any kind of bird.

Birds of prey

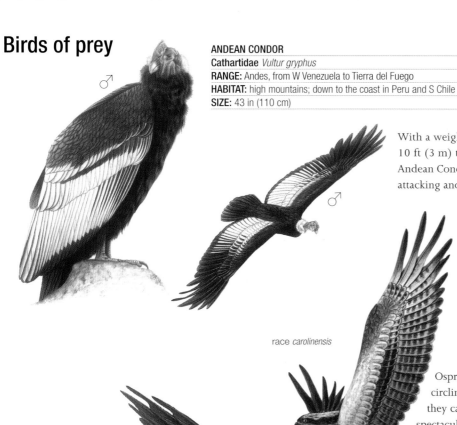

♂

ANDEAN CONDOR
Cathartidae *Vultur gryphus*
RANGE: Andes, from W Venezuela to Tierra del Fuego
HABITAT: high mountains; down to the coast in Peru and S Chile
SIZE: 43 in (110 cm)

♂

With a weight of up to 25 lb (12 kg) and a wingspan of over 10 ft (3 m) this is the largest of all the world's birds of prey. Andean Condors feed extensively on carrion, sometimes also attacking and killing sickly or dying animals.

OSPREY
Pandionidae *Pandion haliaetus*
RANGE: breeds North America, Eurasia (mainly migrants), NE Africa, Australia; winter visitor and non-breeding migrant elsewhere
HABITAT: coasts, rivers, lakes, wetlands
SIZE: 21½–23 in (55–58 cm)

race *carolinensis*

Osprey feed almost exclusively on fish, soaring or circling up to 100 ft (30 m) above the water. When they catch sight of prey near the surface, they make a spectacular headlong plunge, throwing their feet forward at the last moment. The soles of the feet have sharp spines that help the birds grasp slippery fish.

♂

AMERICAN SWALLOW-TAILED KITE
Accipitridae/1 *Elanoides forficatus*
RANGE: SE USA, Mexico S to N Argentina
HABITAT: woodland and forest
SIZE: 23½ in (60 cm)

The American Swallow-tailed Kite feeds entirely on the wing, capturing aerial insects and eating them as it flies along. It will also pluck small lizards and snakes from trees, and snatch eggs and nestlings of small birds, without alighting on the ground. It can even swoop down to the surface of water and take a drink in flight.

AFRICAN FISH EAGLE
Accipitridae/2 *Haliaeetus vocifer*
RANGE: sub-Saharan Africa
HABITAT: coastal and inland waters
SIZE: 29–33 in (74–84 cm)

juv

This handsome fish eagle usually occurs close to water. It is a wonderfully agile flier and, although it can lift fish straight from the surface while still in flight, it usually makes a spectacular plunge into the water with its feet stretched forward.

BALD EAGLE
Accipitridae/2 *Haliaeetus leucocephalus*
RANGE: North America
HABITAT: usually near lakes, rivers, coasts
SIZE: 31–37 in (79–94 cm)

Versatile predators, Bald Eagles catch a variety of live prey including birds, small mammals, and, especially, fish. Pairs remain faithful and maintain their bond each year with spectacular aerial displays in which the 2 birds lock talons and tumble downward through the air.

juv

juv

WHITE-TAILED SEA EAGLE
Accipitridae/2 *Haliaeetus albicilla*
RANGE: W Greenland, Iceland, N, C, and SE
   Europe, N Asia
HABITAT: coasts, lakes, rivers, wetlands
SIZE: 27½–35½ in (70–90 cm)

White-tailed Sea Eagles are skilled hunters of waterfowl, seabirds, and small mammals, and expertly snatch fish from the surface of water with their talons. The huge nest of sticks may be built in the top of a tree, on a crag, or on the ground on a small island if it is free of terrestrial predators.

race *aeruginosus*

MARSH HARRIER
Accipitridae/6 *Circus aeruginosus*
RANGE: W Europe E across Asia, Madagascar, Borneo, Australia
HABITAT: usually lowland wetlands, especially with reedbeds
SIZE: 19–23 in (48–58 cm)

The Marsh Harrier generally nests in thick marsh vegetation, but forages widely over nearby lowland habitats. When the female is incubating and tending the young, the male hunts for them both, calling his mate off the nest when he returns with food and dropping it for her to catch in midair.

BLACK-COLLARED HAWK
Accipitridae/8 *Busarellus nigricollis*
RANGE: Mexico S to Argentina
HABITAT: tropical lowlands, open or semi-open country near water
SIZE: 19–20 in (48–51 cm)

Immature birds are duller than the distinctive adults, with dark streaking. The Black-collared Hawk's principal food is fish; small spines on the undersides of its feet help the bird grasp and hold its prey. An alternative common name is the Fishing Buzzard.

juv

HARRIS' HAWK
Accipitridae/8 *Parabuteo unicinctus*
RANGE: SW USA, Central and South America
HABITAT: lowlands, with or without scattered trees, semi-deserts
SIZE: 19–22 in (48–56 cm)

Primarily a bird of dry, open habitats, Harris' Hawk hunts by gliding at low levels or by swooping suddenly onto prey from a low perch, taking a wide variety of small to medium-sized birds, small rodents, other mammals up to the size of full-grown rabbits, and lizards.

GRAY HAWK
Accipitridae/8 *Buteo nitidus*
RANGE: SW USA, Central and South America
HABITAT: tropical and subtropical woodland and forest
SIZE: 15–17 in (38–43 cm)

juv

The Gray Hawk is a woodland bird, its short wings and long tail allowing it to steer skilfully around trees in pursuit of prey. The usual call is a high-pitched *cree-ee-ee*, but it also utters flutelike cries in flight, apparently during courtship.

RED-SHOULDERED HAWK
Accipitridae/8 *Buteo lineatus*
RANGE: North America, S to C Mexico
HABITAT: mixed or deciduous woodland and nearby open country
SIZE: 16–20 in (41–51 cm)

The Red-shouldered Hawk keeps to cover for most of the time. It takes a wide variety of prey, including birds, small mammals, lizards, snakes, frogs, and toads. Its flight is active, with rapid wing beats followed by periods of gliding. It often calls while in the air.

race *lineatus*

ZONE-TAILED HAWK
Accipitridae/8 *Buteo albonotatus*
RANGE: SW USA, Central and South America
HABITAT: wooded and semi-open country
SIZE: 18–21 in (46–53 cm)

The sexes are similar in plumage, and immatures show copious white spotting below. Their prey include rodents, lizards, amphibians, and birds, which they catch with a rapid swoop. Zone-tailed Hawks are courageous defenders of nests and will swoop at, or even strike, people who come too close.

dark phase juv

pale phase

HAWAIIAN HAWK
Accipitridae/8 *Buteo solitarius*
RANGE: island of Hawaii
HABITAT: varied; especially in light woodland and edges of fields, generally from 2,000–5,000 ft (600–1,500 m), but usually with trees
SIZE: 16–18 in (41–46 cm)

One of Hawaii's many endemic breeding birds. There are 2 color phases. In the light phase, adults are dark brown above, with somewhat paler heads, and whitish below with rusty markings. Immatures are generally paler, except on the wings. Dark phase adult birds are blackish-brown below, with some pale feathering on the throat. Immatures are similar but with irregularly mottled and barred underparts.

race *kriderii*
"Krider's Hawk"

pale phase

race *borealis*

RED-TAILED HAWK
Accipitridae/8 *Buteo jamaicensis*
RANGE: North and Central America, Caribbean
HABITAT: extremely varied, but usually with some tree cover
SIZE: 16–18 in (41–46 cm)

Highly versatile in its hunting methods, the Red-tailed Hawk catches a wide range of prey, including mammals, birds, reptiles, and insects. There are about 14 races of the Red-tailed Hawk, varying in plumage and, to a certain extent, in size.

EURASIAN BUZZARD
Accipitridae/8 *Buteo buteo*
RANGE: Europe E across Asia to the Bering Sea
HABITAT: varied, but usually with some tree cover
SIZE: 20–22½ in (51–57 cm)

The Eurasian Buzzard shows more variation in plumage than any other European bird of prey. Pale forms are present in many populations and very frequent in some, resulting in a bewildering range of plumage. Many of these have white heads, underparts, and underwings.

light phase

dark phase

race *sancti-johannis*
dark phase

ROUGH-LEGGED BUZZARD
Accipitridae/8 *Buteo lagopus*
RANGE: N Europe E across Asia, North America
HABITAT: mainly Arctic or subarctic open terrain
SIZE: 20–24 in (51–61 cm)

The Rough-legged Buzzard is variable in plumage, with several races across its circumpolar range. Its numbers are closely governed by the abundance of small rodents, its main prey. Roughlegged Buzzards are highly migratory, wintering far to the south of their breeding range.

race *lagopus* typical

LONG-LEGGED BUZZARD
Accipitridae/8 *Buteo rufinus*
RANGE: C and SE Europe E to C Asia, N Africa
HABITAT: mainly lowland, open country, often arid or semi-arid
SIZE: 20–26 in (51–66 cm)

The Long-legged Buzzard's plumage is very variable, with both dark and pale phases and intermediates. At close quarters, juvenile birds show pale margins to the feathers on their dark upperparts and are less uniform in appearance than the adults.

typical

race *augur*
"Augur Buzzard"

typical

JACKAL BUZZARD
Accipitridae/8 *Buteo rufofuscus*
RANGE: E and S Africa
HABITAT: varied; mainly hilly country
SIZE: 18–21 in (46–53 cm)

There are 2 principal races, differing in the color of their underparts. Jackal Buzzards fly with markedly raised wings and a rocking, side-to-side action. They hunt both on the wing and from perches. They breed either on cliffs or in trees, using their large stick nests for several years in succession.

race *rufufoscus*

dark phase

typical

GUIANA CRESTED EAGLE
Accipitridae/8 *Morphnus guianensis*
RANGE: Honduras S to N Argentina
HABITAT: tropical lowland forest
SIZE: 31–35 in (79–89 cm)

Uncommon throughout its range, the Guiana Crested Eagle occurs in 2 forms, the less common dark phase having once been regarded as a separate species. The broad, rounded wings and long tail equip the bird for maneuvering around forest trees in pursuit of prey.

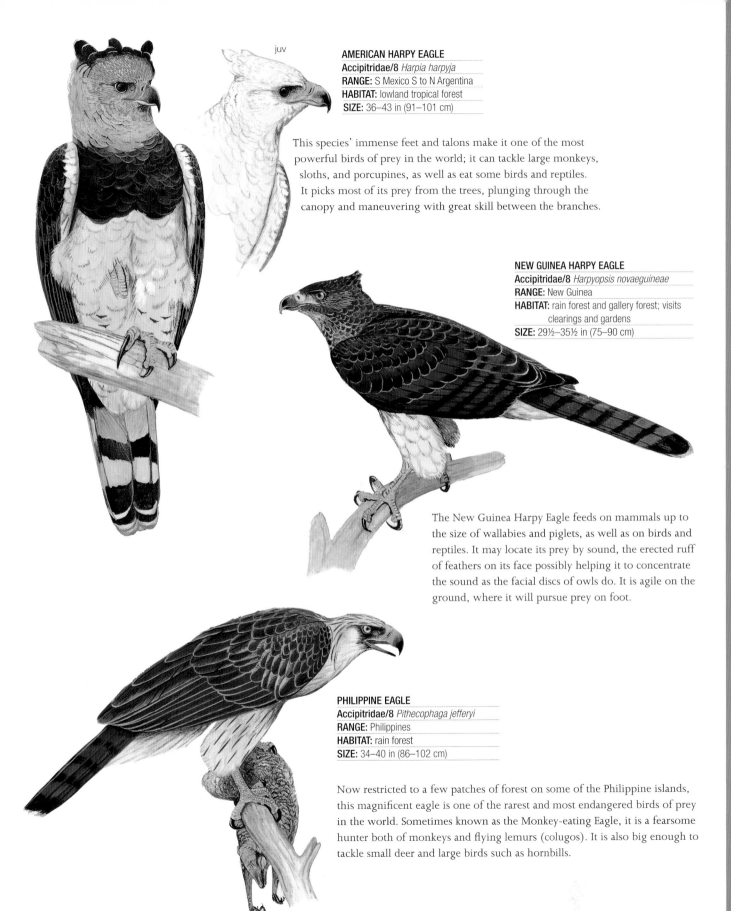

juv

AMERICAN HARPY EAGLE
Accipitridae/8 *Harpia harpyja*
RANGE: S Mexico S to N Argentina
HABITAT: lowland tropical forest
SIZE: 36–43 in (91–101 cm)

This species' immense feet and talons make it one of the most powerful birds of prey in the world; it can tackle large monkeys, sloths, and porcupines, as well as eat some birds and reptiles. It picks most of its prey from the trees, plunging through the canopy and maneuvering with great skill between the branches.

NEW GUINEA HARPY EAGLE
Accipitridae/8 *Harpyopsis novaeguineae*
RANGE: New Guinea
HABITAT: rain forest and gallery forest; visits
clearings and gardens
SIZE: 29½–35½ in (75–90 cm)

The New Guinea Harpy Eagle feeds on mammals up to the size of wallabies and piglets, as well as on birds and reptiles. It may locate its prey by sound, the erected ruff of feathers on its face possibly helping it to concentrate the sound as the facial discs of owls do. It is agile on the ground, where it will pursue prey on foot.

PHILIPPINE EAGLE
Accipitridae/8 *Pithecophaga jefferyi*
RANGE: Philippines
HABITAT: rain forest
SIZE: 34–40 in (86–102 cm)

Now restricted to a few patches of forest on some of the Philippine islands, this magnificent eagle is one of the rarest and most endangered birds of prey in the world. Sometimes known as the Monkey-eating Eagle, it is a fearsome hunter both of monkeys and flying lemurs (colugos). It is also big enough to tackle small deer and large birds such as hornbills.

juv

GOLDEN EAGLE
Accipitridae/9 *Aquila chrysaetos*
RANGE: Europe, N Asia, North America, parts of N Africa
and Middle East
HABITAT: mountains, plains, sea coasts
SIZE: 30–39 in (76–99 cm)

Golden Eagles usually build their nest of branches on cliffs or crags, or in trees. Most pairs have several nests, which they use roughly in rotation. If it is re-used over many successive seasons a nest can grow to a huge size: up to 6 ft (2 m) high and 5 ft (1.5 m) across.

♂

SECRETARY BIRD
Sagittariidae *Sagittarius serpentarius*
RANGE: sub-Saharan Africa
HABITAT: open savanna and grassland
SIZE: 49–59 in (125–150 cm)

Secretary Birds forage for prey on the ground, striding along with a deliberate, measured tread, and are famous for their ability to immobilize and kill snakes. During courtship displays, the birds soar high above the ground, their long legs and tail projecting behind them, and utter weird groaning calls.

COMMON CARACARA
Falconidae/1 *Polyborus plancus*
RANGE: Florida and SW USA, Central, and South America
HABITAT: open or semi-open country
SIZE: 20–24 in (51–61 cm)

The Common Caracara is capable of killing a wide variety of prey, including small mammals, young or disabled birds, fish, frogs, insects, and other invertebrates, as well as being a scavenger and carrion-eater.

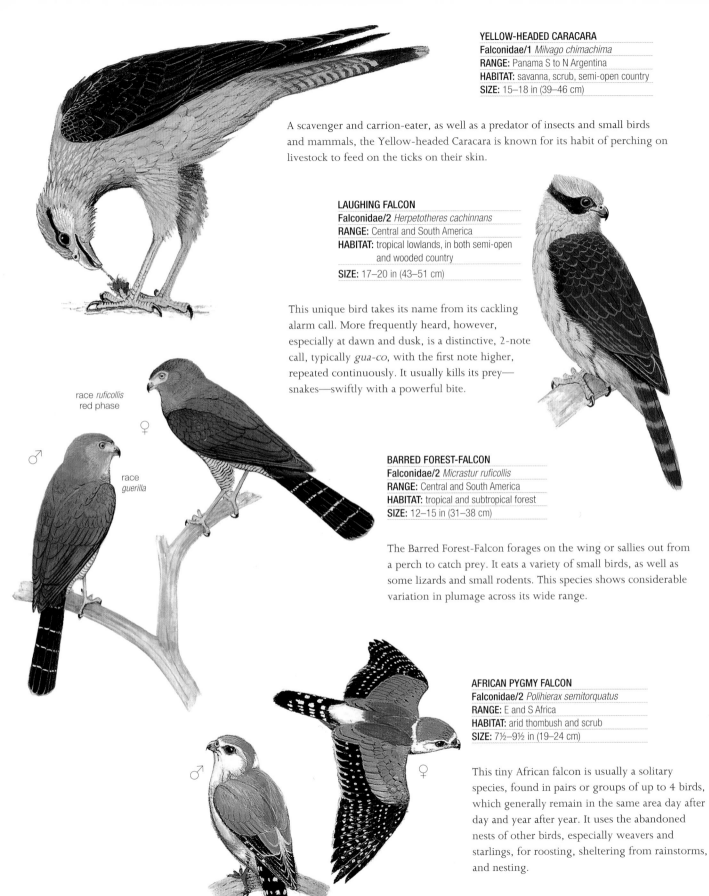

YELLOW-HEADED CARACARA
Falconidae/1 *Milvago chimachima*
RANGE: Panama S to N Argentina
HABITAT: savanna, scrub, semi-open country
SIZE: 15–18 in (39–46 cm)

A scavenger and carrion-eater, as well as a predator of insects and small birds and mammals, the Yellow-headed Caracara is known for its habit of perching on livestock to feed on the ticks on their skin.

LAUGHING FALCON
Falconidae/2 *Herpetotheres cachinnans*
RANGE: Central and South America
HABITAT: tropical lowlands, in both semi-open and wooded country
SIZE: 17–20 in (43–51 cm)

This unique bird takes its name from its cackling alarm call. More frequently heard, however, especially at dawn and dusk, is a distinctive, 2-note call, typically *gua-co*, with the first note higher, repeated continuously. It usually kills its prey—snakes—swiftly with a powerful bite.

race *ruficollis*
red phase

♀

♂

race *guerilla*

BARRED FOREST-FALCON
Falconidae/2 *Micrastur ruficollis*
RANGE: Central and South America
HABITAT: tropical and subtropical forest
SIZE: 12–15 in (31–38 cm)

The Barred Forest-Falcon forages on the wing or sallies out from a perch to catch prey. It eats a variety of small birds, as well as some lizards and small rodents. This species shows considerable variation in plumage across its wide range.

AFRICAN PYGMY FALCON
Falconidae/2 *Polihierax semitorquatus*
RANGE: E and S Africa
HABITAT: arid thornbush and scrub
SIZE: 7½–9½ in (19–24 cm)

♂

♀

This tiny African falcon is usually a solitary species, found in pairs or groups of up to 4 birds, which generally remain in the same area day after day and year after year. It uses the abandoned nests of other birds, especially weavers and starlings, for roosting, sheltering from rainstorms, and nesting.

COLLARED FALCONET
Falconidae/2 *Microhierax caerulescens*
RANGE: India SE to Malaysia
HABITAT: forests with open clearings
SIZE: 5½–7½ in (14–19 cm)

This tiny falcon's main prey is insects, and it frequently catches them in flight by darting out from the perch and returning to eat them on its perch. It is often known as the Red-legged Falconet— an inappropriate name, as the bird has only some chestnut feathering on its black legs.

race *sparverius*

race *sparveroides*
red-chested phase

AMERICAN KESTREL
Falconidae/2 *Falco sparverius*
RANGE: breeds SE Alaska and Canada S to extreme
S South America; N birds winter S to Panama
HABITAT: open country: mountain meadows, grassland, deserts,
open woodland, agricultural land, and urban areas
SIZE: 9–12 in (23–31 cm)

One of the brightest-plumaged of all the kestrels, the American Kestrel is unusual in that, even as juveniles, the sexes have distinct plumages. There is considerable geographical variation in size and in plumage.

COMMON KESTREL
Falconidae/2 *Falco tinnunculus*
RANGE: breeds most of Europe, Africa, Asia; N and E birds winter
from Britain S to S Africa and N India S to Sri Lanka
HABITAT: diverse, from moors to tropical savanna and urban
areas; avoids tundra, dense forest, deserts
SIZE: 12–14 in (31–35 cm)

The Common Kestrel is best known as a hunter of small mammals, hovering for prolonged periods on fast-beating wings as it scans the ground. When prey is spotted, the bird descends in a series of swoops, before finally dropping to snatch it in its feet. It also hunts from a high perch and will sometimes snatch birds in midair.

MAURITIUS KESTREL
Falconidae/2 *Falco punctatus*
RANGE: SW corner of Mauritius
HABITAT: a few areas of dense evergreen forest in rugged gorges and escarpments
SIZE: 11–13 in (28–33 cm)

A remarkable conservation success story, although still vulnerable. Its rather short, rounded wings do not equip the Mauritius Kestrel well for hovering, but give it great maneuverability in the forest canopy.

AUSTRALIAN KESTREL
Falconidae/2 *Falco cenchroides*
RANGE: Australia, Tasmania, New Guinea
HABITAT: open and lightly wooded country, farmland, urban areas
SIZE: 12–14 in (30–35 cm)

This kestrel, also known as the Nankeen Kestrel, has adapted well to artificial landscapes. It hunts in the usual kestrel fashion, including hovering.

NORTHERN HOBBY
Falconidae/2 *Falco subbuteo*
RANGE: breeds Europe, NW Africa, Asia; winters in E and S Africa S to Cape Province, and S to N India and S China
HABITAT: mainly semi-open country with some tree cover
SIZE: 12–14 in (31–36 cm)

The Northern Hobby is a long-winged, aerial hunter. It feeds mainly on flying insects, such as dragonflies, and on birds.

pale phase

ELEONORA'S FALCON
Falconidae/2 *Falco eleonorae*
RANGE: breeds Canary Islands, Morocco, and Mediterranean islands; winters chiefly in Madagascar
HABITAT: breeds on sea cliffs and adjacent rocky tablelands; outside breeding season in wider range of habitats
SIZE: 14–16 in (36–40 cm)

Eleonora's Falcon occurs in 2 main color phases, a pale phase and a dark phase. It breeds in colonies, usually of 5–20 birds, timing the rearing of its young to coincide with the millions of small birds crossing the Mediterranean.

APLOMADO FALCON
Falconidae/2 *Falco femoralis*
RANGE: breeds Mexico to extreme S South America; birds from extreme N and S winter to S and N respectively
HABITAT: open or lightly wooded country
SIZE: 14½–18 in (37–45 cm)

Until the beginning of the 20th century, the Aplomado Falcon bred regularly in southwestern USA, but it became increasingly rare.

GYR FALCON
Falconidae/2 *Falco rusticolus*
RANGE: Greenland, Iceland, and Arctic Europe, Asia, and North America
HABITAT: sea cliffs, uplands, other open country
SIZE: 20–23 in (51–58 cm)

pale phase   gray phase

PEREGRINE FALCON
Falconidae/2 *Falco peregrinus*
RANGE: almost cosmopolitan; absent from Sahara, C Asia, most of South America
HABITAT: mountains, uplands, sea cliffs
SIZE: 14–19 in (36–48 cm)

To many, the Peregrine Falcon is the ultimate predatory bird—a robustly built, fast-flying falcon that typically kills its prey in a spectacular diving stoop.

The largest and most powerful of the falcons, capable of taking prey the size of grouse, ducks, and sometimes even larger birds like buzzards. It occasionally kills mammals as large as hares.

Game birds

AUSTRALIAN BRUSH-TURKEY
Megapodiidae *Alectura lathami*
RANGE: coastal and subcoastal E Australia from Cape York to
mid-New South Wales
HABITAT: rain forest, thick scrub, well-vegetated urban areas
SIZE: 27½ in (70 cm)

The Australian Brush-Turkey uses its feet to rake up
foods from the forest floor, including insects and other
invertebrates, fruits, and seeds. A powerful runner, it flies
only to escape danger or to roost in trees at night.

MALLEE FOWL
Megapodiidae *Leipoa ocellata*
RANGE: inland S Australia, extending to coast in
some areas
HABITAT: eucalypt scrub and woodland (mallee)
SIZE: 23½ in (60 cm)

In late winter and spring, the male and female
build the nest mound of moist leaf litter and
sand, with an egg chamber of wet, rotting litter.
The male maintains a constant temperature of
91.4°F (33°C) in the mound by testing it with the
inside of his bill; he opens or closes the mound to
release or retain the heat produced by fermentation or, later
in the season, to expose or protect it from the fierce sun.

chick emerging from
nest mound

PLAIN CHACHALACA
Cracidae *Ortalis vetula*
RANGE: S Texas to W Nicaragua and NW Costa Rica;
introduced to islands off Georgia
HABITAT: lowland semi-arid scrub forest, thickets, forests
SIZE: 18 in (46 cm)

The Plain Chachalaca is usually located by its call—a
raucous repetition of its name which is taken up by
others in a harsh, rhythmic chorus. In the breeding
season, the pinkish-gray bare skin on each side of
the male's chin turns bright red.

CRESTED GUAN
Cracidae *Penelope purpurascens*
RANGE: Mexico to W Ecuador and N Venezuela
HABITAT: humid forest, scrub, hilly areas up to
3,300 ft (1,000 m)
SIZE: 36 in (91 cm)

Crested Guans are often seen in pairs, walking or running along branches to feed. Although primarily tree-dwelling, they sometimes descend to the ground to eat fallen fruit. In the dry season the males perform a display in which they fly slowly with wings beating rapidly to produce a loud, drumming rattle.

NOCTURNAL CURASSOW
Cracidae *Nothocrax urumutum*
RANGE: NW South America to E Peru
HABITAT: forests
SIZE: 26 in (66 cm)

This species sings on both moonlit and dark nights from high in the forest with a soft dovelike cooing, followed by a pause and a guttural hoot. Its odd specific name, urumutum, is derived from a Brazilian Indian name based on its song. It will descend to the forest floor to feed on ripe fallen fruit, but always retreats to the trees for safety.

red phase

dark phase

GREAT CURASSOW
Cracidae *Crax rubra*
RANGE: Mexico to W Ecuador and W Colombia
HABITAT: humid to semi-arid, undisturbed mature
forest; also scrub
SIZE: 38 in (97 cm)

The Great Curassow normally feeds on the forest floor, but retires to the upper canopy for cover. The song of the male is a long, low, booming sound with a ventriloquial quality. The female is variable in color, the red phase and dark phase being most common.

COMMON TURKEY

Meleagrididae *Meleagris gallopavo*
RANGE: USA, Mexico
HABITAT: forests, clearings, brushland
SIZE: male 48 in (122 cm); female 34 in (86 cm)

Common Turkeys are opportunists with broad tastes; they will eat seeds, nuts, berries, green foliage, and small animals such as grasshoppers and even lizards and salamanders. The birds generally forage on the ground, although they are strong fliers over short distances and roost in trees at night.

SPRUCE GROUSE

Tetraonidae *Dendragapus canadensis*
RANGE: W Alaska to E Canada and N USA
HABITAT: boggy areas in conifer forest with carpets of moss
SIZE: 15–17 in (38–43 cm)

The Spruce Grouse feeds on the buds, twigs, and needles of coniferous trees in winter but switches to berries and other fruits in summer. The male displays energetically in the mating season. Inflating the red skin above his eyes and uttering low-pitched hoots, he struts and whirrs his wings to attract a female.

WILLOW GROUSE

Tetraonidae *Lagopus lagopus*
RANGE: N hemisphere at latitudes above 50° N
HABITAT: treeless tundra, moors, heaths, Arctic willow bogs
SIZE: 14½–16½ in (37–42 cm)

Populations of the Willow Grouse undergo regular 3–10-year cycles, depending on locality. Birds of the British and Irish race *L. l. scoticus*, known as the Red Grouse, which was formerly considered a separate species, do not molt into white plumage like other races.

WESTERN CAPERCAILLIE
Tetraonidae *Tetrao urogallus*
RANGE: N Europe, including Scotland
HABITAT: mature conifer forest
SIZE: male 34 in (87 cm); female 23½ in (60 cm)

In spring, the males perform a dramatic courtship ritual. With tail fanned out and throat feathers puffed up, a male challenges rivals with a song consisting of a series of clicking notes, which accelerate until they run together into a soft drum-roll sound and end in a noise like a cork popping from a wine bottle.

gray phase

RUFFED GROUSE
Tetraonidae *Bonasa umbellus*
RANGE: Alaska, Canada, N USA
HABITAT: deciduous and conifer forest, abandoned farmland
SIZE: 17 in (43 cm)

This game bird is notable for its courtship display. The monogamous male lays claim to a thick stand of aspens and attracts a mate by beating his wings to produce a hollow, accelerating drumming. At the same time, he raises his head crest, extends his neck ruff, and fans his tail to its full extent.

GREATER PRAIRIE CHICKEN
Tetraonidae *Tympanuchus cupido*
RANGE: SC Canada to Gulf of Mexico
HABITAT: grassland
SIZE: 17–19 in (43–48 cm)

Once common on the American prairies, this large grouse has become increasingly rare. In spring the males gather at traditional "booming grounds"—communal courtship arenas—where they inflate their orange neck pouches and perform spectacular stamping dances, accompanied by loud booming cries.

gray phase

♂

♀

CALIFORNIA QUAIL
Phasianidae/1 *Lophortyx californica*
RANGE: British Columbia S to Baja California
HABITAT: brush and grassland, irrigated and fallow arable land
SIZE: 9½–11 in (24–28 cm)

The California Quail forms winter flocks, or coveys, of 200–300 birds. These usually forage together on foot for seeds. The birds rarely fly unless alarmed but, unlike other quails, they roost in dense trees or shrubs rather than on the ground.

race *virginianus*

♂   ♀

race *ridgwayi*
"Masked Bobwhite"

♂

NORTHERN BOBWHITE
Phasianidae/1 *Colinus virginianus*
RANGE: E USA to SW USA and Mexico
HABITAT: open pine forests, clearings
SIZE: 8–11 in (20–28 cm)

This is a social species that forms flocks, or coveys, of 15–30 birds in fall. The birds feed together on the seeds and fruits of grasses, shrubs, and crops. Each covey roosts on the ground in a tight bunch with heads pointing out, and explodes into the air if flushed.

♂   ♀

MONTEZUMA QUAIL
Phasianidae/1 *Cyrtonyx montezumae*
RANGE: S Arizona, New Mexico, Texas, N Mexico
HABITAT: open, grassy, pine, juniper, and oak woodland
SIZE: 7 in (18 cm)

The handsome Montezuma Quail is able to tolerate long periods without rain. Its stout legs are well adapted for digging up moisture-rich bulbs and the tubers of nut grasses; it also eats seeds and insects. Its call is a gentle whistle.

SEE-SEE PARTRIDGE
Phasianidae/2 *Ammoperdix griseogularis*
RANGE: Central Asia, Iran to NW India
HABITAT: arid foothills and semi-desert
SIZE: 9½ in (24 cm)

The See-see Partridge forages in flocks of up to 20 individuals. Single birds are rarely seen except during the mating season, when each male establishes and defends his own breeding territory. The mating system is basically monogamous, but several females may lay their eggs in the same nest.

HIMALAYAN SNOWCOCK
Phasianidae/2 *Tetraogallus himalayensis*
RANGE: E Afghanistan E to W Nepal, NW China
HABITAT: high-altitude mountain slopes
SIZE: 20–22 in (51–56 cm)

The Himalayan Snowcock's predominantly gray and white plumage blends in with the landscape of gray rock and snow. It often has to cover a lot of ground to find enough to eat and may range over an area of up to 250 acres (1 square km) each day.

ROCK PARTRIDGE
Phasianidae/2 *Alectoris graeca*
RANGE: European Alps, Bosnia, Greece, Bulgaria
HABITAT: rocky heaths, pastures, grassland
SIZE: 13–15 in (34–38 cm)

Like many partridges, the Rock Partridge has a variable diet: essentially vegetarian in adulthood, the breeding females and chicks eat quantities of insects, spiders, and other small animals. Rock Partridges are monogamous and often pair for life.

race *castaneiventer*

race *melanogaster*

race *cranchii*

RED-NECKED FRANCOLIN
Phasianidae/2 *Francolinus afer*
RANGE: C and S Africa
HABITAT: forest clearings with brushwood
SIZE: 12–16 in (30–41 cm)

The Red-necked Francolin is a very variable species, with as many as 18 races, found throughout much of Africa south of the Equator. The mated pairs tend to remain within their breeding territories throughout the year, suggesting they mate for life.

INDIAN GRAY FRANCOLIN
Phasianidae/2 *Francolinus pondicerianus*
RANGE: E Iran, India, Sri Lanka
HABITAT: dry plains, thorny scrub
SIZE: 13 in (33 cm)

Its ability to tolerate dry conditions has made the Indian Gray Francolin one of the commonest resident game birds in southern Asia. The breeding season in India is prolonged and nests containing eggs have been recorded in every month of the year.

♂

"Montana" phase

♂

GRAY PARTRIDGE
Phasianidae/2 *Perdix perdix*
RANGE: W and C Europe
HABITAT: open country, farmland
SIZE: 12 in (30 cm)

Originally a bird of open grassland and steppe, the Gray Partridge has adapted well to farmland. Outside the breeding season the birds associate in family flocks, or coveys, but in late winter the breeding adults form monogamous pairs. The "Montana" variety, illustrated along with a more typical adult male, has far more chestnut on its breast and belly.

LONG-BILLED WOOD PARTRIDGE
Phasianidae/2 *Rhizothera longirostris*
RANGE: Malaysia, Sumatra, W Borneo
HABITAT: dry forest, especially bamboo
SIZE: 14 in (36 cm)

This large tropical partridge lives at altitudes of up to 4,000 ft (1,200 m) in remote, dense upland forest, particularly in areas of thick bamboo. This, coupled with its extreme wariness, means that it is rarely seen—although it will occasionally give away its location by calling loudly at night.

MADAGASCAR PARTRIDGE
Phasianidae/2 *Margaroperdix madagarensis*
RANGE: Madagascar
HABITAT: secondary scrub and grassland
SIZE: 12 in (30 cm)

The male Madagascar Partridge is much brighter than the female, indicating an emphasis on courtship that is typical of polygamous species. It often forages on cultivated ground, and in rice fields, where it probably eats rice grain as well as weed seeds and insects.

COMMON HILL-PARTRIDGE
Phasianidae/2 *Arborophila torqueola*
RANGE: N and E India, S Tibet
HABITAT: evergreen forest and scrub
SIZE: 10 in (25 cm)

The Common Hill-Partridge is usually found at altitudes of 5,000–9,000 ft (1,500–2,700 m), in pairs or groups of up to 10 birds. The male has a distinctive black throat pattern that is echoed in reduced form in the plumage of the female.

CRESTED WOOD-PARTRIDGE
Phasianidae/2 *Rollulus roulroul*
RANGE: S Myanmar, Thailand, Malaysia, Sumatra, and Borneo
HABITAT: tropical forest
SIZE: 10 in (25 cm)

The Crested Wood-Partridge has richly colored plumage and, in the male, a red, brushlike crest. It appears to eat more animal material than most partridges.

STONE PARTRIDGE
Phasianidae/2 *Ptilopachus petrosus*
RANGE: Africa, Senegal to Kenya
HABITAT: rocky hills
SIZE: 10 in (25 cm)

This species is well adapted to the arid conditions of areas such as the sub-Saharan Sahel region. However, it prefers dense vegetation among boulder-strewn rocky hills.

CEYLON SPURFOWL
Phasianidae/2 *Galloperdix bicalcarata*
RANGE: Sri Lanka
HABITAT: moist upland forest to 5,000 ft (1,500 m)
SIZE: 13–14 in (33–36 cm)

The Ceylon Spurfowl lives in the dense tropical forests that mantle the foothills and mountains of Sri Lanka, feeding on a variety of seeds, tubers, and berries.

COMMON QUAIL
Phasianidae/3 *Coturnix coturnix*
RANGE: Eurasia
HABITAT: open grassland
SIZE: 7 in (18 cm)

The Common Quail is well known from its distinctive trisyllabic call. It usually forages close to the ground beneath the cover of vegetation, and will run when it is alarmed rather than take flight.

melanistic hybrid   race *colchicus*   typical hybrid

typical hybrid

COMMON PHEASANT
Phasianidae/4 *Phasianus colchicus*
RANGE: Asia; introduced to Europe, Australia, and North America
HABITAT: lowland farmland, woodland, upland scrub
SIZE: male 29½–35½ in (75–90 cm); female 10½–25 in (52–64 cm)

The well-camouflaged females can be hard to spot, but the colorful males are a frequent and conspicuous sight on open farmland.

COMMON PEAFOWL
Phasianidae/4 *Pavo cristatus*
RANGE: Sri Lanka, India, Pakistan, Himalayas; introduced worldwide
HABITAT: forests and semi-open country with streams
SIZE: male 79–90 in (200–229 cm); female 34 in (86 cm)

The dramatic display of the male Common Peafowl (often known as the Peacock) is a familiar sight in parks and gardens throughout the world, where it has been widely introduced as an ornamental bird.

Cranes, rails, and bustards

WHITE-BREASTED MESITE
Mesitornithidae *Mesitornis variegata*
RANGE: 3 tiny areas in W Madagascar
HABITAT: undisturbed dry forest
SIZE: 10 in (25 cm)

All 3 species of mesite are found only in Madagascar and all are endangered. This thrush-sized bird scratches about for insects among the dead leaves that carpet the forest floor. It has been seen only in isolated pockets of remote forest.

race *sylvatica*

LITTLE BUTTONQUAIL
Turnicidae *Turnix sylvatica*
RANGE: S Spain, Africa, S and Southeast Asia, Indonesia, Philippines
HABITAT: dry grassland, scrub; sometimes crops
SIZE: 5–6 in (13–15 cm)

Buttonquails have the peculiar habit of slinking low on the ground and rocking backward and forward on their feet. Shy and secretive birds, the larger female advertises with a low, cooing call, dominates courtship, and mates with several males in succession.

QUAIL PLOVER
Turnicidae *Ortyxelos meiffrenii*
RANGE: a narrow band S of Sahara
HABITAT: very dry, sandy bush
SIZE: 6 in (15 cm)

Restricted to arid areas, the Quail Plover inhabits regions with enough rough, dry grasses to make it very difficult to see as it skulks secretively on the ground. When it flies, it reveals a distinctive black-and-white pattern on its wings.

PLAINS-WANDERER
Pedionomidae *Pedionomus torquatus*
RANGE: inland SE Australia
HABITAT: sparse native grassland
SIZE: 6–6½ in (15–17 cm)

The Plains-wanderer has declined in numbers, due to conversion of much of its habitat to cropland and dense pasture. When danger threatens, it prefers to freeze in a squatting position rather than take to the air.

COMMON CRANE
Gruidae *Grus grus*
RANGE: N temperate Eurasia; winters S to N Africa,
India, and Southeast Asia
HABITAT: breeds in open forest swamps and moorland
bogs; winters in shallow wetlands
SIZE: 43–47 in (110–120 cm)

In its dancing display, performed not only in courtship but also by small groups of birds, the birds walk round in circles, bowing, bobbing, pirouetting, and stopping, bending to pick up small objects and toss them over their heads. All these rituals are interspersed with graceful jumps high into the air.

juv

chick

race *tabida*
"Greater Sandhill Crane"

rust-stained

juv

SANDHILL CRANE
Gruidae *Grus canadensis*
RANGE: breeds NE Siberia, Alaska, Canada,
N USA; winters S USA to C Mexico;
small resident populations in Florida and
Mississippi, Cuba
HABITAT: tundra, marshes, grassland, fields
SIZE: 42 in (107 cm)

Sandhill Cranes may congregate at migration stopovers or on the wintering grounds in flocks of hundreds, creating an extraordinary din with their grating, rattling, trumpetlike calls. They are ground-gleaners, foraging for a wide variety of plants, aquatic invertebrates, insects, worms, frogs, and small mammals. There are 5 races, varying in size.

juv

WHOOPING CRANE
Gruidae *Grus americana*
RANGE: breeds C Canada; winters coastal Texas
HABITAT: breeds on muskeg and prairie pools; prairie and stubble
fields on migration; winters on coastal marshes
SIZE: 51 in (130 cm)

In flight, adult Whooping Cranes show black outer flight feathers that contrast with their otherwise white plumage. The courtship ceremony involves elaborate dances, and the bird's most common call is a whooping or trumpeting *ker-loo*. It is an endangered species.

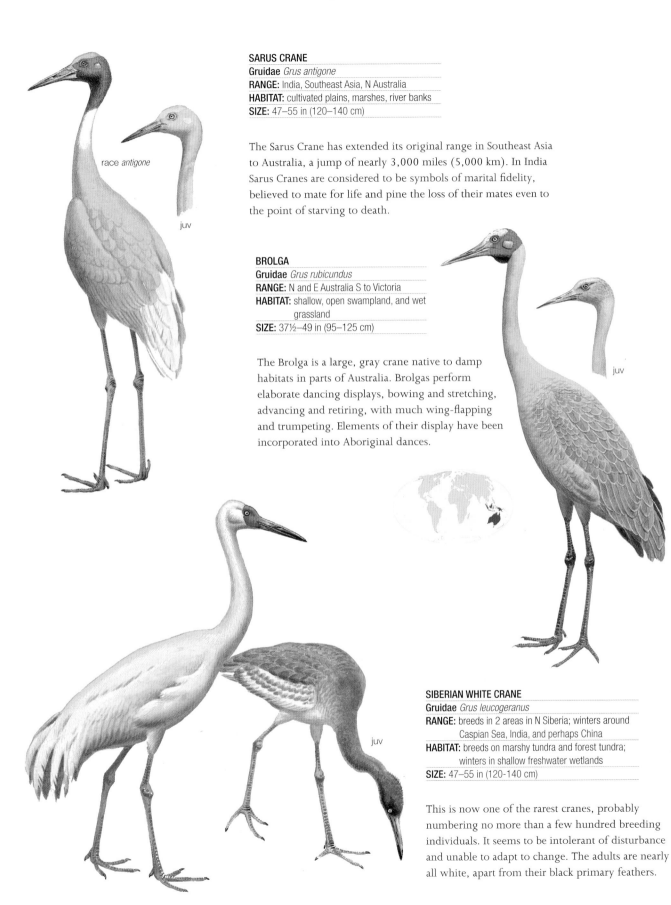

SARUS CRANE
Gruidae *Grus antigone*
RANGE: India, Southeast Asia, N Australia
HABITAT: cultivated plains, marshes, river banks
SIZE: 47–55 in (120–140 cm)

The Sarus Crane has extended its original range in Southeast Asia to Australia, a jump of nearly 3,000 miles (5,000 km). In India Sarus Cranes are considered to be symbols of marital fidelity, believed to mate for life and pine the loss of their mates even to the point of starving to death.

race *antigone*

juv

BROLGA
Gruidae *Grus rubicundus*
RANGE: N and E Australia S to Victoria
HABITAT: shallow, open swampland, and wet grassland
SIZE: 37½–49 in (95–125 cm)

The Brolga is a large, gray crane native to damp habitats in parts of Australia. Brolgas perform elaborate dancing displays, bowing and stretching, advancing and retiring, with much wing-flapping and trumpeting. Elements of their display have been incorporated into Aboriginal dances.

juv

juv

SIBERIAN WHITE CRANE
Gruidae *Grus leucogeranus*
RANGE: breeds in 2 areas in N Siberia; winters around Caspian Sea, India, and perhaps China
HABITAT: breeds on marshy tundra and forest tundra; winters in shallow freshwater wetlands
SIZE: 47–55 in (120-140 cm)

This is now one of the rarest cranes, probably numbering no more than a few hundred breeding individuals. It seems to be intolerant of disturbance and unable to adapt to change. The adults are nearly all white, apart from their black primary feathers.

DEMOISELLE CRANE
Gruidae *Anthropoides virgo*
RANGE: breeds SE Europe and C Asia; winters NE Africa,
India E to Myanmar
HABITAT: breeds on marshes and drier steppes; winters
on open wetlands and agricultural land
SIZE: 35½–39 in (90–100 cm)

juv

On migration, large numbers of these cranes regularly cross
high mountain ranges, including the Himalayas. Wintering
flocks can number many thousands and may cause damage to
arable crops before the harvest. After the harvest, the birds clean
up the spilt grain and take many invertebrates from the ground.

BLACK CROWNED CRANE
Gruidae *Balearica pavonina*
RANGE: Africa, from Senegal to C Ethiopia,
N Uganda, and NW Kenya
HABITAT: open swamps, marshes, grassland
SIZE: 43–51 in (110–130 cm)

A pair or small group of Black Crowned Cranes begin
their display by bowing several times toward one another.
Then, spreading their wings, they proceed to hop and prance,
jumping 3–6 ft (1–2 m) into the air and landing gently on
dangling feet.

juv

race *pavonina*

LIMPKIN
Aramidae *Aramus guarauna*
RANGE: SE USA, Antilles, S Mexico E of Andes
to N Argentina
HABITAT: marshes, open or wooded swamps,
mangroves
SIZE: 23–28 in (58–71 cm)

The Limpkin is a long-legged wading bird that is largely terrestrial
and makes only short, low flights. The call, often given at night,
consists of a variety of shrieks and screams, or melancholy wails and
cries. Limpkins walk with an undulating tread so that they appear to
be limping—hence their common name.

GRAY-WINGED TRUMPETER
Psophiidae *Psophia crepitans*
RANGE: Guianas, E Venezuela to W Ecuador,
N Peru, Brazil N of the Amazon
HABITAT: tropical rain forest
SIZE: 18–21 in (46–53 cm)

Sometimes known as the Common Trumpeter, this bird feeds on the rainforest floor and roosts in flocks of up to 20 individuals. It is largely terrestrial and a poor flier. Like the other members of the family, it utters a variety of booming and trumpeting calls—hence the common name for this group of birds.

GIANT WOOD RAIL
Rallidae *Eulabeornis ypecaha*
RANGE: Brazil, Paraguay, Uruguay, Argentina
HABITAT: wet river valleys with good cover
SIZE: 21 in (53 cm)

Like most rails, this species is a secretive, cautious bird. It feeds alone during the day, using its long bill to probe the soil and plant debris for small animals, but at night the birds often gather in small groups just before roosting and join in a chorus of loud wails and screams.

OKINAWA RAIL
Rallidae *Rallus okinawae*
RANGE: N Okinawa Island, S Japan
HABITAT: dense upland evergreen forest, near
swampy or grassy areas
SIZE: 11 in (28 cm)

Short-winged and effectively flightless, the endangered Okinawa Rail is typical of many species of rail that have evolved on islands. With no native predators to escape from, flight was unnecessary, so the birds abandoned it as a waste of energy.

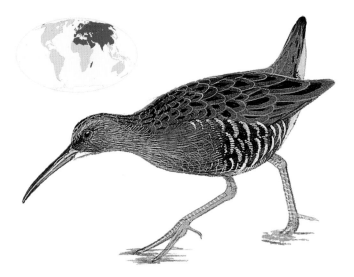

WATER RAIL
Rallidae *Rallus aquaticus*
RANGE: Eurasia, from Iceland to Japan; N Africa
HABITAT: marshes, swamps, wet meadows
SIZE: 11 in (28 cm)

The Water Rail is a shy, skulking bird, particularly in summer, but when the marshes freeze in winter it often emerges to forage across open ground. Although rarely seen during the breeding season, it is often heard then and at other times as it utters a wide range of loud, blood-curdling groans and piglike grunts and squeals, a process known as "sharming."

CLAPPER RAIL
Rallidae *Rallus longirostris*
RANGE: S Canada to N Peru; Caribbean islands
HABITAT: brackish estuaries and salt marsh,
especially with glasswort plants
SIZE: 12½–18 in (32–46 cm)

The species takes its common name from the loud clattering, cackling calls that sound like an old-fashioned clapper or rattle. It nests among salt marsh grasses where it is liable to lose whole clutches of eggs to a single high spring tide. The downy, black chicks, like the adults, can swim well and even submerge by grasping underwater plants with their feet when threatened.

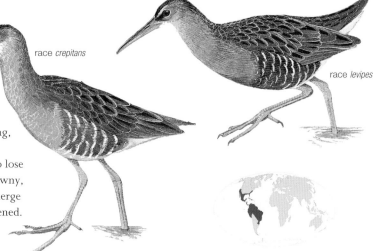

race *crepitans*

race *levipes*

INACCESSIBLE ISLAND RAIL
Rallidae *Atlantisia rogersi*
RANGE: Inaccessible Island (S Atlantic)
HABITAT: tussock grass
SIZE: 5 in (12.5 cm)

This rail, a mere 1¼ oz (35 g) in weight, is the world's smallest flightless bird. It lives rather like a small mammal, constructing runs and burrows through the roots of windy and exposed tussock grass meadows. It lives only on the uninhabited Inaccessible Island, which is almost 2,000 miles (3,200 km) from land both to east and west, and measures only 4½ sq miles (12 sq km).

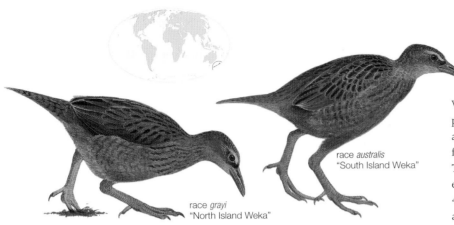

race *grayi*
"North Island Weka"

race *australis*
"South Island Weka"

WEKA

Rallidae *Gallirallus australis*
RANGE: New Zealand
HABITAT: scrubland, forest edge
SIZE: 21 in (53 cm)

Wekas are very large flightless rails with powerful bills and feet. They are inquisitive and omnivorous birds, eating grass, seeds, fruit, mice, birds, eggs, beetles, and snails. They frequently raid rubbish bins and even enter fowl runs to eat the chicks. There are 4 races, distinguished by plumage details and slight differences in size.

ZAPATA RAIL

Rallidae *Cyanolimnas cerverai*
RANGE: Cuba
HABITAT: dense, scrubby marshland
SIZE: 12 in (30 cm)

This little-known and critically endangered rail inhabits only one part of its Caribbean island home—the Zapata Swamp, southeast of Havana. It is a noisy bird with a loud croaking alarm note, making it surprisingly easy to locate. Owing to its unusually short wings, it is a poor flier.

YELLOW RAIL

Rallidae *Coturnicops noveboracensis*
RANGE: E Canada to Mexico; also Siberia, China, Japan
HABITAT: hay meadows and tussock grass near fresh running water
SIZE: 7 in (18 cm)

This is one of the few members of its family to occur in both the Old and New Worlds. The nestlings are very mobile by 2 days after hatching and are able to haul themselves through the vegetation using the well-developed claw on each wing. They are fed by the parents at first, but become independent when they are about 3 weeks old.

AMERICAN BLACK CRAKE

Rallidae *Laterallus jamaicensis*
RANGE: S North America, Caribbean, Central and South America to N Chile
HABITAT: marshes, among reeds and sedges
SIZE: 6½ in (17 cm)

race *murivagans*

race *jamaicensis*

Timid and unpredictable, this tiny bird is extremely hard to follow. At the slightest alarm it will leave its feeding area or nest and vanish noiselessly into the dense vegetation. If it has to flee, it never attempts a long run across open ground, but darts like lightning from one tussock to the next.

CORN CRAKE

Rallidae *Crex crex*

RANGE: Europe, W Asia, N Africa; winters in
sub-Saharan Africa

HABITAT: coarse grassland, hay meadows

SIZE: 10 in (25 cm)

In flight, Corn Crakes can be recognized by their rich chestnut
wing patches. Although their flight appears weak, fluttering,
and brief, with dangling legs, they can fly fast and strongly
when they migrate by night, traveling long distances to their
winter quarters as far away as South Africa.

SORA CRAKE

Rallidae *Porzana carolina*

RANGE: Canada to Venezuela and Peru, including
Caribbean islands

HABITAT: freshwater marshes, also wet meadows in prairie
regions; winters by salt and brackish waters

SIZE: 9 in (23 cm)

In its summer haunts the Sora Crake is a shy bird, rarely
seen and usually detected by its call: a loud, staccato *cuck*
accompanied by sneezing and whinnying sounds. It lays a large
clutch—usually 8–12 eggs—that is incubated by both sexes.

juv

NEW GUINEA FLIGHTLESS RAIL

Rallidae *Amaurornis ineptus*

RANGE: N and S New Guinea

HABITAT: mangrove swamps, bamboo thickets
at edges of rivers

SIZE: 14–15 in (36–38 cm)

This little-known flightless rail has a heavy, hatchet-like bill and strong
feet with which it can defend itself against most predators. It can run
swiftly and may also take to the branches of shrubs or trees to escape
danger. Like many other rails, it has a harsh voice, uttering an
aaah-aaah call rather like the squealing of a pig.

WATER COCK
Rallidae *Gallicrex cinerea*
RANGE: India to Japan, Philippines, Sulawesi (Celebes)
HABITAT: reedy swamps, paddy fields, sugar cane, brackish marshes
SIZE: 17 in (43 cm)

During the breeding season, the male of this largely vegetarian species can be distinguished from his mate by his almost black plumage and a vivid, blood-red frontal shield. In winter he loses this head ornamentation and becomes brown and gray, like the female.

PURPLE SWAMPHEN
Rallidae *Porphyrio porphyrio*
RANGE: Europe, Africa, S Asia, Southeast Asia to Australasia
HABITAT: reedbeds, scrubby marsh margins, tussock swamps
SIZE: 18 in (45 cm)

Largely vegetarian, the Purple Swamphen may become extremely numerous where food is plentiful; scores of birds can often be seen in the early morning when they climb the marsh vegetation to sunbathe as the first rays of dawn penetrate the mist.

race *porphyrio*

race *melanotus*

COMMON MOORHEN
Rallidae *Gallinula chloropus*
RANGE: throughout temperate and tropical Eurasia, Africa, North and South America; but not Australasia
HABITAT: small ponds, rivers, wet marshes
SIZE: 14 in (35 cm)

Possibly the most abundant species of rail in the world, the Common Moorhen is a poor flier and a barely adequate swimmer, preferring to search for food on foot with a delicate, high-stepping gait. Males are highly territorial. The chicks become independent very quickly and often help their parents feed a second brood.

race *chloropus*

mutual retreat display

TAKAHE
Rallidae *Porphyrio mantelli*
RANGE: New Zealand
HABITAT: mountain tussock grassland and (rarely) adjacent woodland
SIZE: 25 in (63 cm)

Once thought to be extinct but rediscovered in 1948, Takahes mate for life, nesting on the ground among tussocks. Introduced predators, such as stoats, take a heavy toll of the eggs and young, and the breeding success rate is low. Captive breeding, conservation, and predator control have helped to preserve the species, but the Takahe remains endangered.

GIANT COOT
Rallidae *Fulica gigantea*
RANGE: Peru, Chile, Bolivia, Argentina
HABITAT: mountain lakes, usually above 11,500 ft (3,500 m) in puna
SIZE: 23½ in (60 cm)

Instead of migrating to lower altitudes in winter, the Giant Coots congregate in small flocks around the widely scattered volcanic springs of the region, where they find pools that are kept clear of ice by the warm water and enough food to see them through until spring.

BLACK COOT
Rallidae *Fulica atra*
RANGE: widespread through Europe, Asia, Japan, and Australasia
HABITAT: large ponds, lakes and marshes, usually at low altitude
SIZE: 17 in (43 cm)

aggressive encounter

The most widespread and common of all the coots. During the spring breeding season, both sexes are extremely territorial. In winter Black Coots flock together in hundreds or even thousands. Juvenile birds are much paler than the adults, with lighter, duller legs, a grayish bill, and brown eyes, and lack the adults' white frontal shield.

SUNGREBE

Heliornithidae *Heliornis fulica*
RANGE: Mexico to Bolivia and Argentina
HABITAT: heavily forested lowland streams,
freshwater ponds and lagoons
SIZE: 11–12 in (28–30 cm)

The Sungrebe, or American Finfoot, frequents the slower backwaters of large streams. The nest is built in a bush over water. When the 2 chicks hatch, they are removed and carried by the male, both on the water and in the air, clamped tightly into pouches beneath each wing.

KAGU

Rhynochetidae *Rhynochetos jubatus*
RANGE: New Caledonia
HABITAT: dense forest
SIZE: 23½ in. (60 cm)

Threatened with extinction, the Kagu is another example of a ground-dwelling island bird that has been virtually wiped out by introduced predators and habitat loss. Both sexes have the flamboyant crest, and during courtship they dance round each other with wings spread to display the black, red and white bars on the slate-gray plumage.

display

SUNBITTERN

Eurypygidae *Eurypyga helias*
RANGE: S Mexico to Bolivia and C Brazil
HABITAT: forested streams, rivers, lakes
SIZE: 18 in (46 cm)

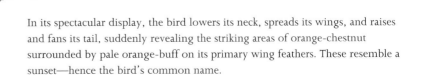

In its spectacular display, the bird lowers its neck, spreads its wings, and raises and fans its tail, suddenly revealing the striking areas of orange-chestnut surrounded by pale orange-buff on its primary wing feathers. These resemble a sunset—hence the bird's common name.

RED-LEGGED SERIEMA
Cariamidae *Cariama cristata*
RANGE: C and E Brazil S through Paraguay to N Argentina
HABITAT: mixed grassland and open scrub
SIZE: 27½ in (70 cm)

The Red-legged, or Crested, Seriema rarely flies, usually escaping danger by running rapidly with its head lowered. It spends all its time on the ground except for roosting and nesting low in trees and bushes. It has an omnivorous diet, which regularly includes small snakes.

courtship display

LITTLE BUSTARD
Otididae *Tetrax tetrax*
RANGE: S Europe, NW Africa E to C Asia
HABITAT: open areas with tall grasses, open
        scrubland, farmland
SIZE: 16–18 in (40–45 cm)

The displays of breeding males include surprisingly loud foot stamps, nasal *prrt* calls, and a hissing sound produced by the short, seventh primary feather when the bird flaps its wings and leaps 3–6 ft (1–2 m) vertically into the air, revealing his white breast and underwings. Outside the breeding season, the male's striking slate-gray chin and throat and black-and-white neck pattern are replaced by buff feathers with dark markings.

chicks

AUSTRALIAN BUSTARD
Otididae *Choriotis australis*
RANGE: N and inland Australia
HABITAT: open woodland, grassland, and shrub steppe
SIZE: 31½–47 in (80–120 cm)

The male Australian Bustard displays by inflating his neck with air, so that the long neck feathers spread out into a great fan, drooping his wings and raising his tail. He struts about in this posture with his head thrown back, uttering loud booming and roaring noises. He mates with any females attracted to his small display mound.

race *undulata*

race *macqueenii*

HOUBARA BUSTARD
Otididae *Chlamydotis undulata*
RANGE: Breeds Canary Islands, N Africa, Middle East, SW and C Asia; Asian breeders winter S to Arabia, Pakistan, Iran, and NW India
HABITAT: semi-desert, arid plains and steppes
SIZE: 21½–25½ in (55–65 cm)

Outside the breeding season, the Houbara Bustard lives in small flocks of 4–10 birds, occasionally more, which feed and roost together. It is an omnivorous bird.

GREAT BUSTARD
Otididae *Otis tarda*
RANGE: Morocco, parts of N, S, and C Europe, Turkey, parts of C Asia
HABITAT: extensive gently undulating grassy plains and steppes, lightly wooded areas, farmland
SIZE: 29½–41 in (75–105 cm)

This is the world's heaviest flying bird: a particularly large male can weigh as much as 40 lb (18 kg). Females are much lighter, at up to 11 lb (5 kg).

race *ruficrista*

CRESTED BUSTARD
Otididae *Eupodotis ruficrista*
RANGE: just S of Sahara, from N Senegal locally to W and E Sudan; E Africa, from Ethiopia to EC Tanzania; S Africa S to N South Africa
HABITAT: arid or semi-arid savanna
SIZE: 19½ in (50 cm)

Males perform dramatic "rocket flights," in which they call with increasing volume, then run forward and fly up vertically to about 100 ft (30 m), before dropping vertically.

race *vigorsii*

VIGORS' BUSTARD
Otididae *Eupodotis vigorsii*
RANGE: W South Africa, S Namibia
HABITAT: dry, open, stony Karoo, semi-desert and desert edge with scattered shrubs and short grass
SIZE: 22–23½ in (56–60 cm)

Also known as the Black-throated Bustard or Karoo Korhaan, Vigors' Bustard is very variable in plumage, particularly in the redness of the upperparts, the grayness of the underparts, and the overall intensity of color.

BENGAL FLORICAN
Otididae *Houbaropsis bengalensis*
RANGE: NE India, Nepal, Cambodia, S Vietnam
HABITAT: plains with tall grasses interspersed with scattered shrubs
SIZE: 26–27 in (66–68 cm)

The Bengal Florican is almost extinct. The female is slightly larger than the male and differs greatly in her plumage from the striking black-and-white male. Males perform courtship displays in which they leap 25–30 ft (8–10 m) into the air, emitting a strange, deep humming sound and uttering loud croaks.

Waders, shorebirds, and seabirds

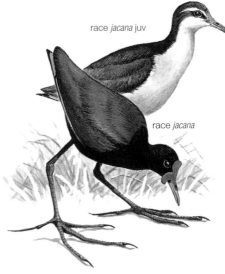

PHEASANT-TAILED JACANA
Jacanidae *Hydrophasianus chirurgus*
RANGE: India to S China, Southeast Asia, Indonesia;
    N population winters in S Asia
HABITAT: well-vegetated fresh water
SIZE: 12 in (31 cm) up to 23 in (58 cm)

non-breeding

Each female mates with 7–10 males in a season and
it is the males' responsibility to incubate the eggs. If
disturbed, a male may remove the eggs to a safer spot
by pressing each one between his throat and breast and
walking backward over the vegetation.

race *jacana* juv

race *hypomelaena*

WATTLED JACANA
Jacanidae *Jacana jacana*
RANGE: Panama S to C Argentina; Trinidad
HABITAT: tropical freshwater ponds, marshes,
    streams with emergent vegetation
SIZE: 8–9 in (20–23 cm)

Female Wattled Jacanas mate with more
than one male in each season and compete
vigorously with one another. Since the males
incubate and care for the young, one female
may even destroy the eggs of a successful rival
in order to gain access to a male.

race *jacana*

GREATER PAINTED-SNIPE
Rostratulidae *Rostratula benghalensis*
RANGE: Africa, Asia, and Australia
HABITAT: well-vegetated freshwater wetlands,
    including marshes, paddy fields
SIZE: 6½–9 in (17–23 cm)

When feeding out in the open, this wading bird will freeze
motionless if danger threatens, holding its position until the threat
has passed. The female is both larger and more brightly colored than
the male. She calls, a soft koht-koht-koht, at dusk and at night, often
while in flight.

CRAB PLOVER
Dromadidae *Dromas ardeola*
RANGE: coasts of Indian Ocean; breeds Gulf of Oman, Gulf of Aden, and Red Sea
HABITAT: sandy beaches and coastal dimes
SIZE: 15–16 in (38–41 cm)

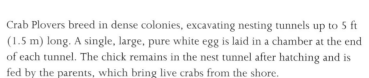

Crab Plovers breed in dense colonies, excavating nesting tunnels up to 5 ft (1.5 m) long. A single, large, pure white egg is laid in a chamber at the end of each tunnel. The chick remains in the nest tunnel after hatching and is fed by the parents, which bring live crabs from the shore.

PALEARCTIC OYSTERCATCHER
Haematopodidae *Haematopus ostralegus*
RANGE: breeds Eurasia; winters S to Africa and Indian Ocean
HABITAT: breeds on coasts and near inland fresh waters; winters only on coasts
SIZE: 16–18 in (40–46 cm)

Like that of other oystercatchers, the stout orange bill of the Palearctic Oystercatcher is triangular in cross-section and reinforced so that it does not bend easily. Outside the breeding season the adults develop a white neck collar, making them similar to an immature bird in its first winter.

AMERICAN BLACK OYSTERCATCHER
Haematopodidae *Haematopus bachmani*
RANGE: Pacific coast of North America, from Alaska to Baja California
HABITAT: rocky coasts and islands, occasionally sandy beaches
SIZE: 15 in (38 cm)

Oystercatchers have loud, piercing calls, which can be heard above the sound of crashing surf, facilitating communication between individuals. Young birds are able to fly in about 35 days but associate with their parents for up to a year, learning the feeding techniques needed to open molluscs and crab shells.

IBISBILL
Ibidorhynchidae *Ibidorhyncha struthersii*
RANGE: Central S Asia
HABITAT: stony, upland river valleys
SIZE: 15–16 in (38–41 cm)

The bold plumage is common to both sexes. The Ibisbill haunts remote mountain regions, where it uses its bill to probe among riverbed stones and rake through gravel to find small fish and invertebrates. During courtship, the rear of the black cap is raised in display to form a slight crest.

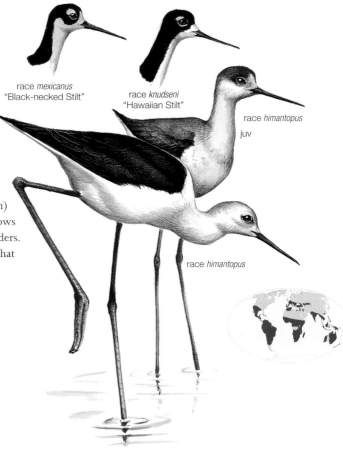

race *mexicanus*
"Black-necked Stilt"

race *knudseni*
"Hawaiian Stilt"

race *himantopus*
juv

race *himantopus*

BLACK-WINGED STILT
Recurvirostridae *Himantopus himantopus*
RANGE: worldwide in tropics, subtropics, and warm temperate latitudes
HABITAT: coastal and inland wetlands
SIZE: 14–16 in (35–40 cm)

The long, bright pink legs of this slender wader extend 7 in (18 cm) beyond the tail when the bird takes to the wing. The leg length allows the Black-winged Stilt to feed in much deeper water than other waders. When feeding on dry terrain, it has to bend its legs awkwardly so that its bill can reach the ground.

BANDED STILT
Recurvirostridae *Cladorhynchus leucocephalus*
RANGE: S Australia
HABITAT: inland salt lakes, estuaries and lagoons
SIZE: 15–16 in (38–41 cm)

The Banded Stilt feeds in flocks, the members of the group sometimes converging to herd their prey. It nests erratically in huge massed colonies, where occasional heavy rains fill desert salt pans. The eggs are laid in a scrape on flat nesting islands left by the receding water.

PIED AVOCET
Recurvirostridae *Recurvirostra avosetta*
RANGE: breeds W and C Eurasia; winters mainly in Africa and the Middle East
HABITAT: saline or brackish wetlands, coastal and inland
SIZE: 16½–18 in (42–45 cm)

The delicately pointed, upturned bill of the Pied Avocet is a highly specialized feeding tool, held slightly open just below the surface of shallow water or very soft mud and swept from side to side as the bird walks slowly forward. The species can also upend in deeper water and sweep its bill to and fro through the mud on the bottom.

chick

RED-NECKED AVOCET
Recurvirostridae *Recurvirostra novaehollandiae*
RANGE: S and inland Australia
HABITAT: lagoons, lakes, marshes, estuaries
SIZE: 16–18 in (40–45 cm)

The Red-necked Avocet haunts shallow waters inland and on the coast. Like Pied Avocets, they forage by sweeping their upturned bills from side to side through shallow water or mud and sometimes stir the water up with their bills to reveal more food. Their partially webbed feet enable them to swim.

STONE-CURLEW
Burhinidae *Burhinus oedicnemus*
RANGE: W and S Europe, SW Asia, N Africa, Middle East, Indian subcontinent
HABITAT: open farmland, heaths, semi-desert
SIZE: 16–17 in (40–44 cm)

The Stone-Curlew lives mainly in dry, open terrain. It can run swiftly across the ground, and is partly nocturnal in habits. In spring, they indulge in circling display flights and call frequently at dusk, often continuing through the night. The far-carrying call is similar to that of the curlew, hence the species' name.

CAPE DIKKOP
Burhinidae *Burhinus capensis*
RANGE: sub-Saharan Africa
HABITAT: open or scrub country
SIZE: 17 in (43 cm)

Unlike other thick-knees, the Cape, or Spotted, Dikkop will nest close to towns and villages, and even in suburban gardens. It is most active at dusk and during the night, resting in the shade of bushes during the heat of the day.

BEACH THICK-KNEE
Burhinidae *Esacus magnirostris*
RANGE: coasts of N Australia, New Guinea, New Caledonia, Solomon Islands, Philippines, Indonesia, Andaman Islands
HABITAT: sandy beaches and inshore reefs
SIZE: 21–23 in (53–58 cm)

Also known as the Beach Stone-Curlew, this species is a plain-colored, large, and heavily built thick-knee that wails mournfully at night. It is almost exclusively a ground-dweller, running to escape danger, and only taking to the air when hard pressed.

EGYPTIAN PLOVER
Glareolidae *Pluvianus aegyptius*
RANGE: W, C, and NE Africa
HABITAT: river valleys and marshes
SIZE: 7½–8 in (19–21 cm)

The Egyptian Plover's breeding habits are unique among waders. The adults bury their 2–3 eggs under a layer of sand about ⅛ in (3 mm) thick. Warmed by the sun, the sand helps to incubate the clutch. If the weather cools, the parents incubate the eggs by sitting on them in the normal way, and they also do so at night. Conversely, if the daytime temperature rises, the adult cools the eggs by shading them with its body or by wetting the sand with water carried in its belly feathers.

CREAM-COLORED COURSER
Glareolidae *Cursorius cursor*
RANGE: N and E Africa, Middle East to W Pakistan; N African birds winter just S of Sahara,
Middle Eastern birds in Arabia, SW Asian birds in NW India
HABITAT: open arid plains with sparse vegetation; margins of cultivated land
SIZE: 8–9 in (21–24 cm)

The pale sandy-brown plumage of this species provides perfect camouflage in its desert habitat. It is much more conspicuous in flight, however, when it reveals the striking black-and-white pattern on the underside of its wings.

AUSTRALIAN PRATINCOLE
Glareolidae *Stiltia isabella*
RANGE: breeds N and inland Australia; most populations winter N to extreme
N Australia, New Guinea and other Papuan islands, Indonesia
HABITAT: bare, open plains, fields, edges of lagoons
SIZE: 8–9 in (20–23 cm)

The Australian Pratincole can tolerate brackish water by excreting excess salt through special nasal glands. The clutch of 2 eggs is laid on the bare ground and incubated by both sexes. Soon after hatching, the chicks are led to the shade of vegetation or burrows.

COMMON PRATINCOLE
Glareolidae *Glareola pratincola*
RANGE: S Eurasia, N Africa; winters S Africa
HABITAT: flood plains, deltas, steppes
SIZE: 9–10 in (23.5–26.5 cm)

Common Pratincoles nest in large colonies on bare or sparsely vegetated ground, each clutch laid in a slight scrape. When a predatory bird appears over the colony, all the adults in the area will fly up and mob it, giving harsh *kirrik* calls until the intruder moves away.

non-breeding

NORTHERN LAPWING

Charadriidae *Vanellus vanellus*
RANGE: breeds temperate Eurasia; most populations migrate
S in winter to Mediterranean, India, China
HABITAT: breeds on open ground, including farmland, freshwater
marshes, saltmarshes; also visits estuarine mud flats
SIZE: 11–12 in (28–31 cm)

The Northern Lapwing is a common and familiar bird
over much of Europe. Its broad, rounded wings produce
a distinctive creaking sound during the wheeling, rolling,
and tumbling display flight. The sounds are accompanied by
a characteristic plaintive cry, from which the bird takes its
alternative English name, Peewit.

SOUTHERN LAPWING

Charadriidae *Vanellus chilensis*
RANGE: South America, mainly E of Andes
HABITAT: savanna, wet grassland, farmland
SIZE: 14½–15 in (37–38 cm)

This plover readily adapts to feeding on cultivated land, taking earthworms, grubs,
and insects. At the slightest intrusion, day or night, it utters its strident alarm calls.
When approached, an incubating bird will slip away from the nest before taking
flight and then make sweeping passes at the intruder while emitting loud cries.

BLACKSMITH PLOVER

Charadriidae *Anitibyx armatus*
RANGE: Kenya to South Africa
HABITAT: margins of fresh and saline wetlands and
adjacent open ground
SIZE: 11–12 in (28–31 cm)

The bold plumage of the adult Blacksmith Plover becomes even more striking
when the bird takes flight, enhanced by the contrast between the black and gray
upperwings and the black-and-white underwings.

non-breeding

AMERICAN GOLDEN PLOVER

Charadriidae *Pluvialis dominica*
RANGE: breeds Arctic North America; winters C South America
HABITAT: breeds on tundra; otherwise coastal mud flats, inland marshes and grassland
SIZE: 9½–11 in (24–28 cm)

There is a striking difference in this bird between the breeding and non-breeding plumage. However, the upperparts of adult and immature have a golden hue all year. The speckling on the back camouflages the incubating bird.

♂

non-breeding

GRAY PLOVER

Charadriidae *Pluvialis squatarola*
RANGE: breeds circumpolar Arctic; winters worldwide on coasts to S
HABITAT: breeds on lowland tundra; winters on coastal mud flats and lagoons
SIZE: 10½–12 in (27–30 cm)

Although the black axilliary feathers, or "armpits," of this bird are seen only in flight, they form a unique and distinctive field character. They are especially useful in winter when the overall gray plumage of the standing bird lacks any obvious distinguishing marks.

RINGED PLOVER

Charadriidae *Charadrius hiaticula*
RANGE: breeds Arctic E Canada and Eurasia; winters Europe and Africa
HABITAT: breeds on shingle beaches and tundra; winters along coasts and some inland wetlands
SIZE: 7–8 in (18–20 cm)

Ringed Plovers are experts at the broken-wing display, in which they pretend to be injured. They flutter with drooped wings and spread tail while calling loudly and plaintively, in an effort to distract a potential predator away from the vulnerable young in the nest.

KILLDEER

Charadriidae *Charadrius vociferus*
RANGE: breeds S Canada to SC Mexico, West Indies, coastal Peru, and extreme N Chile; winters N South America
HABITAT: open expanses near wet areas, ponds, rivers
SIZE: 8–10 in (21–25 cm)

This plover takes its name from its *killdee-killdee* calls. Killdeers make their nest scrapes in an area with short, sparse vegetation or none at all. Bits of grass, pebbles, and other loose material end up in the scrape as a result of a ritual ceremony in which the birds slowly walk away from the nest while tossing the material over their shoulders.

KENTISH PLOVER

Charadriidae *Charadrius alexandrinus*
RANGE: temperate and S Eurasia and North America, South America, Africa
HABITAT: coastal and inland brackish or saline wetlands
SIZE: 6–7 in (15–17.5 cm)

race *alexandrinus*

The 3–4 eggs are laid in a shallow scrape in the sand. Their buff color with fine black marks acts as excellent camouflage. The young, too, are cryptically patterned. When their parents give the alarm call, they flatten themselves to the ground and become indistinguishable from small irregularities in the surface of the sand.

WRYBILL

Charadriidae *Anarhynchus frontalis*
RANGE: New Zealand
HABITAT: breeds along shallow, stony rivers; winters on estuaries, in harbors
SIZE: 8 in (20 cm)

This small plover is unique in that the tip of its bill bends to the right. It feeds by walking in clockwise circles, probing over mud and under pebbles. The bird's winter migration from South Island to North Island takes place in January and it returns to its southern breeding grounds in August.

EURASIAN DOTTEREL

Charadriidae *Eudromias morinellus*
RANGE: breeds Arctic and mountainous Eurasia; winters N Africa
and Middle East
HABITAT: breeds on tundra and mountain plateaus; winters on
open, often stony ground
SIZE: 8–8½ in (20–22 cm)

non-breeding

♀

The bright white eye stripes and white chest band of this bird break up its outline when it is nesting among the short tundra or mountain vegetation of its breeding grounds. The male is solely responsible for incubation and the rearing of young. Each female often lays 2 or more clutches of 3 eggs for different males.

MAGELLANIC PLOVER

Pluvianellidae *Pluvianellus socialis*
RANGE: breeds Tierra del Fuego N through S Patagonia; winters N on the coast of Argentina
HABITAT: shores of lakes, ponds, lagoons; winters by river mouths and bays
SIZE: 8 in (20 cm)

Magellanic Plovers nest near shallow fresh or brackish water. The sexes share incubation of the eggs; usually only one chick survives. Uniquely among waders, the chick is fed partly by regurgitation from the parents' bills; they continue to feed it for at least 12 days after it has fledged.

non-breeding

♂

BAR-TAILED GODWIT

Scolopacidae *Limosa lapponica*
RANGE: breeds Eurasian Arctic; winters S to S Africa and Australasia
HABITAT: breeds on marshy and scrubby tundra; winters on estuaries
SIZE: 14½–16 in (17–41 cm)

The rich mahogany-chestnut summer plumage of this species provides good camouflage for nesting birds against the colored mosses and low scrub of the Arctic tundra. The thin, slightly upturned bill is approximately 20 percent longer in the female than in the male.

WESTERN CURLEW
Scolopacidae *Numenius arquata*
RANGE: breeds temperate and N Eurasia; winters S
to Africa, India, Southeast Asia
HABITAT: breeds on open vegetated land; winters
mainly on coastal wetlands
SIZE: 19½–23½ in (50–60 cm)

The distinctive long, decurved bill of the Western Curlew is
perfectly adapted for probing deeply into soft mud in search of
food. During courtship, the male indulges in a shallow, gliding
flight accompanied by a rich, bubbling and trilling song, which
can also be heard outside the breeding season.

GREATER YELLOWLEGS
Scolopacidae *Tringa melanoleuca*
RANGE: breeds N North America, non-breeders S along
coasts; winters SW Canada to extreme South
America; vagrant elsewhere
HABITAT: breeds on tundra; otherwise coastal mudflats
and marshes, shores of inland lakes
SIZE: 14 in (36 cm)

The Greater Yellowlegs nests in muskeg country,
along the tundra-forest edge and on the high tundra
of North America, migrating south for the winter. It
feeds mainly in shallow waters, wading in to sweep
its bill with a sideways motion or dash about after
visible prey.

SPOTTED SANDPIPER
Scolopacidae *Actitis macularia*
RANGE: breeds North America; winters S from Mexico to S Brazil
HABITAT: open and wooded areas, usually near water
SIZE: 7½ in (19 cm)

The Spotted Sandpiper's main call is a clear, whistled *peet-weet*. Its curious
flight, with short glides on down-bowed wings alternating with groups
of shallow, flickering wing beats, is shared only by its close relative, the
Common Sandpiper *A. hypoleucos.*

RUDDY TURNSTONE
Scolopacidae *Arenaria interpres*
RANGE: breeds circumpolar Arctic, and N temperate region in Scandinavia; winters S worldwide to C Argentina, South Africa, and Australia
HABITAT: breeds on tundra and coastal plains; winters on coasts
SIZE: 8–10 in (21–26 cm)

Flocks of these birds walk busily over heaps of seaweed on the shore, flicking pieces with the bill, quickly grabbing any morsel of food that appears. Invertebrates and their larvae make up the main part of their diet.

non-breeding

non-breeding

RED-NECKED PHALAROPE
Scolopacidae *Phalaropus lobatus*
RANGE: breeds circumpolar Arctic and N temperate regions; winters in the tropics
HABITAT: breeds on freshwater marshes, including uplands; marine in winter
SIZE: 7–7½ in (18–19 cm)

Like the other 2 species of phalarope, Red-necked Phalaropes are adapted for swimming, rather than merely wading, with lobed toes to propel them through water. The female is more brightly colored than the male; his duller plumage camouflages him while incubating and rearing the young.

COMMON SNIPE
Scolopacidae *Gallinago gallinago*
RANGE: breeds N temperate North America and Eurasia; many winter widely to S
HABITAT: freshwater and coastal wetlands
SIZE: 10–10½ in (25–27 cm)

When displaying over the breeding territory, the male Common Snipe circles high in the air and then dives groundward, holding out his outer tail feathers at a sharp angle to the rest of his tail. The air rushing past makes them vibrate and give out a bleating sound, often known as "drumming."

RED KNOT
Scolopacidae *Calidris canutus*
RANGE: breeds Arctic Canada and Siberia; winters South
America, S Africa, and Australia
HABITAT: breeds on tundra; winters on estuaries
and beaches
SIZE: 9–10 in (23–25 cm)

non-breeding

The Red Knot undergoes a marked change in plumage through the year,
from its rich chestnut-orange breeding dress to the pale gray of winter.
Although the rather duller, white-bellied female helps with incubation,
she departs soon after, leaving the male to rear the brood.

non-breeding

DUNLIN
Scolopacidae *Calidris alpina*
RANGE: circumpolar Arctic and N temperate regions; winters
S to subtropics
HABITAT: breeds on tundra, moorland, marshes; winters on
estuaries or inland wetlands
SIZE: 6–8½ in (16–22 cm)

The Dunlin is the most common small wader of the northern
hemisphere. This species is very variable in size, birds of
southern and western races being far smaller than those of
some of the east Siberian and New World races.

SPOON-BILLED SANDPIPER
Scolopacidae *Eurynorhynchus pygmeus*
RANGE: breeds NE Siberia; winters coasts of SE India
to Myanmar, coastal SE China
HABITAT: breeds on coastal marshy tundra; winters on
muddy coasts and brackish lagoons
SIZE: 5½–6 in (14–16 cm)

chick

The spoon-shaped bill of this species is an adaptation for feeding. The bird forages in
soft mud or shallow water, sweeping its bill from side to side as it walks. The broadened
bill tip is already obvious in the newly hatched young. The Spoon-billed Sandpiper is in
danger of extinction.

RUFF

Scolopacidae *Philomachus pugnax*
RANGE: breeds N Eurasia; winters Mediterranean, S Africa, India, and Australia
HABITAT: lowland freshwater wetlands, marshes and wet pastures
SIZE: 8–12½ in (20–32 cm)

In the breeding season, the male Ruff develops remarkable plumes, variable in both color and pattern, around his head and neck. Groups of rival males form "leks" at which they display to one another and advertise to visiting females.

variants

non-breeding

typical

LONG-TAILED SKUA

Scolopacidae *Stercorarius longicaudus*
RANGE: breeds circumpolar high Arctic; winters in S hemisphere
HABITAT: breeds on Arctic tundra and marshes; winters at sea
SIZE: 19½–23 in (50–58 cm)

During the breeding season, this species concentrates on hunting lemmings, rather than parasitizing other seabirds. The breeding performance of the skuas is closely linked to the abundance of lemmings: in years when lemmings are scarce, the skuas may not breed at all, or will fail to rear any young.

non-breeding

COMMON GULL

Laridae *Larus canus*
RANGE: temperate and N Eurasia and NW North America
HABITAT: breeds in marshes and wet scrubland; winters on
the shores of seas and large lakes
SIZE: 16–18 in (40–46 cm)

Common Gulls nest in colonies, sometimes on the ground, but often in the tops of bushes or scrub. In winter, the birds gather in large roosts on estuarine mudflats or large fresh waters. They may feed along the shore or fly well inland to forage, returning to the roosting site in the evening.

race *argenteus*

HERRING GULL

Laridae *Larus argentatus*
RANGE: circumpolar N, temperate, and Mediterranean
HABITAT: varied; coastal and inland, including urban areas
SIZE: 22–26 in (56–66 cm)

The Herring Gull's nest is an untidy gathering of vegetation and scraps of garbage. Soon after they have hatched in the nest, the young peck instinctively at the prominent red spot on the lower mandible of their parents' bills, inducing the adult bird to regurgitate the food in its crop.

first winter

GREAT BLACK-BACKED GULL

Laridae *Larus marinus*
RANGE: coastal NE North America, SW Greenland, and NW Europe
HABITAT: coasts, locally inland waters and moors
SIZE: 28–31 in (71–79 cm)

The Great Black-backed Gull is a highly predatory gull, especially in the breeding season when it may live almost exclusively on seabirds and, if they are available, rabbits. At other times of the year, it often obtains food by scavenging. Breeding may take place in loose colonies or the birds may build solitary nests.

non-breeding

FRANKLIN'S GULL

Laridae *Larus pipixcan*
RANGE: breeds on North American prairies; winters on coasts of Central and South America
HABITAT: breeds in freshwater marshes; winters on coasts
SIZE: 13–15 in (33–38 cm)

The soft gray upperparts and white underparts of this gull have earned it the local name of Prairie Dove. The young hatch with either a gray or a brown downy coat, although these two color phases do not persist in the adult plumage.

non-breeding

ROSS'S GULL
Laridae *Rhodostethia rosea*
RANGE: Arctic Siberia, Canada, and Greenland
HABITAT: breeds on Arctic tundra and scrub; winters at sea
SIZE: 12–12½ in (30–32 cm)

Ross's Gull in its breeding plumage has white underparts suffused with pink. For a long time the breeding grounds were quite unknown; they were finally discovered in northern Siberia in 1905. More recently, breeding has been confirmed in northern Canada and in Greenland.

BLACK-LEGGED KITTIWAKE
Laridae *Rissa tridactyla*
RANGE: circumpolar Arctic and temperate coasts
HABITAT: coastal and open sea
SIZE: 15–18 in (39–46 cm)

first winter

Often known simply as the Kittiwake, this bird traditionally nests in large colonies on narrow cliff ledges, building a nest of seaweed lined with grass; as the seaweed dries, it cements itself to the rock. The young, when they hatch, have strong claws on their toes, enabling them to cling to their precarious home.

non-breeding

SWALLOW-TAILED GULL
Laridae *Creagrus furcatus*
RANGE: breeds Galapagos Islands and Colombia; winters off NW South America
HABITAT: breeds on coasts; winters on open sea
SIZE: 21½–23½ in (55–60 cm)

With its dark gray head, boldly patterned wings, and deeply forked tail, the Swallow-tailed Gull has a particularly striking appearance. Its eyes are much larger than those of most gulls and are more forward-facing, giving the bird binocular vision—an adaption that helps the birds find food at night.

juv

non-breeding

SABINE'S GULL
Laridae *Xema sabini*
RANGE: circumpolar Arctic
HABITAT: breeds Arctic coasts and islands;
winters on the open sea
SIZE: 13–14 in (33–36 cm)

Presumably as a defense against predators, parents lead their young away from the nest as soon as they hatch. The adults also perform a distraction display if danger threatens their chicks. Both these types of behavior are more typical of waders than of gulls.

non-breeding

BLACK TERN
Sternidae *Chlidonias nigra*
RANGE: breeds central S Eurasia and North America;
winters in tropics mainly N of Equator
HABITAT: breeds on marshes and pools; winters on coasts
SIZE: 8½–9½ in (22–24 cm)

Instead of hovering above the water and then diving into it, like many other species of tern, the Black Tern and the other "marsh terns" of the genus *Chlidonias* hover and then swoop down to peck aquatic insects and their larvae from the water's surface in mid-flight.

CASPIAN TERN
Sternidae *Hydroprogne caspia*
RANGE: worldwide, but breeding range is fragmentary
HABITAT: breeds on coastal and inl and marshes; winters on coasts
SIZE: 19–23 in (48–59 cm)

The Caspian Tern is the largest of the terns, with an orange-red, daggerlike bill. Its range covers all 5 continents, but the breeding areas are hundreds of miles apart—probably because the species requires remote coastal and marshland nesting sites with rich feeding areas close by.

ARCTIC TERN

Sternidae *Sterna paradisaea*
RANGE: breeds circumpolar Arctic and sub-Arctic; winters
S to Antarctic Ocean
HABITAT: breeds on coasts; winters at sea
SIZE: 13–15 in (33–38 cm)

From their breeding grounds in the Arctic, the birds fly south to winter
in the seas just north of the Antarctic pack-ice, a round trip of more than
20,000 miles (32,000 km) every year. Like some other terns, they vigorously
defend their nests against predators by dive-bombing and actually striking the
intruders around the head with their beaks.

juv

SOOTY TERN

Sternidae *Sterna fuscata*
RANGE: tropical and subtropical latitudes
HABITAT: breeds on coasts and islands; winters on the open sea
SIZE: 17–18 in (43–45 cm)

The Sooty Tern takes its alternative name, Wideawake Tern, from its loud,
repeated call of *ker-wacky-wacky*, and perhaps also from its nocturnal feeding
habits. The bird hardly ever seems to alight on the water, but obtains its food
by swooping down and pecking from the surface. It seems likely that it actually
sleeps on the wing.

ROYAL TERN

Sternidae *Thalasseus maximus*
RANGE: breeds on coasts of Central America and W Africa;
winters on coasts to S
HABITAT: coastal and marine
SIZE: 18–21 in (46–53 cm)

Colonies are often large, with up to several
thousand pairs. The young are looked after by
their parents for an unusually long time: adults
have been observed still feeding chicks that are
5 months old.

BLACK SKIMMER
Rynchopidae *Rynchops niger*
RANGE: S North America, Caribbean, and South America
HABITAT: coastal and riverine marshes
SIZE: 16–19½ in (40–50 cm)

The lower mandible of the Black Skimmer's bill is flattened and is a third as long again as the rounded upper mandible. When feeding, the bird flies close to the surface of the water, with only the tip of the lower mandible submerged. As soon as this encounters prey, such as small fish and shrimps, the bird throws its head downward and snaps its bill shut.

LITTLE AUK
Alcidae *Alle alle*
RANGE: North Atlantic and adjacent Arctic
HABITAT: breeds on coastal scree and in rock crevices; otherwise on open sea
SIZE: 8–10 in (20–25 cm)

Breeding colonies may contain several million pairs of Little Auks, their nests placed deep among the fallen rocks of coastal scree. Colonies are constantly patrolled by the species' main predators, Glaucous Gulls, which wait their chance to snatch unwary birds as they enter or leave their nest-holes.

bridled form

COMMON GUILLEMOT
Alcidae *Uria aalge*
RANGE: circumpolar Eurasia and North America
HABITAT: open sea; breeds on coastal cliffs
SIZE: 16–17 in (40–43 cm)

Common Guillemots breed in large colonies on narrow cliff ledges. Each pair's single egg is markedly pointed so that it will roll in a circle if pushed and not fall off the ledge. The chicks leave the nest site when they are only about 3 weeks old, accompanying their parents out to sea in search of food.

non-breeding

BLACK GUILLEMOT

Alcidae *Cepphus grylle*

RANGE: North Atlantic and adjacent Arctic

HABITAT: breeds on coasts; winters mainly in
coastal waters

SIZE: 12–14 in (30–36 cm)

In contrast to its pale, mottled winter plumage, the breeding dress of the Black Guillemot is a bold jet-black, save for a broad white patch on the upper side of the wing and white on the inner half of the underwing. The bird also has bright red legs and feet that show up distinctly in clear water and on land.

non-breeding

MARBLED MURRELET

Alcidae *Brachyramphus marmoratus*

RANGE: N Pacific, S to Japan and California

HABITAT: inshore marine; breeds in woodland and tundra near the coast

SIZE: 9½–10 in (24–25 cm)

Although it is an abundant species, the breeding habits of the Marbled Murrelet are virtually unknown, as only a few solitary nests have ever been found. Two of these were several miles inland in forested areas; two others were in hollows in the open tundra of small subarctic islands.

ATLANTIC PUFFIN

Alcidae *Fratercula arctica*

RANGE: N Atlantic and adjacent Arctic

HABITAT: open sea; breeds on coasts

SIZE: 11–12 in (28–30 cm)

The depth of its bill, and especially its sharp edges, enable the Atlantic Puffin to catch and hold fish. A dozen or more can be held at one time and, as each fish is caught, it is held between the tongue and the upper mandible, freeing the lower mandible for further catches.

Doves and pigeons

COMMON GROUND-DOVE
Columbidae *Columbina passerina*
RANGE: S USA and Caribbean to Ecuador and Brazil; Bahamas
HABITAT: open country, roadsides, farms, grassland
SIZE: 6½ in (16.5 cm)

Largely terrestrial, Common Ground-Doves forage on the ground. When they do fly, their bright chestnut primary wing feathers are apparent. Their usual call is a soft, cooing whistle. The female is generally duller than the male.

INCA DOVE
Columbidae *Scardafella inca*
RANGE: locally from SW USA to N Costa Rica
HABITAT: towns, open areas, farms, riverside scrub, cactus, mesquite
SIZE: 8 in (20 cm)

This tiny dove reveals the rich chestnut color of its primary wing feathers when it takes flight. Its usual call is a series of 2-note coos, but it also utters a variety of soft or throaty display, threat, and alarm calls.

WHITE-TIPPED DOVE
Columbidae *Leptotila verreauxi*
RANGE: S Texas and Mexico S to W Peru, C Argentina, and Uruguay; Trinidad and Tobago, Aruba
HABITAT: arid to semi-arid environments; open woodland, plantations
SIZE: 11 in (28 cm)

This solitary, terrestrial dove, also known as the White-fronted Dove, feeds mostly on seeds it finds on the ground, but it also eats some insects. Its voice has been likened to the sound produced when a person blows across the top of a narrow-mouthed bottle.

RUDDY QUAIL DOVE
Columbidae *Geotrygon montana*
RANGE: Mexico, Central America S to Bolivia and Brazil; Caribbean
HABITAT: humid lowland forest
SIZE: 9 in (23 cm)

Although it appears as a beautifully colored bird in good light, the colors blend into the shadows of the forest floor, allowing the Ruddy Quail Dove to remain undetected from only a few yards away. The repetitive call is a deep, booming coo.

NICOBAR PIGEON
Columbidae *Caloenas nicobarica*
RANGE: Nicobar and Andaman islands, E through Indonesia and the Philippines to New Guinea and the Solomon Islands
HABITAT: forested islands
SIZE: 13 in (33 cm)

juv

The Nicobar Pigeon occurs only on small islands over its extensive range. It forages alone on the ground for fallen fruits, seeds, and nuts. It can even eat hard nuts that humans can open only with a hammer. This is made possible by the bird's muscular gizzard.

LUZON BLEEDING HEART
Columbidae *Gallicolumba luzonica*
RANGE: Luzon and Polillo islands (Philippines)
HABITAT: forests
SIZE: 11–12 in (28–30 cm)

Of all the 5 species of bleeding heart dove, this bird most lives up to its name. The bright red oval patch on its breast forms a groove between surrounding pink "blood-stained" feathers and has misled many people into believing the bird is seriously injured. It is an important element in the bird's courtship displays.

Blue Crowned Pigeon

VICTORIA CROWNED PIGEON
Columbidae *Goura victoria*
RANGE: N New Guinea, Biak and Yapen islands
HABITAT: lowland rain forest
SIZE: 26 in (66 cm)

Victoria Crowned Pigeons forage on the ground in small flocks, searching for fallen fruit, berries, and seeds. A male defends his territory by opening one wing, ready to strike buffeting blows on any intruder, while fanning and tilting his tail. In courtship he performs a bowing display, nodding his lowered head and fanning his tail up and down while giving a booming call. Male and female then preen each other.

PHEASANT PIGEON
Columbidae *Otidiphaps nobilis*
RANGE: New Guinea and offshore islands, Aru Islands
HABITAT: foothill and mountain rain forest
SIZE: 18 in (46 cm)

The ground-dwelling Pheasant Pigeon keeps to the undergrowth, but it can run fast and will fly heavily and noisily to escape danger. In courtship, the male performs a bowing display with his tail raised and gives a loud, growling call. The female responds by preening his head.

juv

TOOTH-BILLED PIGEON
Columbidae *Didunculus strigirostris*
RANGE: Upolu and Savaii islands (Samoa)
HABITAT: wooded mountainsides at altitudes of 1,000–4,500 ft (300–1,400 m)
SIZE: 13 in (33 cm)

Its massive hooked bill reminiscent of the bill of its distant relative, the extinct Dodo *Raphus cucullatus*, the Tooth-billed Pigeon is itself now critically endangered. Formerly believed to be strictly a ground feeder, it has recently been found to feed frequently on fruits in trees.

AFRICAN GREEN PIGEON
Columbidae *Treron calva*
RANGE: sub-Saharan Africa
HABITAT: forests, riverine woods, savanna
SIZE: 11 in (28 cm)

The overall dark olive-green plumage of this small pigeon provides perfect camouflage in its typical forest habitat. There are some 18 races of this species. Plumage color varies from darker green in more forested areas to a paler, yellowish green in drier regions.

race *magnificus*

race *puella*

WOMPOO FRUIT-DOVE
Columbidae *Ptilinopus magnificus*
RANGE: E coast of Australia, from Cape York to N New South Wales,
lowland New Guinea
HABITAT: rain forest
SIZE: 14–18 in (35–45 cm)

Despite its striking and beautiful coloration, this pigeon is difficult to locate in the forest canopy, unless it calls with the deep double coo that gives it its common name. Wompoo Fruit-Doves feed in the canopy, eating a variety of fruits, and often reveal their presence by the sound of falling fruit.

MADAGASCAR BLUE PIGEON
Columbidae *Alectroenas madagascariensis*
RANGE: Madagascar
HABITAT: evergreen forest
SIZE: 10 in (25 cm)

Parties of up to 12 or more of these pigeons move through the forests of Madagascar, keeping mainly to the treetops and feeding exclusively on fruit. Although few nests have been found, the breeding season appears to be a prolonged one, lasting at least from July to March.

GREEN IMPERIAL PIGEON
Columbidae *Ducula aenea*
RANGE: India, Southeast Asia, Philippines, Indonesia, New Guinea
HABITAT: evergreen forest, mangrove swamps; also more open country with scattered woods
SIZE: 17–18 in (43–46 cm)

The principal food of this pigeon is soft fruits, often varieties containing hard stones. Instead of the muscular gizzard and long gut of most members of its family, it has a relatively soft stomach and short, wide gut, through which the stones pass intact. The seed within is able to germinate and form new trees in the course of time.

juv

TOP-KNOT PIGEON
Columbidae *Lopholaimus antarcticus*
RANGE: E coast of Australia
HABITAT: rain forest
SIZE: 16½–18 in (42–45 cm)

The Top-knot Pigeon feeds on a variety of rain forest fruits, including those of palms. It feeds only in the tree canopy, where it scrambles about among the foliage. They are nomadic birds, making long seasonal movements in search of food.

NEW ZEALAND PIGEON
Columbidae *Hemiphaga novaeseelandiae*
RANGE: New Zealand
HABITAT: forests; also woodland patches in farmland
SIZE: 20 in (51 cm)

This is a large, heavy, colorful pigeon, with back and neck plumage that may appear gray, bronze-purple, or green, depending on the light. It eats a range of fruits, flowers, and green vegetation, including leaves and grass.

Parrots

KAKAPO
Psittacidae *Strigops habroptilus*
RANGE: New Zealand, originally widespread, now reduced to 2 introduced populations on Little Barrier Island and Codfish Island
HABITAT: forest and scrub; may depend on fruiting yellow-wood trees for breeding
SIZE: 25 in (63 cm)

Nocturnal, ground-dwelling, and the heaviest of all parrots, the critically endangered Kakapo is the only parrot to have become completely flightless. The males gather at traditional mating grounds, or "leks," in late summer and advertise for mates with loud booming calls that may be heard over ½ mile (1 km) away.

KEA
Psittacidae *Nestor notabilis*
RANGE: South Island (New Zealand)
HABITAT: mountain forest and ridges often above snow line; coastal forest in winter
SIZE: 18 in (46 cm)

The Kea uses its elongated upper bill (longer in the male) to tear into carrion, fruit, leaves, and insects. Its name reflects its call, which is unforgettable when heard echoing among the mist-veiled mountain tops. The male is polygamous and will often breed with several females at the same time.

VULTURINE PARROT
Psittacidae *Gypopsitta vulturina*
RANGE: NE Brazil
HABITAT: dry and periodically flooded forest
SIZE: 9 in (23 cm)

This odd-looking parrot owes its name to its distinctive bare forehead. It is possible that, as in vultures, this enables the bird to feed without matting its head plumage.

RED-TAILED BLACK COCKATOO
Psittacidae *Calyptorhynchus magnificus*
RANGE: N and W Australia, with isolated inland populations
HABITAT: scrub, open woods, river forest
SIZE: 19½–24 in (50–61 cm)

A feeding group of Red-Tailed Black Cockatoos will often make themselves obvious by audibly snapping their bills as they split nuts to eat the seeds and scatter the husks on the ground beneath the trees. The distinctive helmetlike crest of both sexes is raised when they are alighting and when they are alarmed or excited.

PALM COCKATOO
Psittacidae *Probosciger aterrimus*
RANGE: New Guinea, including some smaller islands, NE Australia
HABITAT: edges of rain forest bordering on savanna, in lowlands up to 2,500 ft (750 m)
SIZE: 19½–25 in (50–63 cm)

This is the largest of all cockatoos and the largest Australian parrot. It is also notable for its dramatic displays before the beginning of the breeding season. The male—slightly larger than the female—grips a stick with his foot and pounds a tree trunk to produce a loud drumming.

GALAH
Psittacidae *Eolophus roseicapillus*
RANGE: most of Australia
HABITAT: eucalypt woodland, watercourse vegetation, and grassland
SIZE: 14 in (35 cm)

The commonest cockatoo—indeed, one of the commonest of all parrots—in Australia, the Galah is sometimes known as the Roseate Cockatoo. The pairs bond for life and share the incubation and feeding of the young.

SULPHUR-CRESTED COCKATOO
Psittacidae *Cacatua galerita*
RANGE: Melanesia, New Guinea, N and E Australia
HABITAT: lowland forest, savanna and partly cleared
land up to 5,000 ft (1,500 m)
SIZE: 15–19½ in (38–50 cm)

This handsome, noisy parrot often associates in
large flocks outside the breeding season. While the
flock is feeding on the ground, a few birds stand
sentinel in nearby trees and warn of danger with
loud raucous cries. At dusk the flock returns to
a habitual roost. During the breeding season the
flocks break up.

COCKATIEL
Psittacidae *Nymphicus hollandicus*
RANGE: Australia, throughout interior
HABITAT: open scrub, woods, near water
SIZE: 12½ in (32 cm)

This slender cockatoo, which is sometimes called the Quarrion, usually
forages for fruits and seeds in pairs or small groups. Both sexes are
crested, but the male's facial markings are brighter. They usually
breed after rainfall, at any time of year.

BUFF-FACED PYGMY PARROT
Psittacidae *Micropsitta pusio*
RANGE: N and E New Guinea lowlands and offshore
islands, Bismarck Archipelago
HABITAT: lowland forest, regrowth, and remnant trees
SIZE: 3 in (8 cm)

One of 6 very similar pygmy parrots found on New Guinea
and neighboring islands, the Buff-Faced Pygmy Parrot is
exceptional among birds in feeding on lichen and fungi, but it
will also eat fruits, seeds, and insects, picking them out of the
bark as it works its way over the trunk and branches.

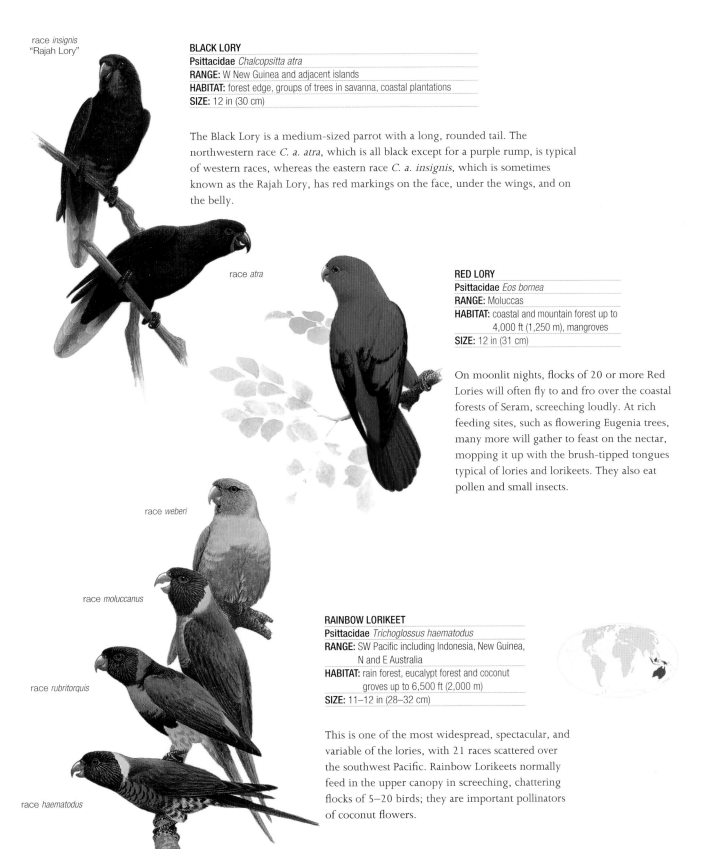

race *insignis*
"Rajah Lory"

BLACK LORY
Psittacidae *Chalcopsitta atra*
RANGE: W New Guinea and adjacent islands
HABITAT: forest edge, groups of trees in savanna, coastal plantations
SIZE: 12 in (30 cm)

The Black Lory is a medium-sized parrot with a long, rounded tail. The northwestern race *C. a. atra*, which is all black except for a purple rump, is typical of western races, whereas the eastern race *C. a. insignis*, which is sometimes known as the Rajah Lory, has red markings on the face, under the wings, and on the belly.

race *atra*

RED LORY
Psittacidae *Eos bornea*
RANGE: Moluccas
HABITAT: coastal and mountain forest up to 4,000 ft (1,250 m), mangroves
SIZE: 12 in (31 cm)

On moonlit nights, flocks of 20 or more Red Lories will often fly to and fro over the coastal forests of Seram, screeching loudly. At rich feeding sites, such as flowering Eugenia trees, many more will gather to feast on the nectar, mopping it up with the brush-tipped tongues typical of lories and lorikeets. They also eat pollen and small insects.

race *weberi*

race *moluccanus*

race *rubritorquis*

RAINBOW LORIKEET
Psittacidae *Trichoglossus haematodus*
RANGE: SW Pacific including Indonesia, New Guinea, N and E Australia
HABITAT: rain forest, eucalypt forest and coconut groves up to 6,500 ft (2,000 m)
SIZE: 11–12 in (28–32 cm)

This is one of the most widespread, spectacular, and variable of the lories, with 21 races scattered over the southwest Pacific. Rainbow Lorikeets normally feed in the upper canopy in screeching, chattering flocks of 5–20 birds; they are important pollinators of coconut flowers.

race *haematodus*

BLACK-CAPPED LORY
Psittacidae *Lorius lory*
RANGE: lowland New Guinea and offshore islands
HABITAT: undisturbed rain forest, swamp forest
SIZE: 11 in (28 cm)

race *somu*

race *lory*

This stocky, rather shy bird has a ringing, melodious cry, quite unlike the usual screeching of parrots. During the courtship display, the perching male faces his mate in an upright posture with his wings open and head turned to one side, and bobs his body up and down.

♂

JOSEPHINE'S LORY
Psittacidae *Charmosyna josefinae*
RANGE: W and C New Guinea
HABITAT: mountain forest, at 2,500–6,500 ft (800–2,000 m)
SIZE: 9½ in (24 cm)

This slender, quiet, long-tailed parrot flies in pairs or small groups, alighting to gather pollen and nectar from tree blossom, or climbing slowly through the tendrils of a clinging vine to feed at the large white flowers.

COLLARED LORY
Psittacidae *Phigys solitarius*
RANGE: Fiji Islands
HABITAT: rain forest, disturbed forest, plantations, coconut palms, urban trees
SIZE: 8 in (20 cm)

Feeding flocks of these small lories often congregate around coconut palms, landing on the fronds and working their way down to the nectar-rich flowers in short, fluttering leaps, displacing other birds such as honeyeaters, which may already be feeding.

PURPLE-CROWNED LORIKEET
Psittacidae *Glossopsitta porphyrocephala*
RANGE: SW and S Australia (not Tasmania)
HABITAT: dry open woods, mallee scrub
SIZE: 6 in (16 cm)

Outside the breeding season, small nomadic flocks of Purple-crowned Lorikeets visit flowering and fruiting trees to feed on fruits; they also harvest pollen and nectar from the blossoms, using comb-like fringes on their tongues. The nests are usually in unlined hollows in eucalypts, with knot-hole entrances, often in loose colonies.

WHISKERED LORIKEET
Psittacidae *Oreopsittacus arfaki*
RANGE: W, C, and NE New Guinea
HABITAT: mountain forest, at 6,500–12,300 ft
          (2,000–3,750 m)
SIZE: 6 in (15 cm)

This bird, also known as the Plum-faced Lorikeet, often forages in small mixed flocks in the company of flowerpeckers, honeyeaters, and other lorikeets. In display the male struts back and forth along a branch, calling excitedly, then bobs and thrusts his head toward the female.

DOUBLE-EYED FIG PARROT
Psittacidae *Opopsitta diophthalma*
RANGE: New Guinea, W Papuan islands, and
          NE Australia
HABITAT: subtropical and tropical rain forest
          up to 5,300 ft (1,600 m)
SIZE: 6 in (15 cm)

race *coxeni*

race *marshalli*

True to their name, these small green parrots feed mainly on the seeds of figs, although they also eat other fruits, as well as nectar and insects. The males are more colorful than the females and their head color varies among the 8 races.

imm

RED-CHEEKED PARROT
Psittacidae *Geoffroyus geoffroyi*
RANGE: Lesser Sundas, Moluccas, New Guinea, NE Australia
HABITAT: wide range of lowland forest, including secondary forest, rain forest, mangroves, savanna, up to 2,500 ft (800 m)
SIZE: 8–10 in (20–25 cm)

Red-cheeked Parrots usually forage in pairs or groups of up to 30, but sometimes gather in great feeding aggregations around rich food sources. After feeding all day, the big flock splits up into smaller groups that spend the night in communal roosts.

BLUE-CROWNED RACKET-TAILED PARROT
Psittacidae *Prioniturus discurus*
RANGE: Philippines, Jolo Island (Sulus)
HABITAT: forests, clearings, banana groves
SIZE: 10½ in (7 cm)

The Blue-crowned Racket-tailed Parrot is widely distributed through the Philippines, with 5 races showing color variations. These birds are most commonly seen in undisturbed forest, flying high above the canopy in small, noisy flocks.

race *discurus*

race *platenae*

ECLECTUS PARROT
Psittacidae *Eclectus roratus*
RANGE: Lesser Sundas, Solomon Islands, New Guinea, NE Australia
HABITAT: lowland rain forest and dense savanna up to 3,300 ft (1,000 m)
SIZE: 15–18 in (38–45 cm)

The male and female Eclectus Parrot's plumage differs dramatically: whereas the male is bright green with blue and red patches, the female is crimson with a blue belly. When they are feeding among the green foliage, this makes her more conspicuous than her mate, something that is unique among parrots.

CRIMSON ROSELLA
Psittacidae *Platycercus elegans*
RANGE: E Australia except Tasmania
HABITAT: eucalypt forest, woods, and gardens up to 6,000 ft (1,900 m); in N restricted to mountain forests above 1,500 ft (450 m)
SIZE: 14 in (36 cm)

Both sexes have the same rich red and blue plumage; in immature birds much of the red is replaced by green. The adults occur in pairs or small groups and stay in the same area throughout the year, but the immature birds are nomadic, wandering in flocks of up to 30.

AUSTRALIAN KING PARROT
Psittacidae *Alisterus scapularis*
RANGE: E Australia except Tasmania
HABITAT: dense forest; visits open woodland and parkland outside breeding season
SIZE: 17 in (43 cm)

Male Australian King Parrots have brilliant scarlet plumage, whereas females are largely green. They breed in dense forest, frequently nesting in trees with very deep cavities; the entrance may be over 33 ft (10 m) up the tree, but the 3–6 eggs are often laid close to ground level.

RED-FRONTED PARAKEET
Psittacidae *Cyanoramphus novaezelandiae*
RANGE: New Zealand, New Caledonia
HABITAT: mature forest, tall scrub on treeless islands
SIZE: 10–11 in (25–28 cm)

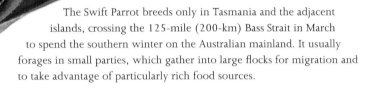

Also known as the Red-Crowned Parakeet, this species is rare on the mainland and only common on islands free of mammalian predators.

SWIFT PARROT
Psittacidae *Lathamus discolor*
RANGE: breeds Tasmania; winters SE Australia
HABITAT: eucalypt woodland and parkland
SIZE: 10 in (25 cm)

The Swift Parrot breeds only in Tasmania and the adjacent islands, crossing the 125-mile (200-km) Bass Strait in March to spend the southern winter on the Australian mainland. It usually forages in small parties, which gather into large flocks for migration and to take advantage of particularly rich food sources.

BUDGERIGAR
Psittacidae *Melopsittacus undulatus*
RANGE: throughout inland Australia
HABITAT: tussock grassland, arid and semi-arid
        scrub and woodland close to water
SIZE: 6½ in (7 cm)

imm

In the wild, the budgerigar is a gregarious, wide-ranging nomad that often travels in large flocks that rarely stay in one place for long. Wild birds are always green. They breed at any time of year when food is abundant, usually after rains.

♂

NIGHT PARROT
Psittacidae *Geopsittacus occidentalis*
RANGE: arid and semi-arid regions of central Australia
HABITAT: low succulent vegetation bordering salt lakes;
        tussock grasses when in seed
SIZE: 9 in (23 cm)

Thought for many years to be extinct, the Night Parrot is classed as endangered. It spends most of its time on the ground, feeding singly or in pairs on the seeds of grasses and shrubs.

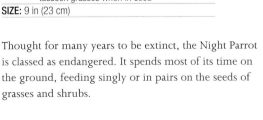

VASA PARROT
Psittacidae *Coracopsis vasa*
RANGE: Madagascar, Comoro Islands
HABITAT: forest and savanna below 3,300 ft (1,000 m)
SIZE: 20 in (50 cm)

These noisy, conspicuous parrots are usually seen in small flocks. Their flight, often high above the forest canopy, is distinctive and rather crowlike, with slow, flapping wing beats. It is thought that the breeding season lasts from at least October to December.

PEACH-FACED LOVEBIRD
Psittacidae *Agapornis roseicollis*
RANGE: SW Angola, Namibia (not NE),
　　　　　N Cape Province
HABITAT: dry wooded steppe, usually in
　　　　　belts of trees along watercourses
SIZE: 6 in (15 cm)

As with other lovebirds, pairs of Peach-faced Lovebirds preen each other attentively—hence their name—and nest in colonies. The male feeds his mate as she broods the eggs and young.

GRAY PARROT
Psittacidae *Psittacus erithacus*
RANGE: C Africa, Sierra Leone E to Kenya and NW Tanzania
HABITAT: lowland forest, wooded savanna, mangroves
SIZE: 13 in (33 cm)

In eastern Gabon vast flocks of over 5,000 Gray Parrots gather at traditional roosting sites each night, perching on the fronds of oil palms. Elsewhere the roosts are smaller, but it is common to find more than 100 birds in a single tree.

BLUE-CROWNED HANGING PARROT
Psittacidae *Loriculus galgulus*
RANGE: Malaya, Singapore, Sumatra, Borneo
　　　　　and some adjacent islands
HABITAT: light woodland in lowlands,
　　　　　plantations, orchards, gardens
SIZE: 5 in (12 cm)

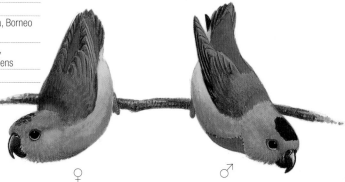

When they climb, Blue-crowned Hanging Parrots take extremely long strides, turning the whole body as they stretch each leg forward. They may also hold their tails stiffly against a branch as a prop, like woodpeckers, and grasp twigs with their bills.

ROSE-RINGED PARAKEET
Psittacidae *Psittacula krameri*
RANGE: C Africa E to Uganda, India, Sri Lanka; introduced
to Middle and Far East, North America, England,
Netherlands, Belgium, West Germany
HABITAT: woodland, farmland
SIZE: 16 in (41 cm)

Rose-ringed Parakeets often associate in flocks of 1,000 or more to feast on crops of grain or ripening fruit. During the breeding season the flocks split up; each pair nests in a tree cavity after an elaborate courtship ritual in which the female twitters and rolls her eyes at the strutting male, rubs bills with him, and accepts gifts of food.

HYACINTH MACAW
Psittacidae *Anodorhynchus hyacinthinus*
RANGE: C Brazil, E Bolivia, NE Paraguay
HABITAT: dry forest along watercourses, wet forest edges,
among palms
SIZE: 37½–39 in (95–100 cm)

The endangered Hyacinth Macaw is the largest of all the parrots and feeds mainly on palm fruits and nuts. When disturbed, these majestic macaws screech loudly, circle overhead with their long tails streaming, then settle in the tops of tall trees.

BLUE-AND-YELLOW MACAW
Psittacidae *Ara ararauna*
RANGE: E Panama to N Bolivia and SE Brazil
HABITAT: forests along watercourses and swampy
regions up to 1,500 ft (500 m)
SIZE: 34 in (86 cm)

The large Blue-and-yellow Macaw has been seen eating at least 20 species of plant, many containing substances that are distasteful or toxic to humans, but apparently not to them. These macaws, and others, are often attracted to mineral licks where they eat clay, which may help to detoxify the noxious compounds in their diet.

SCARLET MACAW
Psittacidae *Ara macao*
RANGE: S Mexico, Central America to N Bolivia and C Brazil
HABITAT: lowland forest, to 1,300 ft (400 m)
SIZE: 33½ in (85 cm)

At sunrise Scarlet Macaws fly from their communal roosting sites to scattered feeding grounds in the forest. They are noisy in flight, uttering loud metallic screeches, but they always feed in silence. At dusk they return to their roosts, flying wing tip to wing tip through the thickening twilight.

MONK PARAKEET
Psittacidae *Myiopsitta monachus*
RANGE: C Bolivia, Paraguay, and S Brazil to C Argentina; introduced to USA, Puerto Rico
HABITAT: open woods, savanna, arid acacia scrub, cultivated land
SIZE: 11½ in (29 cm)

Uniquely among parrots, the Monk Parakeet builds a bulky nest of dry, often thorny twigs in the upper branches of a tree. They use the nests throughout the year for roosting as well as breeding, each pair incubating a clutch of 5–8 eggs on a bed of twigs.

race *luchsi*

race *monachus*

SUN CONURE
Psittacidae *Aratinga solstitialis*
RANGE: NE South America
HABITAT: savanna
SIZE: 12 in (30 cm)

A series of shrill, 2-note screeches will often draw attention to this brilliantly colored, gregarious parrot, which frequently gathers in large noisy flocks to feed on blossoms, fruits, seeds, and nuts in the treetops. It uses cavities in palm trees as nesting sites.

SPECTACLED PARROTLET
Psittacidae *Forpus conspicillatus*
RANGE: E Panama, Colombia, W Venezuela
HABITAT: open woods, forest edges and clearings, savanna
SIZE: 5 in (12 cm)

As they feed, Spectacled Parrotlets keep up a constant chatter and twitter of soft, finchlike calls, quite unlike the raucous screeches of larger parrots. Males are brighter than females, with blue markings on the wing, rump, lower back, and behind the eye.

YELLOW-CROWNED AMAZON
Psittacidae *Amazona ochrocephala*
RANGE: C Mexico, Trinidad, S to Amazon basin and E Peru; introduced to S California and S Florida
HABITAT: deciduous and humid lowland forest, open woods, savanna, pine ridges
SIZE: 14 in (35 cm)

race *ochrocephala*

race *tresmariae*

Yellow-crowned Amazons are opportunist feeders that gather in small groups in the treetops to forage for a wide variety of seeds, berries, fruits, and flowers. At dusk they return to their habitual roosts, flying with characteristic shallow wing beats below body level, rather like those of a duck.

ST VINCENT AMAZON
Psittacidae *Amazona guildingii*
RANGE: St Vincent (Lesser Antilles)
HABITAT: humid forest at 1,150–2,000 ft (350-600 m)
SIZE: 16–18 in (40–46 cm)

This large, picturesque, and colorful Amazon parrot is found only in the forests of the island of St Vincent, where it has suffered badly from habitat loss. The adult plumage is variable and virtually no 2 birds are exactly alike, but there are 2 basic color phases: the yellow-brown phase illustrated, and the green phase, which has the upper parts mainly dusky green, the base of the primaries green, and the underwing coverts and undersides of the flight feathers green.

HAWK-HEADED PARROT
Psittacidae *Deroptyus accipitrinus*
RANGE: South America N of the Amazon, W to SE Colombia and NE Peru
HABITAT: mixed forest and savanna
SIZE: 14 in (35 cm)

Sometimes known as the Red-fan Parrot, this bird has long red and blue feathers on its nape, which can be raised to form a ruff, giving it a uniquely hawklike appearance. It is also distinctive in flight, flying low through the forest, skimming the treetops, giving a few shallow flaps followed by a short glide, with its wings held angled slightly downward, its rounded gray-black tail feathers spread, and its head raised. It sometimes calls with a variety of chattering notes and soft whistles.

Turacos, Hoatzins, and Cuckoos

GREAT BLUE TURACO
Musophagidae *Corythaeola cristata*
RANGE: W Africa from Guinea to Nigeria, Congo Basin to
Kenya and Tanzania
HABITAT: lowland rain forest, patches of forest in savanna,
mountain forest
SIZE: 29½ in (75 cm)

By far the largest of the turacos, this bird's alternative name
is the Giant Turaco. It is adept at running along branches but
is a poor flier. Most flights are merely glides from tall trees and
often end abruptly in low vegetation; the bird then climbs quickly
back to the treetops.

GRAY GO-AWAY BIRD
Musophagidae *Corythaixoides concolor*
RANGE: S Africa, N to Angola and the Democratic
Republic of the Congo
HABITAT: dry, open woodland, parks, gardens
SIZE: 19 in (48 cm)

A loud, nasal, descending *g'wa-ay g'wa-ay* is often the first
indication that this bird is about. Also known as the Gray
Lourie, it is a greedy, untidy feeder, dropping many fruits,
pods, and flowers of the figs that make up its diet.

juv

VIOLET TURACO
Musophagidae *Musophaga violacea*
RANGE: W Africa, Senegal to Cameroon
HABITAT: tall forest, riverside forest
SIZE: 17 in (43 cm)

The red in the plumage of this and other turacos is
produced by a copper-based pigment called turacin.
The Violet Turaco's main call is a long series of deep,
gargling *cou-cou-vhou* notes that run into each other,
producing a pulsing roar when, as is nearly always the
case, 2 birds call in a slightly asynchronous duet.

race *corythaix*
"Knysna Turaco"

GREEN TURACO
Musophagidae *Tauraco persa*
RANGE: patchy from Senegal E to the Democratic Republic of the
Congo, Tanzania, and S to South Africa
HABITAT: evergreen forest, forested savanna, abandoned
cultivation, gardens
SIZE: 16½ in (42 cm)

The brilliant green plumage in this and other *Tauraco* species is not
due to iridescence, but to a unique green pigment, turacoverdin,
which contains copper. Green Turacos feed in groups in the
treetops, gorging themselves on fruit. If one begins to call the rest
will follow, producing a chorus of growling, guttural cries. In the
nesting season the birds become very territorial.

PRINCE RUSPOLI'S TURACO
Musophagidae *Tauraco ruspolii*
RANGE: 2 locations in Ethiopia
HABITAT: juniper forest with dense undergrowth,
scrub, acacia
SIZE: 16 in (41 cm)

This elusive turaco has been found only within 2 small
areas in Ethiopia. It has typical cackling, growling, and
gobbling calls, but it is secretive and difficult to find; it is
classified as vulnerable.

HOATZIN
Opisthocomidae *Opisthocomus hoazin*
RANGE: Amazon and Orinoco river basins and rivers
of the Guianas, from Guyana and Brazil to
Ecuador and Bolivia
HABITAT: flooded and riverside forest
SIZE: 23½ in (60 cm)

The Hoatzin is a poor flier, usually gliding from tree to
tree, clumsily flapping up to reach its goal and clambering
through the foliage using its large but weak wings for
support. It is the only tree-dwelling bird in which the chicks
habitually leave the nest soon after hatching.

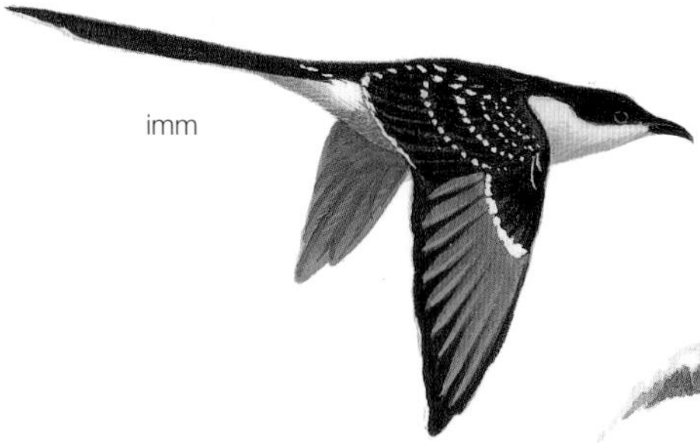

imm

GREAT SPOTTED CUCKOO
Cuculidae *Clamator glandarius*
RANGE: breeds SW Europe to Asia Minor, Africa; N populations winter in N Africa and S of Sahara, S populations winter in C Africa
HABITAT: open woods, bushy heath, scrub
SIZE: 16 in (40 cm)

The Great Spotted Cuckoo lays its eggs in the nests of various species of crow. Unlike that of the Eurasian Cuckoo, the nestling does not throw the eggs or chicks of its foster parent out of the nest, but usually successfully competes for food with the chicks or smothers them.

EURASIAN CUCKOO
Cuculidae *Cuculus canorus*
RANGE: breeds Europe, Asia S to Nepal, China, Japan; winters in Africa
HABITAT: farmland with hedgerows, woods, heaths and moors
SIZE: 13 in (33 cm)

Most females resemble the males, but in addition to the common gray phase females also have a rare rufous phase. Juvenile birds also show a similar variation, with the rufous phase more common than in the female.

♀

rufous phase

♂

young being fed by Dunnock

♂

imm rufous-backed phase

DIDRIC CUCKOO
Cuculidae *Chrysococcyx caprius*
RANGE: sub-Saharan Africa
HABITAT: savanna woodland, farmland, plantations
SIZE: 7–8 in (18–20 cm)

Males are brighter than females and are fond of high, open perches from which they can pounce on their insect prey. Immature Didric Cuckoos have 2 color phases: a rufous-backed phase and a green-backed phase.

race
scolopacea

♂

♀

♀

race
cyanocephala

COMMON KOEL
Cuculidae *Eudynamys scolopacea*
RANGE: N and E Australia, India, Southeast Asia to New Guinea and Solomon Islands
HABITAT: forests with fruiting trees
SIZE: 15–18 in (39–46 cm)

In the breeding season this cuckoo can often be heard calling—the male uttering loud, shrill whistles and the characteristic *ko-el* call, while the female responds with short, piercing whistles. Like most cuckoos, they lay their eggs in the nests of other birds: in India, the hosts are crows, while in Australia they include large honeyeaters and orioles.

CHANNEL-BILLED CUCKOO
Cuculidae *Scythrops novaehollandiae*
RANGE: breeds N and E Australia; winters New Guinea to Sulawesi (Celebes)
HABITAT: open forest, swamp woodland
SIZE: 23–25½ in (58–65 cm)

This bulky bird generally lays its eggs in the nests of crows and butcherbirds such as the Pied Currawong, *(Strepera graculina)*. When the young hatch they do not throw out the other nestlings, but simply take most of their food.

YELLOW-BILLED CUCKOO
Cuculidae *Coccyzus americanus*
RANGE: S Canada, USA S to Central America; winters in South America
HABITAT: open woods, streamside thickets
SIZE: 12 in (31 cm)

The handsome Yellow-billed Cuckoo is surprisingly agile among the trees as it forages for fruit and insects; it has a taste for hairy tent caterpillars and when these are abundant the Yellow-billed Cuckoos are often not far behind. Unlike Old World cuckoos, these birds build their own nests—small, flimsy affairs placed in bushes or trees.

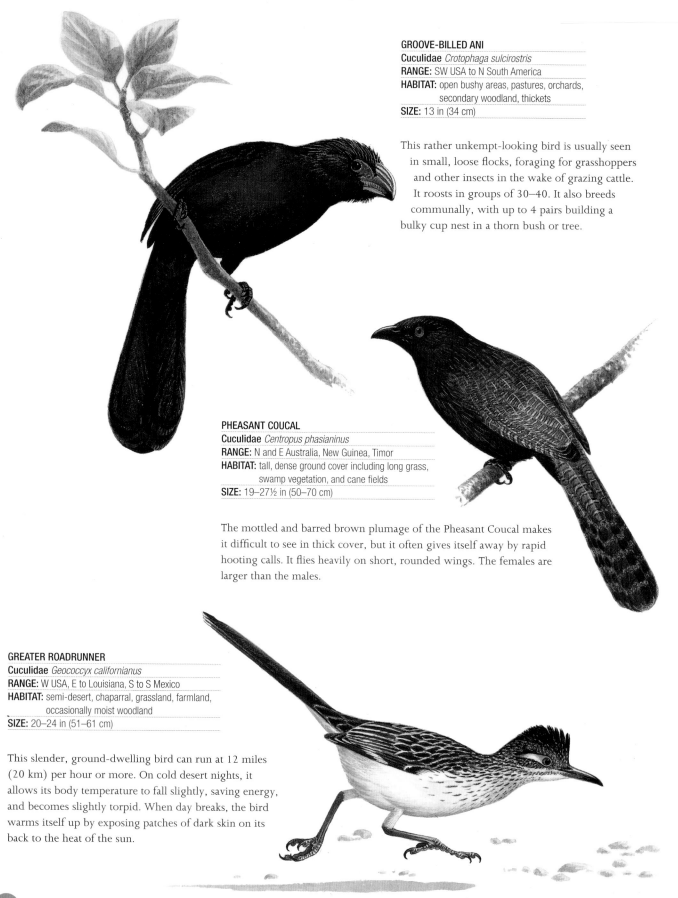

GROOVE-BILLED ANI
Cuculidae *Crotophaga sulcirostris*
RANGE: SW USA to N South America
HABITAT: open bushy areas, pastures, orchards, secondary woodland, thickets
SIZE: 13 in (34 cm)

This rather unkempt-looking bird is usually seen in small, loose flocks, foraging for grasshoppers and other insects in the wake of grazing cattle. It roosts in groups of 30–40. It also breeds communally, with up to 4 pairs building a bulky cup nest in a thorn bush or tree.

PHEASANT COUCAL
Cuculidae *Centropus phasianinus*
RANGE: N and E Australia, New Guinea, Timor
HABITAT: tall, dense ground cover including long grass, swamp vegetation, and cane fields
SIZE: 19–27½ in (50–70 cm)

The mottled and barred brown plumage of the Pheasant Coucal makes it difficult to see in thick cover, but it often gives itself away by rapid hooting calls. It flies heavily on short, rounded wings. The females are larger than the males.

GREATER ROADRUNNER
Cuculidae *Geococcyx californianus*
RANGE: W USA, E to Louisiana, S to S Mexico
HABITAT: semi-desert, chaparral, grassland, farmland, occasionally moist woodland
SIZE: 20–24 in (51–61 cm)

This slender, ground-dwelling bird can run at 12 miles (20 km) per hour or more. On cold desert nights, it allows its body temperature to fall slightly, saving energy, and becomes slightly torpid. When day breaks, the bird warms itself up by exposing patches of dark skin on its back to the heat of the sun.

Owls

BARN OWL
Tytonidae *Tyto alba*
RANGE: Americas, Europe, Africa, Arabia, India, Southeast Asia, Australia
HABITAT: mainly open or semi-open lowlands, including farmland
SIZE: 13–14 in (33–35 cm)

Barn Owls hunt mostly on the wing, low down, with a characteristic light, buoyant action, frequent changes of direction and, sometimes, periods of hovering. They can locate and capture their prey solely by using their phenomenal sense of hearing.

race *alba*

BAY OWL
Tytonidae *Phodilus badius*
RANGE: N India, Southeast Asia
HABITAT: mainly tropical forest
SIZE: 9–13 in (23–33 cm)

The Bay Owl's short wings and long tail are typical of an owl that hunts in thick cover and it is known to prey on small mammals, birds, lizards, amphibians, and insects. They may also eat fish.

race *pallescens*

GREAT HORNED OWL
Strigidae *Bubo virginianus*
RANGE: North America, except tundra regions of Alaska and Canada, S to Tierra del Fuego
HABITAT: lowlands to tree line in deciduous or coniferous boreal, temperate and tropical forests, prairies, deserts, farmland, and occasionally suburban areas
SIZE: 17–18 in (43–46 cm)

The Great Horned Owl has been separated into many races, which vary both in size and in color. The largest are found at high latitudes and altitudes and the smallest in tropical lowland forests and deserts. The song consists of a series of booming hoots and it has a range of calls including barks, growls, and screams.

race *virginianus*

BROWN FISH OWL
Strigidae *Bubo zeylonensis*
RANGE: Middle East (rare); India and Southeast Asia
HABITAT: forest and woodland along streams and lakes
SIZE: 21–22½ in (54–57 cm)

Brown Fish Owls have bare legs and feet, with many tiny, sharp spines on the soles of their toes that enable them to grasp wet, slippery prey. They hunt from trees overhanging the water, from rocks or by wading in the shallows, and have also been seen flying over the surface and taking fish from the water.

NORTHERN EAGLE OWL
Strigidae *Bubo bubo*
RANGE: N Africa, Eurasia (not British Isles)
HABITAT: mainly wild, broken country, often in hills with tree cover, but not dense forests; also desert edge
SIZE: 23½–29½ in (60–75 cm)

race bubo

Northern Eagle Owls are able to take mammals up to the size of young Roe Deer and birds as big as cock Capercaillies *Tetrao urogallus*. The male's song is a deep double hoot, audible over ½ mile (1 km) or more away in still conditions.

PEL'S FISHING OWL
Strigidae *Scotopelia peli*
RANGE: sub-Saharan Africa, excluding SW
HABITAT: forested river banks, wetlands
SIZE: 20–24 in (51–61 cm)

This is the largest and most widely distributed of the 3 African fishing owls. Its calls are a series of resounding hoots, repeated at 10-second intervals for several minutes at a time and audible up to 2 miles (3 km) away. Its legs and feet are unfeathered, as are those of the other fishing owls.

SNOWY OWL
Strigidae *Nyctea scandiaca*
RANGE: circumpolar Arctic
HABITAT: mainly on tundra; also in other wild habitats, from coastal islands to moorland
SIZE: 21–26 in (53–66 cm)

There is a particularly great difference in size between the sexes, females being up to 20 percent larger than males. Also unusual is the marked difference in plumage between the almost all-white male and the strongly barred and chevroned female. Over much of its breeding range it feeds largely on lemmings.

juv

HAWK OWL
Strigidae *Surnia ulula*
RANGE: N Eurasia, North America, mainly subarctic
HABITAT: boreal and mountain forest with easy access to clearings and forest edge
SIZE: 14–15 in (36–39 cm)

This is one of a relatively small number of owls that are habitually active during the daytime. In summer, the prey consists almost entirely of small voles, some other mammals, and small birds; in winter the Hawk Owl may take a greater proportion of birds. Its numbers can vary dramatically depending on the availability of its prey.

AFRICAN WOOD OWL
Strigidae *Strix woodfordi*
RANGE: sub-Saharan Africa, except extreme S
HABITAT: forests, plantations
SIZE: 12–14 in (30–35 cm)

The African Wood Owl is a big-headed, cryptically colored, highly nocturnal wood owl. It generally hunts from a low perch, taking most of its prey from the ground, but also picks insects off vegetation while in flight and is surprisingly agile at hawking for flying insects.

race *sylvatica*
rufous phase

EURASIAN TAWNY OWL
Strigidae *Strix aluco*
RANGE: Europe, N Africa, parts of W Asia, China, Korea, Taiwan
HABITAT: chiefly woodland or areas with some trees, including urban areas
SIZE: 14½–15 in (37–39 cm)

The male's hoot is slightly lower pitched and more clearly phrased than that of the female; often the female replies with a *kewick* call, a variant of which is used by both sexes as a contact call. This combination is popularly represented as *tu-whit, to-woo* and wrongly ascribed to a single bird. Between 10 and 15 races of the Eurasian Tawny Owl are recognized, with distinct reddish-brown and gray color phases in most regions.

chick

race *alucco*
gray phase

PEARL-SPOTTED OWLET
Strigidae *Glaucidium perlatum*
RANGE: sub-Saharan Africa
HABITAT: woodland and savanna
SIZE: 6½–7 in (17–18 cm)

race
nebulosa

GREAT GRAY OWL
Strigidae *Strix nebulosa*
RANGE: N Europe, N America, N Asia
HABITAT: dense, mature boreal forest
SIZE: 25½–27½ in. (65–70 cm)

This magnificent northern forest owl has a wingspan of over 5 ft (1.5 m), and feeds largely on voles. It is often active in daylight and is also capable of finding and capturing its prey in deep snow, apparently by hearing alone. This is one of a number of owls that is exceptionally bold in defense of its nest.

The Pearl-spotted Owlet is the most diurnal of the African owls, regularly hunting during the day. Prominent "false eyes" on the rear of its head are a useful identification feature. It prefers open bush-type savanna and shuns areas where the ground cover is other than sparse.

gray phase

rufous phase

NORTHERN PYGMY OWL

Strigidae *Glaucidium gnoma*
RANGE: W North America (N to Alaska, E to Rocky
Mountains) S to Guatemala
HABITAT: dense woodland in mountains and foothills
SIZE: 6½ in (17 cm)

The tiny Northern Pygmy Owl is strong and ferocious out of all proportion to its size and sometimes takes prey much larger than itself. It has a pair of prominent white-edged black patches at the back of its head resembling eyes, which may help the owls to survive by confusing predators and prey. There are 2 color phases—a gray one and a reddish-brown one.

young in
nest-hole

ELF OWL

Strigidae *Micrathene whitneyi*
RANGE: SW USA S to Baja California and N
Mexico; winters in Mexico
HABITAT: deserts, riparian areas, mountain oak,
and mixed pine and oak forests
SIZE: 5–6 in (13.5–14.5 cm)

The world's smallest owl, the Elf Owl's short tail and less robust shape distinguish it from other Lilliputian, "earless" owls, the Northern Pygmy Owl and the Ferruginous Pygmy Owl. Unlike the pygmy owls, the Elf Owl is strictly nocturnal. Noisy chirps and puppylike yips, often in a series, are its most common calls.

LITTLE OWL

Strigidae *Athene noctua*
RANGE: Europe, N Africa, Middle East, Asia
HABITAT: varied open or semi-open areas
SIZE: 8–9 in (21–23 cm)

race *lilith*

race *vidalii*

The Little Owl shows considerable variation in color, ranging from the dark, strongly marked race *A.n. vidalii* from western Europe to the very pale desert races such as the Middle Eastern race *A. n. lilith*. It is quite active during the day and is much more terrestrial than most owls, often foraging on foot and also sometimes nesting in holes in the ground, including rabbit burrows.

race *hypugaea*

BURROWING OWL

Strigidae *Athene cunicularia*
RANGE: extreme SW Canada, W USA, Florida, Central America
and South America (except the Amazon Basin)
HABITAT: grassland, deserts, farmlands with low-growing or
sparse vegetation, airports, golf courses
SIZE: 7–10 in (18–25 cm)

The Burrowing Owl can be distinguished from other small owls in its range by its long, sparsely feathered legs. Burrowing Owls lay their eggs in a burrow in the ground, often one excavated by a small mammal. They have a mellow *toot tooo* territorial song; adults utter a harsh rattle if a predator approaches the nest and the young make a sound like a rattlesnake when cornered.

juv at
entrance

NORTHERN SAW-WHET OWL
Strigidae *Aegolius acadicus*
RANGE: E and C North America from Nova Scotia S to N Midwest USA; W North America from S Alaska to S California; also extends S in E and W mountain ranges, in W as far as S Mexico
HABITAT: coniferous, deciduous, and mixed deciduous and coniferous forests and woods, riverside thickets
SIZE: 6½–7 in (17–19 cm)

juv

This relatively tame owl is a smaller version of the more widespread Tengmalm's, or Boreal, Owl of northern Europe, Siberia, Alaska, and Canada. The odd name refers to the bird's song, which resembles the sound of a saw-blade being sharpened.

PAPUAN HAWK-OWL
Strigidae *Uroglaux dimorpha*
RANGE: sparsely distributed throughout New Guinea; Yapen Island
HABITAT: lowland rain forest, rarely reaching as high as 5,000 ft (1.500 m)
SIZE: 12–13 in (30–33 cm)

As its name suggests, the Papuan Hawk-Owl is more hawklike than other owls, with a slim build, small head, and a very long tail accounting for half its total length. It is a rare and little-known species, whose calls and nesting habits remain to be discovered.

BOOBOOK OWL
Strigidae *Ninox novaeseelandiae*
RANGE: Australia, Tasmania, Lesser Sundas, Moluccas, S New Guinea, Norfolk Island, New Zealand
HABITAT: forest, woodland, scrub, urban trees
SIZE: 10–14 in (25–35 cm)

race *ocellata*

race *leucopsis*

This common small brown owl's familiar double hoot is reminiscent of the call of the European Cuckoo. Boobook Owls feed mainly on insects, sometimes caught around town lights, and also on small mammals, birds, and geckos. By day they roost in thick foliage or sometimes in tree hollows, caves, or buildings.

race *otus*
cryptic posture

LONG-EARED OWL
Strigidae *Asio otus*
RANGE: breeds Europe, parts of N Africa, N Asia, N America; birds from extreme N migrate S, some beyond breeding range in America and Far East
HABITAT: woods, forests, copses, shelterbelts, mature scrub
SIZE: 14–14½ in (35–37 cm)

Like Scops and Screech Owls, Long-Eared Owls often adopt an extraordinary elongated cryptic posture when perched in trees during the daytime and look exactly like broken branches. Compared with the Eurasian race *A. o. otus*, most North American Long-eared Owls of the race *A. o. wilsonianus* are more barred than streaked below, have a more golden-red facial disc, and yellow rather than orange-red eyes.

SHORT-EARED OWL
Strigidae *Asio flammeus*
RANGE: N Europe, N Asia, North and South America; N populations migrate E, W, or S, some far to S of breeding range
HABITAT: moors, heath, grassland, marshes, and other open habitats
SIZE: 14½–15 in (37–39 cm)

Often hunting by day (especially in winter), Short-eared Owls are easily seen—unlike most owls. The male's song is a series of low, muted hoots, often uttered during aerial display flights. Like the Long-eared Owl, this species displays in flight by clapping its wing tips rapidly beneath its body; the sound thus produced carries surprisingly far.

JAMAICAN OWL
Strigidae *Pseudoscops grammicus*
RANGE: Jamaica
HABITAT: woodland, parklike areas
SIZE: 12–14 in (30–36 cm)

Found only on the island of Jamaica, very little is known of its biology. This strictly nocturnal owl hunts in both open country and woodland. The voice of the Jamaican Owl is a guttural growl, sometimes interpreted as a *wow*, and an occasional high-pitched, tremulous *whoooo*.

brown individual

EURASIAN SCOPS OWL
Strigidae *Otus scops*
RANGE: breeds S Europe, N Africa, E to SW Siberia; N populations and some S ones winter in tropical Africa
HABITAT: open woodland, parks, orchards, gardens, roadside trees, town squares
SIZE: 7½–8 in (19–20 cm)

This small, superbly camouflaged owl may be either gray-brown or red-brown in basic color. It is far more often heard than seen, its song—a monotonously repeated single, plaintive, whistling, note—being one of the most characteristic sounds of the Mediterranean night.

gray individual

rufous phase

gray phase

EASTERN SCREECH OWL
Strigidae *Otus asio*
RANGE: E North America from extreme S Quebec and Ontario to E Montana and C Texas and from S Canada to the tip of Florida and NE Mexico
HABITAT: open forest, riverside woodland, orchards and other cultivated land, parks and gardens with large trees
SIZE: 7½–9 in (19–23 cm)

The Eastern Screech Owl's primary song is a tremulous descending whinny. It also utters a quickly repeated, monotonous *who-who-who* all on one pitch. Twitters and barks are given in agitation. Small mammals and birds and large insects form their chief prey, but these owls sometimes kill birds larger than themselves.

CRESTED OWL
Strigidae *Lophostrix cristata*
RANGE: S Mexico to Bolivia, E Ecuador, Amazonian Brazil E of Andes
HABITAT: forest, tall, second growth, and patches of woodland bordering streams and rivers, chiefly in tropical lowlands
SIZE: 15–16 in (38–40 cm)

During the day the Crested Owl roosts in thick cover, often near a stream. Although the sexes are alike, this owl has 2 color phases, one uniform dark brown, the other pale buff. Its calls are brief, beginning with 3–4 low stuttering notes followed by a deep-throated growl.

juv

SPECTACLED OWL
Strigidae *Pulsatrix perspicillata*
RANGE: S Mexico to NW Argentina and S Brazil
HABITAT: lowland forest, savanna, plantations
SIZE: 17–18 in (43–46 cm)

Female Spectacled Owls are generally larger than males. In contrast to their parents, the young are white with brown wings and have brown spectacles. Its call includes a gruff *bu-hu-hu*, a descending whistled call, and a series of 6–8 low resonant hoots with a slight popping quality.

Nocturnal insect eaters

OILBIRD
Steatornithidae *Steatornis caripensis*
RANGE: Panama to N South America, Trinidad
HABITAT: humid forest, caves
SIZE: 19 in (48 cm)

Flocks of these birds feed together at night, often traveling long distances from the caves where they roost and nest to find the oily fruits of laurels, palms, and incense trees. They do not settle on the trees, but gather the fruit in flight with their long hooked bills and store it in their stomachs, digesting it during the day when they are back in the caves. In the pitch darkness of the cave they find their way by echolocation.

nestling

TAWNY FROGMOUTH
Podargidae *Podargus strigoides*
RANGE: Australia and Tasmania
HABITAT: open forest, rain forest edge, urban trees
SIZE: 14–21 in (35–53 cm)

The Tawny Frogmouth roosts by day on the branch of a tree, where its cryptic, mottled gray plumage looks like bark. It feeds at night on small ground animals. It varies geographically in size and color; females of some races have an uncommon rufous phase.

♂
race
brachyrus

♂
race
phalaenoides

dark brown phase

gray phase

COMMON POTOO
Nyctibiidae *Nyctibius griseus*
RANGE: W Mexico to Uruguay, West Indies
HABITAT: lowland tropical forest, forest edge, open woods along streams, mangroves
SIZE: 14–16 in (36–41 cm)

Named for its melancholy 2-note call, the Common Potoo feeds by night, flying up from a favored perch to capture insects on the wing in its large mouth. By day it normally perches motionless on a branch. Its intricately patterned cryptic plumage varies from grayish to dark brown.

gray phase

AUSTRALIAN OWLET-NIGHTJAR
Aegothelidae *Aegotheles cristatus*
RANGE: Australia, Tasmania, S New Guinea
HABITAT: open forest and woodland
SIZE: 8–10 in (21–25 cm)

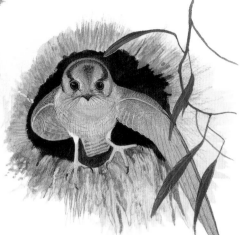

rufous phase
roost hole

The Australian Owlet-Nightjar is a delicate, mottled gray or rufous bird, with short wings, large eyes, very soft plumage, and a mothlike flight. It feeds by night; by day it roosts alone in a crevice or hole, but will some times sun itself at the entrance and often utters its churring call in daylight.

race *minor*

COMMON NIGHTHAWK
Caprimulgidae *Chordeiles minor*
RANGE: breeds in North America (except extreme N) and West Indies; winters in South America S to Argentina
HABITAT: open fields, gravelly areas, grassland, savanna, semi-desert, towns
SIZE: 9½ in (24 cm)

The white patches on the wings of the Common Nighthawk are conspicuous as it swoops through the twilight in pursuit of flying insects. The bird's color varies from dark brown in the eastern North American race *C. m. minor* to paler grayish brown in the Great Plains race *C. m. sennetti*: these color differences are subtle in adults but striking in juveniles.

COMMON POORWILL
Caprimulgidae *Phalaenoptilus nuttallii*
RANGE: breeds in W USA and Mexico; winters S to C Mexico
HABITAT: arid and semi-arid country, prairie, scrub woodland, pine forest
SIZE: 8 in (20 cm)

The smallest of the North American nightjars, the Common Poorwill resembles a large moth in flight. The male has bolder white tips to his tail than the female. The name "poorwill" is derived from its simple 2-note whistle. In desert areas during winter, the Common Poorwill becomes torpid and enters a state resembling hibernation. This is most unusual among birds.

WHIP-POOR-WILL
Caprimulgidae *Caprimulgus vociferus*
RANGE: breeds in E USA and S Canada, also SW USA and Mexico; winters from Mexico through Central America to Panama
HABITAT: deciduous, mountain, and mixed pine-oak forests and woods
SIZE: 10 in (25 cm)

The Whip-poor-will feeds at night and by twilight, pursuing insects on the wing and flying close to the ground, its wide mouth gaping to scoop up prey. Whip-poor-wills tend to synchronize their breeding with the full moon, presumably to make hunting easier when they are feeding the young.

EUROPEAN NIGHTJAR
Caprimulgidae *Caprimulgus europaeus*
RANGE: breeds in Europe, E to C Asia, and N to S Scandinavia; winters in Africa
HABITAT: scrub, heathland, recently felled woodland
SIZE: 11 in (28 cm)

This bird's song is a persistent, monotonous churring, accompanied by wing claps during the male's evening display flights in the breeding season. The tiny bill gives little indication of the huge gape, which is fringed with stiff bristles to improve its efficiency as a snare. The bird always hunts on the wing.

STANDARD-WINGED NIGHTJAR
Caprimulgidae *Macrodipteryx longipennis*
RANGE: tropical Africa
HABITAT: open forest
SIZE: 11 in (28 cm)

The male's second primary flight feathers become elongated to 18–21 in (45–53 cm) in the breeding season, and he uses them in his courtship display as flaglike "standards," circling slowly around a potential mate, with his wings vibrating rapidly and the standards blowing up over his back. Once they have done their job they usually break off, allowing the bird to fly normally again.

courtship display flight

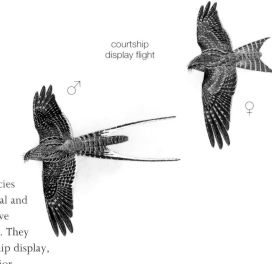

courtship display flight

SCISSOR-TAILED NIGHTJAR
Caprimulgidae *Hydropsalis brasiliana*
RANGE: E Peru, Brazil S of Amazon, Paraguay, Uruguay, N and C Argentina
HABITAT: lowland forest, dry woods, clearings
SIZE: male 20 in (51 cm); female 12 in (30 cm)

Like the Standard-winged Nightjar, this species has elongated feathers, in this case the central and outermost feathers of the tail. Both sexes have them, but they are much longer in the male. They are probably important in the bird's courtship display, but little is known about its breeding behavior.

Swifts, tree swifts, hummingbirds

BLACK SWIFT
Apodidae *Nephoecetes niger*
RANGE: W North America from Alaska to California and
Central America S to Costa Rica, West Indies;
winters in tropical America
HABITAT: mountains
SIZE: 7 in (18 cm)

This is the largest and rarest North American
breeding swift. Like all swifts, it hawks for
insects on the wing. It nests on cliffs and in
canyons and often chooses a site behind a
waterfall, so that it has to fly in and out through
the cascading water. This provides excellent
defense against predators.

EDIBLE-NEST SWIFTLET
Apodidae *Aerodramus fuciphagus*
RANGE: Malaysia, Indonesia
HABITAT: tropical forest with caves, limestone areas,
sandstone sea cliffs
SIZE: 4 in (10 cm)

nest site

BROWN SPINETAILED SWIFT
Apodidae *Hirundapus gigantea*
RANGE: India, Southeast Asia, Indonesia
HABITAT: forested valleys, grassy hilltops
SIZE: 8 in (21 cm)

Despite its heavy-bodied
appearance, this bird is
a spectacularly fast and
acrobatic performer in the air. It uses
its speed and agility to catch flying insects
and, like many other swifts, it spends much
of its life on the wing. A courting pair will
even mate in flight.

All swifts use dried saliva to cement
their nesting materials together, but
the cave swiftlets use more than
most. The nests of this species are
cups of almost pure saliva and are
collected in great quantities for
use in Chinese bird's-nest soup.
They breed in vast colonies in
the high recesses of large caves, using
echolocation to navigate in the dark.

nest

CHIMNEY SWIFT
Apodidae *Chaetura pelagica*
RANGE: breeds E USA and S Canada; winters in
Central and NE South America
HABITAT: open and wooded areas, often in towns
SIZE: 5 in (13 cm)

This small, dark swift nests and roosts in huge colonies, sometimes numbering several
thousand birds, which may overlap like shingles on a roof. The nest is made of thin
twigs, which the bird snatches in its feet while in flight.

WHITE-THROATED SWIFT
Apodidae *Aeronautes saxatilis*
RANGE: N Central America and W USA
HABITAT: mountains and sea cliffs
SIZE: 6½ in (17 cm)

LESSER SWALLOW-TAILED SWIFT
Apodidae *Panyptila cayennensis*
RANGE: S Mexico to Peru and Brazil
HABITAT: aerial, over many types of terrain
SIZE: 5 in (13 cm)

This species is only a summer visitor to much of its range in the USA. It often breeds high in the mountains, and has been recorded nesting at 13,000 ft (4,000 m). The clutch size is large for a swift, with as many as 6 eggs.

nest

With its deeply forked tail, this is the most swallowlike of all the true swifts, although in the air it usually holds its tail closed in a single point. Its flight is fast and agile, if slightly erratic, as it coasts and then accelerates with rapid wing beats.

AFRICAN PALM SWIFT
Apodidae *Cypsiurus parvus*
RANGE: sub-Saharan Africa, except much of Ethiopia, Somalia, and S Africa
HABITAT: aerial, near palms
SIZE: 6 in (15 cm)

nest

Always found in association with palms, this swift's nest is little more than a pad of feathers and plant down, glued to the vertical underside of a palm frond with saliva. The 2 eggs are also glued to the nest and the nestlings have long curved claws, enabling them to cling on tightly as the palm fronds are whipped about during windy weather.

ALPINE SWIFT
Apodidae *Tachymarptis melba*
RANGE: Mediterranean and S Asia to India, also S and E Africa; N birds winter in Africa S to South Africa and in India
HABITAT: aerial over hilly country
SIZE: 8½ in (22 cm)

More than twice the size of the Eurasian Swift, this powerful swift is usually seen hunting high over the rocky terrain. Alpine Swifts are monogamous, retaining the same mate for several years, but they breed in colonies of up to 170 pairs. They rarely fly in bad weather, preferring to roost in the colony.

EURASIAN SWIFT
Apodidae *Apus apus*
RANGE: most of Europe, parts of N Africa and C Asia, and
  E almost to Pacific; winters in tropical Africa
HABITAT: aerial; breeds in buildings and rock crevices
SIZE: 5½ in (14 cm)

The Eurasian Swift feeds, drinks, sleeps, and mates on the wing, returning to earth only to lay its eggs and feed its chicks. A young bird may spend up to 4 years in the air, from the moment it leaves the nest to the day it returns to the colony to rear its own family.

CRESTED TREE SWIFT
Hemiprocnidae *Hemiprocne longipennis*
RANGE: India, Southeast Asia
HABITAT: open woods, clearings, gardens
SIZE: 6 in (15 cm)

nest

True swifts spend nearly all their time in the air, but the Crested Tree Swift is well able to perch and often alights on treetops to rest and preen, sitting bolt upright with its crest raised. It is most active at dawn and dusk and can often be seen hunting in loose flocks.

LONG-TAILED HERMIT
Trochilidae *Phaethornis superciliosus*
RANGE: E Mexico to Bolivia and Brazil
HABITAT: lowland forest understorey and tall
  secondary growth
SIZE: 6 in (15 cm)

The Long-tailed Hermit's downcurved bill allows it to extract nectar from large flowers such passion flowers, but it also gleans insects and spiders from leaves and cobwebs. The males form singing assemblies, or "leks," and compete with each other to attract mates. The best singers usually mate with all the available females.

at nest

REDDISH HERMIT
Trochilidae *Phaethornis ruber*
RANGE: Colombia and Venezuela to N Bolivia and S Brazil
HABITAT: humid forest undergrowth, forest edge, secondary
  woodland, scrub
SIZE: 3½ in (9 cm)

Like other hermits, this small hummingbird prefers to fly along a circuit of food sources instead of establishing a feeding territory. It has an insectlike, weaving flight that generates an audible humming—the origin of their common name.

WHITE-TIPPED SICKLEBILL
Trochilidae *Eutoxeres aquila*
RANGE: Costa Rica to W Ecuador and NE Peru
HABITAT: forest understorey, forest edge, secondary growth
SIZE: 5 in (13 cm)

This hummingbird probes the curved blooms of plants such as certain heliconias with its downcurved bill. It prefers to feed at hanging bunches of flowers, clinging to them with its feet as it sips the nectar. In the process it becomes dusted with pollen and cross-pollinates other heliconia flowers.

VIOLET SABREWING
Trochilidae *Campylopterus hemileucurus*
RANGE: S Mexico to W Panama
HABITAT: mountain forest, in understorey and at edges, especially near streams
SIZE: 6 in (15 cm)

This hummingbird is named for the glittering violet plumage of the male and the thickened and flattened shafts of the outer 2 primary feathers. The female is mainly gray and, unusually for a hummingbird, smaller. It can often be located while feeding by its explosive twittering.

RUBY-TOPAZ HUMMINGBIRD
Trochilidae *Chrysolampis mosquitus*
RANGE: Trinidad and Tobago, N and C South America
HABITAT: arid open country, gardens, lowlands up to 5,750 ft (1,750 m)
SIZE: 3½ in (9 cm)

The glittering male courts his mate alone, putting on a spectacularly beautiful display in which he circles rapidly around her with widely fanned tail and raised crown feathers. He is very aggressive at this time and will even attack birds of prey. The nest is a tiny lichen-covered cup lined with plant down.

FRILLED COQUETTE
Trochilidae *Lophornis magnifica*
RANGE: E and C Brazil
HABITAT: forest, scrub, parkland
SIZE: 2 in (7 cm)

During courtship the male and female hover together, dancing up and down in the air. After mating, the female builds a simple cup-shaped nest in low vegetation, fastening it down by working the fibers of the bottom and one side around the supporting twig.

race *townsendi*

FORK-TAILED WOODNYMPH
Trochilidae *Thalurania furcata*
RANGE: NW and C South America from W Ecuador to E Bolivia and Paraguay
HABITAT: humid forest and forest edge in lowlands and foothills
SIZE: male 4 in (10 cm); female 3 in (8 cm)

Unusually for a hummingbird, the female is considerably smaller than her mate. This has its drawbacks: small hummingbirds may have to eat up to half their body weight in food every day to maintain their body heat. At night hummingbirds often become torpid, regaining their normal temperature when the sun raises the air temperature the following day.

race *polytmus*

GLITTERING-THROATED EMERALD
Trochilidae *Amazilia fimbriata*
RANGE: N South America, E of Andes to S Bolivia and S Brazil
HABITAT: shrubby secondary growth, forest edge, up to 1,650 ft (500 m)
SIZE: 3 in (8 cm)

STREAMERTAIL
Trochilidae *Trochilus polytmus*
RANGE: Jamaica
HABITAT: semi-arid lowlands to high mountains, including man-made habitats
SIZE: 10 in (25 cm)

The male is the most spectacular of all Jamaican hummingbirds. He has glittering green plumage with two 6-in (15-cm) black tail feathers. During the mating display he will fly before a perched female in short pendulums, chirping rhythmically, or perch near her and wave his fluttering streamers from side to side.

This tiny hummingbird feeds mainly on nectar. It often perches on bare, exposed twigs, calling with a soft tapping note like 2 small pebbles being struck together. It nearly always nests low down, attaching its nest to a fork in a bush or the tip of a low tree branch.

CRIMSON TOPAZ

Trochilidae *Topaza pella*
RANGE: Guianas, SE Venezuela, NE Brazil, E Ecuador
HABITAT: rain forest
SIZE: male 8 in (20 cm); female 7 in (18 cm)

Over a third of the male's length is accounted for by 2 long, slender, inward-curving tail feathers. With their relatively short bills, these birds are less specialized than long-billed hummingbirds and will take nectar from a wide variety of flowers, as well as catching insects.

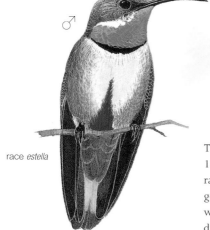

race *estella*

ANDEAN HILLSTAR

Trochilidae *Oreotrochilus estella*
RANGE: Andes from Ecuador to Argentina, Chile, and N Peru
HABITAT: rocky gorges, grassy low scrubby growth with grasses, high plateaux
SIZE: 5 in (13 cm)

The Andean Hillstar lives in the harsh climate and sparse vegetation above 13,000 ft (4,000 m). It uses its disproportionately large feet to perch rather than hover when it is feeding on nectar. Females feed in abundant gorges containing high concentrations of blooms close to nest sites, whereas males tend to feed in open areas where the flowers are more dispersed. Courtship thus brings the male into the female's territory, which is the reverse of the situation in most hummingbirds.

GIANT HUMMINGBIRD

Trochilidae *Patagona gigas*
RANGE: Andes from Ecuador to Chile and Argentina
HABITAT: mountain scrub and river bank forest, cultivated land
SIZE: 7½–8 in (19–20 cm)

This is the largest of all hummingbirds. Its long pointed wings occasionally perform a flap-sail flight pattern, and its wing beats are noticeably slower than those of other hummingbirds when hovering before flowers to glean food.

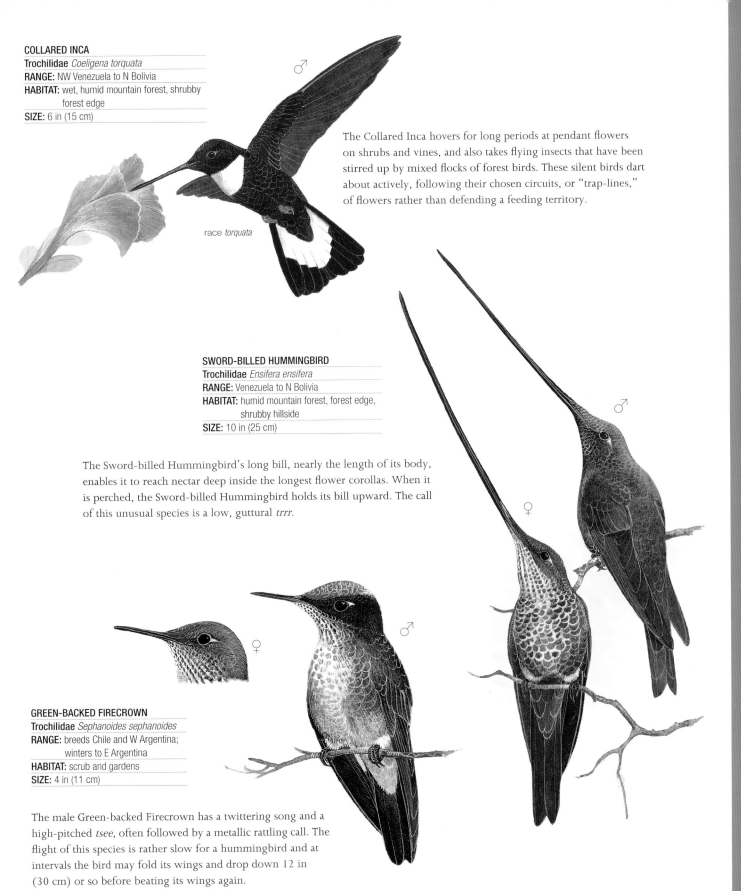

COLLARED INCA
Trochilidae *Coeligena torquata*
RANGE: NW Venezuela to N Bolivia
HABITAT: wet, humid mountain forest, shrubby forest edge
SIZE: 6 in (15 cm)

♂

race *torquata*

The Collared Inca hovers for long periods at pendant flowers on shrubs and vines, and also takes flying insects that have been stirred up by mixed flocks of forest birds. These silent birds dart about actively, following their chosen circuits, or "trap-lines," of flowers rather than defending a feeding territory.

SWORD-BILLED HUMMINGBIRD
Trochilidae *Ensifera ensifera*
RANGE: Venezuela to N Bolivia
HABITAT: humid mountain forest, forest edge, shrubby hillside
SIZE: 10 in (25 cm)

♂

♀

The Sword-billed Hummingbird's long bill, nearly the length of its body, enables it to reach nectar deep inside the longest flower corollas. When it is perched, the Sword-billed Hummingbird holds its bill upward. The call of this unusual species is a low, guttural *trrr*.

♀

♂

GREEN-BACKED FIRECROWN
Trochilidae *Sephanoides sephanoides*
RANGE: breeds Chile and W Argentina; winters to E Argentina
HABITAT: scrub and gardens
SIZE: 4 in (11 cm)

The male Green-backed Firecrown has a twittering song and a high-pitched *tsee*, often followed by a metallic rattling call. The flight of this species is rather slow for a hummingbird and at intervals the bird may fold its wings and drop down 12 in (30 cm) or so before beating its wings again.

GLOWING PUFFLEG
Trochilidae *Eriocnemis vestitus*
RANGE: NW Venezuela to E Ecuador and N Peru
HABITAT: high mountain forest edge, scrub
SIZE: 3½ in (9 cm)

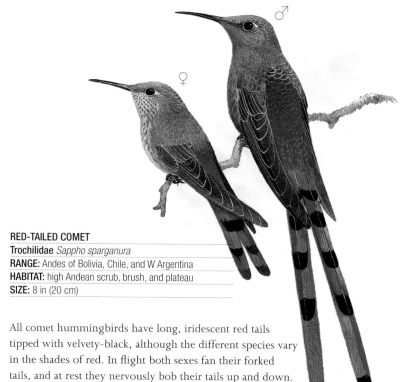

In good light this bird's brilliant colors, particularly its upper tail coverts, really do glow, while its spectacular white leg muffs make it look as though each leg is wrapped in fresh cotton.

BLACK-TAILED TRAINBEARER
Trochilidae *Lesbia victoriae*
RANGE: Colombia and Ecuador S to S Peru
HABITAT: grassy slopes and shrubby areas, upper subtropical and temperate zones of the Andes
SIZE: male up to 10 in (25 cm); female up to 5½ in (14 cm)

The male's song is a rattling trill that descends at the end; it changes to simple high-pitched chip notes while he is foraging. The deeply forked tail is much longer in the male than in the female, measuring up to over half his total length.

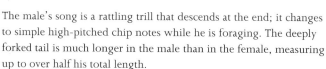

RED-TAILED COMET
Trochilidae *Sappho sparganura*
RANGE: Andes of Bolivia, Chile, and W Argentina
HABITAT: high Andean scrub, brush, and plateau
SIZE: 8 in (20 cm)

All comet hummingbirds have long, iridescent red tails tipped with velvety-black, although the different species vary in the shades of red. In flight both sexes fan their forked tails, and at rest they nervously bob their tails up and down.

BEARDED HELMETCREST
Trochilidae *Oxypogon guerinii*
RANGE: NW Venezuela, N and C Colombia
HABITAT: bushy or grassy slopes above 10,000 ft (3,000 m)
SIZE: 4 in (11 cm)

The female Bearded Helmetcrest lacks the unique crest and white beard of the male, but both are well camouflaged to blend into their open environment. Bearded Helmetcrests forage at low flowering shrubs by hovering or clinging briefly to sip nectar from the blossoms or capture visiting insects.

race *querinni*

LONG-TAILED SYLPH
Trochilidae *Aglaiocercus kingi*
RANGE: Venezuela, Colombia, Ecuador, Peru, and Bolivia
HABITAT: from 3,000–10,000 ft (900–3,000 m) in tropical and subtropical humid forest and scrub, gardens, plantations
SIZE: male 7 in (18 cm); female 4 in (10 cm)

The Long-tailed Sylph feeds forages by "trap-lining" —making a regular circuit of flowers within a territory. It also takes nectar or insects while hovering or briefly perching, and will dart out to capture tiny insects. It can reach speeds of 30–47 mph (50–75 km/h).

MARVELLOUS SPATULETAIL
Trochilidae *Loddigesia mirabilis*
RANGE: N Peru
HABITAT: subtropical forest and scrub
SIZE: male 11½ in (29 cm); female 4 in (10 cm)

Now endangered, the Marvellous Spatuletail has only 4 fully developed tail feathers, compared with the 10 typical of other hummingbirds. Particularly marvellous are the 2 outermost tail feathers of the male, each of which has a long, bare shaft ending in a broad spatule, or racquet, which curve inward to cross over one another.

RUBY-THROATED HUMMINGBIRD
Trochilidae *Archilochus colubris*
RANGE: breeds E North America; winters coastal SE USA to NW Costa Rica
HABITAT: woodland and swamp
SIZE: 3½ in (9 cm)

Males leave their breeding territories immediately after the nesting season, and females follow soon after the young have fledged. The young migrate alone. Male Ruby-throated Hummingbirds defend nectar resources as breeding territories with highly stylized pendulum displays; females defend the nest area. Outside the breeding season, both sexes defend nectar sources vigorously.

feeding chicks

AMETHYST WOODSTAR
Trochilidae *Calliphlox amethystina*
RANGE: South America E of Andes to S Peru, N Bolivia, Paraguay, NE Argentina
HABITAT: tropical forest, scrub, savanna, grassland
SIZE: 2–3 in (6–8 cm)

The Amethyst Woodstar is one of the smallest of all hummingbirds, and females are smaller than males. It forages well into the canopy and often perches high. Its hovering wings, beating at up to 80 times per second, make a distinctive insectlike buzz.

at nest

BEE HUMMINGBIRD
Trochilidae *Calypte helenae*
RANGE: Cuba and Isle of Pines
HABITAT: forest and forest edge, gardens; occasionally in fairly open country
SIZE: 2 in (6 cm)

This threatened species is the smallest bird in the world, the male being slightly smaller than the female; its body measures only ½ in (1.25 cm), the bill and tail making up the total length. It weighs no more than ¹⁄₁₅ oz (2 g).

CALLIOPE HUMMINGBIRD
Trochilidae *Stellula calliope*
RANGE: breeds W North America; winters SW Mexico
HABITAT: mountain meadows, edges of coniferous forest
SIZE: 3 in (8 cm)

The smallest bird breeding in the North American continent north of Mexico, juveniles resemble females, lacking the male's magenta-striped gorget and possessing cinnamon underparts. Northward migration in early spring usually follows the Pacific coast, since snow on high mountains restricts the availability of nectar and insect foods. Southward migration in late summer follows mountain ridges, with late wildflowers being the main food source.

Mousebirds, trogons, kingfishers, and relatives

RESPLENDENT QUETZAL
Trogonidae *Pharomachrus mocinno*
RANGE: S Mexico to W Panama
HABITAT: humid cloud forest, usually at 4,000–10,000 ft (1,200–3,000 m)
SIZE: 14–15 in (35–38 cm)

The male Resplendent Quetzal's upper tail coverts form a train of filmy streamers up to 3 ft (1 m) long that undulate and flutter during normal flight as well as in aerial courtship displays. They generally keep to the canopy, where their green upperparts provide surprisingly effective camouflage in the leafy shade.

BAR-TAILED TROGON
Trogonidae *Apaloderma vittatum*
RANGE: mountains of C Africa, from Nigeria to Mozambique
HABITAT: forest
SIZE: 11 in (28 cm)

Although silent for much of the time, the Bar-tailed Trogon has a characteristic sharp *wup* note that it repeats with increasing volume about 12 times. It is a sedentary, territorial species, but the size of individual territories varies considerably.

COLLARED TROGON
Trogonidae *Trogon collaris*
RANGE: tropical Mexico S to W Ecuador, N Bolivia, and E Brazil; Trinidad
HABITAT: humid and wet forest and forest edges; also riverine forest in Amazonia
SIZE: 10 in (25 cm)

The most widespread of the New World trogons, this species is typical of the family both in color and pattern. Collared Trogons often sit motionless for extended periods, but will sally out from perches to snatch insects or pluck hanging fruit.

ORANGE-BREASTED TROGON

Trogonidae *Harpactes oreskios*
RANGE: Myanmar to Vietnam, Java, Borneo
HABITAT: evergreen forest, bamboo; also sparse woodland
SIZE: 12 in (30 cm)

♂

This species sometimes takes insects from the ground; it also flutters to snatch prey from twigs and can catch winged insects in flight. Across its range, this species is less confined to wet evergreen forest than most other Southeast Asian trogons.

SPECKLED MOUSEBIRD

Coliidae *Colius striatus*
RANGE: C, E, and S Africa
HABITAT: woodland, scrub, gardens, hedges
SIZE: 12–14 in (30–36 cm)

race *striatus*

Mousebirds take their name from their striking, rodentlike appearance. Members of family groups follow each other with alternate whirring and gliding flight, their extremely long tails, up to 8½ in (22 cm) long, projecting stiffly behind them. Speckled Mousebirds use their robust, arched, hooked bills to feed on all kinds of vegetable matter.

♀

♂

BELTED KINGFISHER

Alcedinidae *Megaceryle alcyon*
RANGE: breeds through most of North America; winters in ice-free areas S to West Indies and N Colombia
HABITAT: streams, rivers, ponds, marshes
SIZE: 12 in (30 cm)

This solitary kingfisher prefers clear waters with overhanging trees, wires, or other perches. It usually hovers and dives for fish, but will also prey on insects, crayfish, frogs, snakes, and even the occasional mouse. A loud, dry, rattling call often announces its presence.

LESSER PIED KINGFISHER
Alcedinidae *Ceryle rudis*
RANGE: Africa, Middle East, S Asia
HABITAT: lakes, broad rivers, estuaries
SIZE: 10 in (25 cm)

By hovering rather than perching as it watches for fish, the Lesser Pied Kingfisher can hunt over broad stretches of water. It is the only kingfisher species that regularly fishes far offshore. The breeding pair receive help with the nesting chores from up to 4 full-grown, non-breeding adults—sometimes offspring from the previous year, but often unrelated.

GREEN KINGFISHER
Alcedinidae *Chloroceryle americana*
RANGE: extreme S USA S to W Peru, C Argentina, and Uruguay; Trinidad, Tobago
HABITAT: streams bordered by shrubby habitat or forest, some mountain streams
SIZE: 7½ in (19 cm)

Generally solitary, the Green Kingfisher would easily go unnoticed as it watches for prey were it not for its characteristic habit of frequently raising its head and bobbing its tail. It utters a low, but distinctive *choot* or *chew* call and a descending series of *tew-tew-tew* notes. Its alarm call is a soft, ticking rattle.

RIVER KINGFISHER
Alcedinidae *Alcedo atthis*
RANGE: breeds Europe, NW Africa, Asia, Indonesia to Solomon Islands; winters in S of range
HABITAT: clear, slow-moving streams and small rivers, canals, ditches, reeds, marshes; coasts in winter
SIZE: 6 in (16 cm)

This bird and the Belted Kingfisher are the most northerly breeding species of kingfisher. The River Kingfisher is aggressively territorial, defending a ½–3 mile (1–5 km) stretch of stream in winter, even from its mate. In spring it will drive away both rivals and small songbirds. It rarely feeds away from water and is an expert fisher.

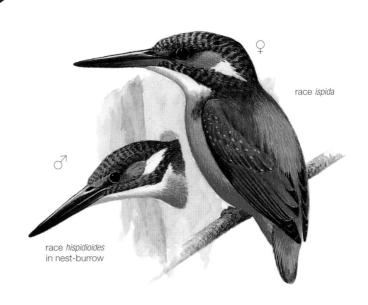

race *ispida*

race *hispidioides*
in nest-burrow

AFRICAN PYGMY KINGFISHER
Alcedinidae *Ceyx picta*
RANGE: tropical Africa
HABITAT: grassy glades near forest edge, streams,
lakeshores, dry woodland
SIZE: 5 in (12 cm)

This bird is one of the world's smallest kingfishers.
Although it takes some of its prey from water, it feeds
mainly on dry land, where it catches insects, millipedes,
spiders and, occasionally, even small frogs.

LAUGHING KOOKABURRA
Alcedinidae *Dacelo novaeguineae*
RANGE: E and SE Australia; introduced to Tasmania
and SW Australia
HABITAT: open forest, urban trees
SIZE: 16–18 in (40–45 cm)

This giant kingfisher has a loud, rollocking territorial call that sounds like
maniacal human laughter. It feeds on a variety of terrestrial invertebrates,
reptiles, small mammals, birds, and nestlings. Although they are not
closely associated with water, they will sometimes catch fish with
plunging dives.

race
novaeguineae

SHOVEL-BILLED KINGFISHER
Alcedinidae *Clytoceyx rex*
RANGE: mainland New Guinea
HABITAT: forest
SIZE: 12½ in (32 cm)

The Shovel-billed Kingfisher is often seen on the
ground, foraging on exposed mud banks. It digs for
insects, snails, earthworms, and small vertebrates
and forages in mangroves for crabs. The tail, which is
brown in females and blue in males, is often cocked
when the bird is perched.

STORK-BILLED KINGFISHER

Alcedinidae *Halcyon capensis*
RANGE: Southeast Asia, E Pakistan, India, Nepal, Sri Lanka
HABITAT: rivers and streams in wooded lowlands, paddy fields; sometimes at wooded lakes or on the coast, especially among mangroves
SIZE: 13–14 in (33–36 cm)

This is one of 3 species of stork-bill in Southeast Asia. They are among the biggest of the world's many kingfisher species, exceeded in size only by the kookaburras, the Shovel-billed Kingfisher, and 3 giant *Megaceryle* species.

BLUE-BREASTED KINGFISHER

Alcedinidae *Halcyon malimbica*
RANGE: tropical W Africa
HABITAT: rain forest, gallery forest, mangroves
SIZE: 10 in (25 cm)

This large kingfisher is the forest-dwelling counterpart of the better-known Woodland Kingfisher *H. senegalensis* of Africa's savanna woodlands. The latter has a loud, trilling "laughing" song lasting about 3 seconds. The Blue-breasted Kingfisher has a similar song, but it is greatly slowed down, with 7–10 long, plaintive whistles.

nest in termite colony

♂

SACRED KINGFISHER

Alcedinidae *Halcyon sancta*
RANGE: Australia, Tasmania, Indonesia, New Guinea, Solomon Islands, some SW Pacific islands, New Zealand
HABITAT: open forest and woodland
SIZE: 7½–9 in (19–23 cm)

This kingfisher is a land-dweller that often occurs far from water. The color of the bird's breast can vary considerably from season to season. The female is similar to the male, but with a duller, greener crown, back, wings, and tail, and usually with paler underparts.

COMMON PARADISE KINGFISHER
Alcedinidae *Tanysiptera galatea*
RANGE: New Guinea, offshore islands, Moluccas
HABITAT: lowland rain forest, swamp forest, gallery forest,
patches of scrub, plantations
SIZE: 13–17 in (33–43 cm)

race *doris*

The Common Paradise Kingfisher perches low in the forest understorey,
slowly pumping its tail, which is two-thirds the length of its body.
It feeds on insects, worms, and lizards. Adults are highly sedentary,
maintaining small territories that they strongly defend.

race *galatea*

juv

BLUE-CROWNED MOTMOT
Momotidae *Momotus momota*
RANGE: E Mexico to NW Peru, NW Argentina, and
SE Brazil; Trinidad, Tobago
HABITAT: rain forest, deciduous forest, coffee and
cocoa plantations, semi-open habitats
SIZE: 16 in (41 cm)

Alone or in pairs, this motmot perches with an
upright stance, swinging its racquet-tipped tail from
side to side like a pendulum. The racquet shape results
from the preening of segments of the inherently weak
vane from the long central tail feathers.

CUBAN TODY
Todidae *Todus multicolor*
RANGE: Cuba and Isle of Pines
HABITAT: bushy ravines, thickets on mountain
slopes, grazed open woodland
SIZE: 4 in (11 cm)

This tody feeds mainly on flying insects, darting out
from a favorite perch to capture them with an audible
snap of its bill. Its call is a rapid, staccato rattle. Todies are
renowned for their voracious appetites and for the rapid
rate at which they feed their young.

AUSTRALIAN BEE-EATER

Meropidae *Merops ornatus*
RANGE: Australia, New Guinea, Lesser Sundas
HABITAT: light woodland, scrub, grassland, sandy pasture, arable land
SIZE: 8–11 in (21–28 cm)

Also known as the Rainbow Bird, this is the only bee-eater that occurs in Australia. Its winter range extends across the islands to the north, and some birds migrate up to 2,500 miles (4,000 km). Australian Bee-eaters feed on a variety of large insects, catching their prey in flight. They are gregarious birds throughout the year, and groups of 30–40 may breed co-operatively.

juv

EUROPEAN BEE-EATER

Meropidae *Merops apiaster*
RANGE: breeds NW Africa, Europe, SW Asia, S Africa; winters W and SE Africa
HABITAT: warm, wooded, and cultivated lowland
SIZE: 10–10½ in (25–27 cm)

Ringing has shown that some individuals migrate 10,000 miles (16,000 km) between their summer and winter quarters. In Europe, their principal food is bumblebees, but the birds feed largely on honeybees and dragonflies in Africa. Thousands of European Bee-eaters are killed each year by bee-keepers.

juv

race *nubicus*
"Northern Carmine Bee-eater"

CARMINE BEE-EATER

Meropidae *Merops nubicus*
RANGE: breeds N and S tropics of Africa; winters nearer the Equator
HABITAT: open bushy savanna, river plains, open pastures, tilled fields with trees or hedges, marshes, mangroves
SIZE: 14–15 in (36–39 cm)

Carmine Bee-eaters nest in huge colonies. They hunt on the wing, flying far to find swarms of locusts, bees, ants, and cicadas. They are attracted to bush fires, where they can catch fleeing grasshoppers. They also hunt by riding on the backs of ostriches, storks, cattle, and other animals, snatching prey that the animals disturb from the grass.

EUROPEAN ROLLER
Corachdae *Coracias garrulus*
RANGE: breeds Mediterranean, E Europe to W Siberia; winters tropical Africa
HABITAT: open forest, especially with clearings and patches of heathland; also parks, well-wooded farmland
SIZE: 12–12½ in (30–32 cm)

juv

European Rollers feed principally on insects, although they have also been known to eat snails and frogs. Rollers take their name from their aerobatic, rolling display flights and this species is no exception, rocking from side to side as it dives steeply down and even performing aerial somersaults.

juv

EASTERN BROAD-BILLED ROLLER
Corachdae *Eurystomus orientalis*
RANGE: N and E Australia, New Guinea, Southeast Asia, India, China
HABITAT: woodland
SIZE: 11½ in (29 cm)

This species is often known as the Dollarbird in the Far East and Australia, owing to the large, coinlike mark on each wing. They feed on large beetles and other flying insects. If they cannot swallow their victims in flight, they will take them back to the perch and batter their bodies against the wood to soften them.

SCALY GROUND-ROLLER
Corachdae *Brachypteracias squamigera*
RANGE: NE and C Madagascar
HABITAT: deep rain forest with scant undergrowth
SIZE: 12 in (30 cm)

This vulnerable species dwells in the shade of the forest floor, where it feeds mainly on insects and small lizards. It is a rather heavy, slow bird that moves only a few steps between lengthy pauses or uses its short, rounded wings to make whirring flights to low perches.

♂

CUCKOO-ROLLER
Leptosomatidae *Leptosomus discolor*
RANGE: Madagascar and Comoro Islands
HABITAT: forest and scrub
SIZE: 17 in (42 cm)

These birds are relatively common in savanna with scattered tall trees from sea level up to 6,500 ft (2,000 m), but cannot survive in newly cleared areas which are gradually eroding their natural range. They take locusts, stick insects, beetles, and larvae, along with larger prey such as chameleons.

race *epops*

HOOPOE
Upupidae *Upupa epops*
RANGE: Europe, Asia, Africa, Madagascar; N birds winter in the tropics
HABITAT: woodland, savanna, parks, lawns, orchards, farmland
SIZE: 11 in (28 cm)

The Hoopoe's striking plumage, its mobile crest, its far-carrying *hoo-poo-poo* call, and its association with human settlement make it a familiar bird. Daytime migrants are so conspicuous that, despite pungent, defensive secretions, they are a favorite prey of Eleonora's and Sooty Falcons.

GREEN WOOD-HOOPOE
Phoeniculidae *Phoeniculus purpureus*
RANGE: sub-Saharan Africa
HABITAT: woodland, thorn bushes
SIZE: 15–16 in (38–41 cm)

The most widespread of Africa's 8 species of wood-hoopoe, Green Wood-Hoopoes indulge in remarkable social territorial displays: several times each hour, they will cackle loudly, rock back and forth in an exaggerated manner, preen, and pass pieces of bark from one to another.

EASTERN YELLOW-BILLED HORNBILL
Bucerotidae *Tockus flavirostris*
RANGE: NE Africa
HABITAT: dry woodland savanna
SIZE: 19½–23½ in (50–60 cm)

This hornbill has a rare mutual association with the dwarf mongoose, in which each helps the other locate food and watch for predators. It displays in pairs, holding its wings fanned and head bowed, and uttering hoarse clucking calls.

GREAT INDIAN HORNBILL
Bucerotidae *Buceros bicornis*
RANGE: India E to Thailand, S to Sumatra
HABITAT: tropical rain forest
SIZE: 39–47 in (100–120 cm)

In flight, this large hornbill's "whooshing" wing beats can be heard over ½ mile (1 km) away. Much of the rain forest habitat in western India and mainland Asia has been felled, making this spectacular bird a vulnerable species.

race *bicornis*

MALABAR PIED HORNBILL
Bucerotidae *Anthracoceros coronatus*
RANGE: India
HABITAT: monsoon forest
SIZE: 29½–31½ in (75–80 cm)

The eggs are incubated by the female in a natural tree hole. The male carries fruit to his incarcerated mate, storing them in his crop and regurgitating them one at a time through a narrow slit in the nest wall.

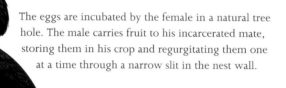

race *corontus*

SOUTHERN GROUND HORNBILL
Bucerotidae *Bucorvus cafer*
RANGE: Africa S of the Equator
HABITAT: open savanna and grassland
SIZE: 35½–51 in (90–130 cm)

This, the largest of the hornbills, differs from most other species in being carnivorous and largely terrestrial, and in not sealing the entrance to its nest. Groups of up to 11 birds occupy territories of about 40 square miles (100 sq km). Only the dominant pair breeds, but the other group members help in territorial defense, in lining the nest with dry leaves, and in feeding the breeding female and single chick.

Toucans, woodpeckers, and relatives

PARADISE JACAMAR
Galbulidae *Galbula dea*
RANGE: S Venezuela and Guianas S to N Bolivia
HABITAT: humid tropical forest and forest edge, savanna, margins of watercourses
SIZE: 12 in (30 cm)

This jacamar's central tail feathers are up to 7 in (18 cm) long, making the tail longer than the bird's body. Its iridescent plumage flashes copper, bronze, and blue as the bird darts about in the sunlight after insects. The sexes have similar plumage. The song is a series of peeping notes.

GREAT JACAMAR
Galbulidae *Jacamerops aurea*
RANGE: Costa Rica S through N South America to N Bolivia
HABITAT: humid tropical forest, secondary growth woodland, edges of water
SIZE: 12 in (30 cm)

This is the largest of the jacamar species. The heavy bill is nearly 2 in (5 cm) long. Immatures are similar to adults, but less iridescent. Their vocalizations include loud whistles and a variety of soft call notes.

♂

WHITE-NECKED PUFFBIRD
Bucconidae *Notharchus macrorhynchos*
RANGE: S Mexico to N South America, N Bolivia, SE Brazil, Paraguay, N Argentina
HABITAT: humid tropical forest, open secondary growth, savanna
SIZE: 10 in (25 cm)

Both sexes share the contrasting black-and-white plumage, but immature birds have buff-gray on the forehead and underparts. This species is usually quiet, but occasional calls include a series of weak twitters or purring notes. Both sexes help to excavate the nesting cavity in arboreal termite mounds.

race
hyperhynchus

RUSTY-BREASTED NUNLET

Bucconidae *Nonnula rubecula*
RANGE: S Venezuela, N Peru, N Brazil S to Paraguay and N Argentina
HABITAT: humid tropical forest; especially seasonally flooded forest
SIZE: 6 in (15 cm)

Sleeker in appearance than most puffbirds, Rusty-breasted Nunlets are generally quiet, unlike their noisy relatives, the nunbirds. Very little is known of their breeding biology, but they probably nest in burrows that they dig in the ground or in termite nests, like other puffbirds.

COLLARED PUFFBIRD

Bucconidae *Bucco capensis*
RANGE: N South America S to N Peru
HABITAT: humid tropical forest
SIZE: 8 in (20 cm)

This little-known puffbird's stout bill is well adapted for dealing with large insects. Its song is a series of *ca-will* notes, rather like that of the Common Poorwill *Phalaenoptilus nuttallii*. Collared Puffbirds are largely insectivorous, but probably eat some small vertebrates as well.

WHITE-FRONTED NUNBIRD

Bucconidae *Monasa morpheus*
RANGE: Central America, W Venezuela S to N Bolivia, Amazonian Brazil
HABITAT: humid tropical forest, river edges, swamps, secondary growth forest
SIZE: 12 in (30 cm)

SWALLOW-WINGED PUFFBIRD

Bucconidae *Chelidoptera tenebrosa*
RANGE: N South America E of the Andes S to N Bolivia and S Brazil
HABITAT: forest edge, savanna, scrub
SIZE: 6 in (15 cm)

Common along waterways from sea level up to at least 3,300 ft (1,000 m), this species forages above the forest, sallying from its perch in fast pursuit of flying insects, returning at a more leisurely pace with its prey. Its voice consists of weakly whistled *pi-pu* and *pit-wit-wit* calls.

race
morpheus

White-fronted Nunbirds change perches frequently, sallying out to catch flying insects or glean prey from foliage on the ground. They are more vocal than other puffbirds, uttering a wide variety of rolling, churring, and whistling notes.

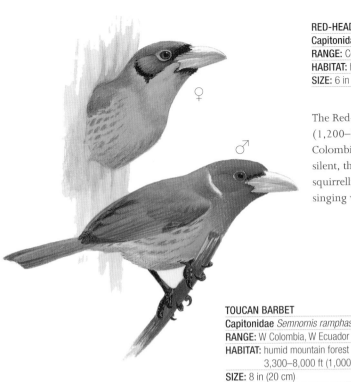

RED-HEADED BARBET
Capitonidae *Eubucco bourcierii*
RANGE: Costa Rica, Panama, Colombia, Ecuador, W Venezuela, N Peru
HABITAT: humid mountain forest
SIZE: 6 in (15 cm)

The Red-headed Barbet usually lives at altitudes of 4,000–8,000 ft (1,200–2,400 m), but on the western slopes of the Andes in Colombia it may be found at 1,300 ft (400 m). Although usually silent, they are known to give low, cicadalike rattling calls and squirrellike sputters and chatters. The males have been heard singing with a prolonged, toadlike trill.

TOUCAN BARBET
Capitonidae *Semnornis ramphastinus*
RANGE: W Colombia, W Ecuador
HABITAT: humid mountain forest and forest edge at 3,300–8,000 ft (1,000–2,400 m)
SIZE: 8 in (20 cm)

This near threatened species is the largest and most heavily built of the American barbets. Its song is a rhythmic series of loud, resonant, almost honking notes that may continue for several minutes. If disturbed, the bird will snap its bill loudly.

BLUE-THROATED BARBET
Capitonidae *Megalaima asiatica*
RANGE: N India, Southeast Asia
HABITAT: light mixed forest, gardens
SIZE: 9 in (23 cm)

race
davisoni

The noisy Blue-throated Barbet is common from the Himalayan foothills down to low-level plains. It prefers groves of fig trees around villages and wooded slopes, where it searches for fruit. It also eats large insects, which it strikes against a branch before swallowing.

race
olivacea

race
woodwardi

GREEN BARBET
Capitonidae *Cryptolybia olivacea*
RANGE: E Kenya, Tanzania, Malawi, S Africa
HABITAT: mountain forest to coastal woods
SIZE: 8 in (20 cm)

The Green Barbet is found in just a few isolated areas. Roosting holes may accommodate 4–5 birds, and other adults may help breeding pairs excavate nest-holes. Its song is a series of up to 29 notes, with both male and female singing together, either at the same tempo or with one at twice the speed of the other.

YELLOW-RUMPED TINKERBIRD
Capitonidae *Pogoniulus bilineatus*
RANGE: sub-Saharan Africa
HABITAT: evergreen forest thickets
SIZE: 4 in (10 cm)

This widespread species, also known as the Golden-rumped Tinkerbird, has 10 races across tropical Africa. It prefers dense forest and riverside trees, where it eats a wide variety of berries and seeds. Its song consists of groups of 3–5 notes given in a series lasting several minutes.

race
jacksoni

race
leucolaima

DOUBLE-TOOTHED BARBET
Capitonidae *Lybius bidentatus*
RANGE: W Africa E to Ethiopia and Kenya; S as far as N Angola
HABITAT: clearings, forest edge, parkland
SIZE: 9 in (23 cm)

The Double-toothed Barbet is named for the 2 prominent sharp projections on the upper mandible of its bill. When several Double-toothed Barbets gather together, they flick and droop their tails and call a variety of low, grating sounds. Their song is a prolonged, buzzing trill.

race
erythrocephalus

RED-AND-YELLOW BARBET
Capitonidae *Trachyphonus erythrocephalus*
RANGE: E Ethiopia, Kenya, N Tanzania
HABITAT: woods, bushy areas, grassland with scattered trees
SIZE: 9 in (23 cm)

This ground-loving barbet, often found under bushes or foraging around termite mounds and banks of bare earth, is a gregarious species and up to 10 may feed together or gather to mob a snake or some other predator. Up to 4 adult and 5 younger birds may attend each nest as communal helpers.

imm ♂

BLACK-THROATED HONEYGUIDE
Indicatoridae *Indicator indicator*
RANGE: Senegal to Ethiopia, and S to South Africa
HABITAT: woodland, open country with scattered trees, rarely dense forest
SIZE: 8 in (20 cm)

When it locates a nest of bees, the Black-throated Honeyguide flicks its tail and chatters noisily to attract the attention of a human or a Honey Badger, or Ratel, and guide it to the hive. It falls silent while its "helper" breaks open the nest to get at the honey, then feeds on the bee grubs and wax. The Black-throated Honeyguide's eggs are laid among those of hole-nesting birds such as bee-eaters and woodpeckers. The naked, blind hatchling attacks the host's young with the hook on its bill, killing them so as to monopolize the food supply.

INDIAN HONEYGUIDE
Indicatoridae *Indicator xanthonotus*
RANGE: Himalayas, from Pakistan to N Myanmar
HABITAT: forests, especially near cliffs and rock faces
SIZE: 6 in (15 cm)

♂

This olive-brown sparrow-sized bird is also known as the Yellow-rumped Honeyguide. The female bird is slightly smaller and duller than the male. The males defend territories that are centered on the nests of giant honeybees. Wax is an important component of the species' diet, but it is not known whether the Indian Honeyguide guides mammals to hives.

race *prasinus*

EMERALD TOUCANET
Ramphastidae *Aulacorhynchus prasinus*
RANGE: C Mexico through SE Peru to NW Venezuela
HABITAT: highland forest, highland and lowland forest edge, clearings
SIZE: 12–13 in (30–33 cm)

Emerald Toucanets are active, excitable birds, often cocking their tails and stretching their necks. They are also noisy, calling to each other with a variety of loud croaks, barks, and rattles. The penetrating "song" of the Emerald Toucanet is said to resemble the sound of a crosscut saw.

GROOVE-BILLED TOUCANET
Ramphastidae *Aulacorhynchus sulcatus*
RANGE: N Colombia, N Venezuela
HABITAT: humid forest, forest edge, secondary woodland
SIZE: 14 in (36 cm)

Similar to the Emerald Toucanet in both appearance and habits, pairs or small flocks of these birds forage together in noisy, energetic fashion, feeding on fruit, insects, or nestling birds anywhere from the high forest canopy to the smaller trees of the understorey.

GOLDEN-COLLARED TOUCANET
Ramphastidae *Selenidera reinwardtii*
RANGE: NW South America E of the Andes
HABITAT: lowland rain forest, forest edge
SIZE: 13 in (33 cm)

Unusually for toucans, the sexes differ markedly in appearance. Like other toucans, the Golden-collared Toucanet feeds mainly on berries and other fruits, generally swallowing them whole and disgorging the pips later, thus helping to disperse the seeds throughout the forest. Its normal call is a low, guttural, froglike croak.

GREEN ARACARI
Ramphastidae *Pteroglossus viridis*
RANGE: Colombia, N Bolivia, Venezuela, Guianas, Brazil
HABITAT: lowland rain forest
SIZE: 12 in (30 cm)

Green Aracaris forage through the canopy in small groups, seeking fruiting trees. They straggle through the foliage in single file, often leaping from branch to branch instead of flying, calling to one another with loud rattling cries. The female's head and throat are chestnut, whereas the male's head and throat are black.

RED-NECKED ARACARI
Ramphastidae *Pteroglossus bitorquatus*
RANGE: lower Amazonia S of Amazon in Brazil
HABITAT: rain forest, forest edge, scrub
SIZE: 15 in (38 cm)

race *bitorquatus*

Also known as the Double-collared Aracari, this species is distinguished by its bright yellow breast band. It is an opportunist feeder. Loose bands of 2–5 birds move through the forest in search of fruiting trees, picking up a variety of small animals, eggs, and nestlings on the way.

PLATE-BILLED MOUNTAIN TOUCAN
Ramphastidae *Andigena laminirostris*
RANGE: NW South America, from SW Colombia through W Ecuador
HABITAT: humid and wet mountain forest and forest edge
SIZE: 20 in (51 cm)

GUIANAN TOUCANET
Ramphastidae *Selenidera culik*
RANGE: NE Amazonia, Guianas, and N Brazil S to lower reaches of Amazon
HABITAT: lowland rain forest, forest edge
SIZE: 14 in (35 cm)

The Guianan Toucanet has a longer bill than the other lowland toucanets and a shorter tail and wings. Both sexes have conspicuous yellow tufts behind each eye, which may play a role in the birds' courtship display.

This toucan is unique in having an additional yellow plate on each side of its upper mandible, the function of which, if any, is not known. It lives in humid mountain forests, from 1,000 ft (300 m) to 10,500 ft (3,200 m), but is uncommon throughout its range and is now under threat.

BLACK-BILLED MOUNTAIN TOUCAN
Ramphastidae *Andigena nigrirostris*
RANGE: N South America, Colombia to NE Ecuador
HABITAT: mountain forest, cloud forest, forest edge,
open areas with scattered trees
SIZE: 20 in (51 cm)

This is the most northerly of the mountain toucans, most often seen in wet mountain forest between 6,500 and 10,00 ft (2,000 and 3,000 m). It normally associates in pairs or small groups, communicating with other birds with nasal yelping calls and hollow rattlings of its great black bill.

TOCO TOUCAN
Ramphastidae *Ramphastos toco*
RANGE: E South America, Guianas through Brazil to N Argentina
HABITAT: open woodland, river forest, forest edge, plantations, palm
groves; avoids continuous lowland forest
SIZE: 24 in (61 cm)

KEEL-BILLED TOUCAN
Ramphastidae *Ramphastos sulfuratus*
RANGE: tropical Mexico to N Colombia and NW Venezuela
HABITAT: tropical lowland forest, forest edge, open areas
with scattered trees, plantations
SIZE: 18–22 in (45–56 cm)

The Keel-billed Toucan has a distinctive, strongly undulating flight pattern, with intensive bursts of flapping alternating with short glides. Its voice is a series of mechanical clicks, like that of a tree frog. Young birds are much duller than adults and their bills continue to grow for some weeks after they fledge.

The Toco Toucan is the largest toucan, with a bill up to 7½ in (19 cm) long. Toco Toucans are unusual in that they avoid dense rain forest, preferring more open habitats. They generally forage in loose flocks, flying from site to site with their characteristic undulating flap-glide flight pattern, and communicating with toadlike croaks.

NORTHERN WRYNECK
Picidae *Jynx torquilla*
RANGE: breeds Eurasia to N Africa; winters C Africa and S Asia
HABITAT: open forest, parkland
SIZE: 6–6½ in (16–17 cm)

When disturbed at its nest, the Northern Wry-neck twists and writhes its neck into strange positions—hence its common name. These contortions resemble the movements of a snake and, when combined with snakelike hissing sounds, serve as an effective deterrent to small predators.

WHITE WOODPECKER
Picidae *Melanerpes candidus*
RANGE: S Suriname and Brazil to E Bolivia,
Paraguay, W Uruguay, N Argentina
HABITAT: open woods, palm groves, savanna,
chaco woodland
SIZE: 10½ in (27 cm)

The sociable White
Woodpecker's flight pattern
is less undulating than that
of other woodpeckers, and it
will travel long distances to
reach favored foraging sites.
It eats some insects, but feeds
mainly on plant matter.

GUIANAN PICULET
Picidae *Picumnus minutissimus*
RANGE: Guianas
HABITAT: lowland forest edge, savanna,
coffee plantations
SIZE: 3½ in (9 cm)

There are 27 species of piculet, all
bewilderingly similar in appearance and all, like
the wrynecks, lacking the stiffened, proplike tail
feathers of the true woodpeckers. The Guianan
Piculet, also known as the Arrowhead Piculet,
forages in pairs for small insects on twigs and
branches of small trees and shrubs.

RUFOUS PICULET
Picidae *Sasia abnormis*
RANGE: Myanmar, Thailand S through Malaya to Sumatra,
Borneo, W Java, and other Indonesian islands
HABITAT: lowland forest, dense second growth, bamboo
thickets, river bank vegetation
SIZE: 3½ in (9 cm)

This restless little bird is fond of habitats near water and its toes
have prominent ridges on their undersides that probably help it
cling to smooth, wet branches. Unlike most members of the family,
it has only 3 toes, not 4.

juv

RED-HEADED WOODPECKER
Picidae *Melanerpes erythrocephalus*
RANGE: E USA and S Canada
HABITAT: open woods, parks, scattered trees
SIZE: 7½ in (19 cm)

Both male and female of this handsome and highly aggressive species have
the completely red head that the juveniles lack until the spring following their
year of hatching. Unusually for woodpeckers, the species catches flying insects
in midair and swoops down to capture insects from the ground, rather than
gleaning them from tree surfaces.

ACORN WOODPECKER
Picidae *Melanerpes formicivorus*
RANGE: NW Oregon S to Baja California, SW USA S to W Panama and N Colombia
HABITAT: oak savanna, parkland, mixed pine and oak woods
SIZE: 8 in (20 cm)

acorns wedged
in tree holes

The Acorn Woodpecker's presence is easily detected by its characteristic food larders. Tree surfaces, utility poles, fenceposts, and the sides of buildings are excavated and acorns, nuts, insects, and fruits firmly wedged in for future use.

race *formicivorus*

race *ruber*

RED-BREASTED SAPSUCKER
Picidae *Sphyrapicus ruber*
RANGE: NW North America
HABITAT: coastal evergreen and some mountain coniferous forest, aspen and pine forest
SIZE: 7½ in (19 cm)

juv

The male and female Red-breasted Sapsucker are indistinguishable in appearance. Sapsuckers excavate tiny holes in trees with a high sugar concentration, from which they can extract sap. Exploratory holes are in horizontal rows; when a good supply of sweet sap is found, vertical rows and even grid-shaped patterns are excavated. Insects complete their diet.

NUBIAN WOODPECKER
Picidae *Campethera nubica*
RANGE: EC Africa
HABITAT: savanna
SIZE: 7 in (18 cm)

The Nubian Woodpecker's loud, far-reaching series of metallic calls increases in tempo and ends with a squeaky trill. When one bird begins to call, its mate very often joins in, and their outburst may elicit vocal responses from neighboring pairs.

GROUND WOODPECKER
Picidae *Geocolaptes olivaceus*
RANGE: South Africa
HABITAT: upland grassland in rocky country
SIZE: 11 in (28 cm)

This unusual woodpecker has completely forsaken the trees. It forages on the ground, pecking and probing for ants and their larvae, and hopping among rocks to probe crevices. On the rare occasions when it does take to the air, it flies heavily and for short distances, its red rump feathers showing conspicuously.

CARDINAL WOODPECKER

Picidae *Dendropicos fuscescens*
RANGE: sub-Saharan Africa
HABITAT: open forest, forest clearings and edges, savanna, brush
SIZE: 5–6 in (13–15 cm)

race *lepidus*

race *hemprichii*

Also known as the Little Woodpecker, the Cardinal Woodpecker probes and taps tree crevices to reveal subsurface insects; it also gleans insects from tree surfaces. Foraging birds move rapidly over the branches and twigs of trees and bushes, often hanging upside down, wings beating to maintain their position, as they investigate every nook and cranny.

race *pinetorum*
♂ ♀
juv

GREAT SPOTTED WOODPECKER

Picidae *Picoides major*
RANGE: N Eurasia to Middle East and N Africa
HABITAT: deciduous and coniferous forest from Arctic taiga to Mediterranean scrub
SIZE: 8½–9 in (22–23 cm)

Most Great Spotted Woodpeckers are sedentary, but some northern populations may migrate south in winter to find food. Although rather secretive at times, these birds often betray their presence with a loud *tchick* call.

HAIRY WOODPECKER

Picidae *Picoides villosus*
RANGE: Alaska and Canada, S to Central America, W Panama, and Bahamas
HABITAT: coniferous and deciduous forest
SIZE: 7–9½ in (18–24 cm)

♂
race *septentrionalis*

race *sanctorum*

Northern populations of Hairy Woodpecker may migrate south for food in winter, but most birds are sedentary. Hairy Woodpeckers forage on trunks and major limbs of trees for surface and subsurface insects, berries, and seeds. Their calls include a loud *peek* location call and a rattling call.

♂
race *crissoleucus*

♂
race *funebris*

THREE-TOED WOODPECKER

Picidae *Picoides tridactylus*
RANGE: N North America S to N USA, N Eurasia S to S Scandinavia, S Siberia, W China, N Japan; isolated mountain populations farther S
HABITAT: damp, dense coniferous forest
SIZE: 8½ in (22 cm)

This species is unusual in having only 3 toes on each foot, heavily barred flanks, and yellow rather than red on the crown of the male. Its range is closely linked to the distribution of spruce trees and the bark beetles that infest them.

SCARLET-BACKED WOODPECKER
Picidae *Veniliornis callonotus*
RANGE: SW Colombia, W Ecuador, NW Peru
HABITAT: arid scrub, dry forest
SIZE: 5½ in (14 cm)

♂

Within its limited range, this stunning species shows considerable geographical variation in the amount of barring on the breast. Females lack the red tips on the black crown feathers, but are otherwise very similar to males.

GOLDEN-OLIVE WOODPECKER
Picidae *Piculus rubiginosus*
RANGE: Mexico to Argentina; Trinidad, Tobago
HABITAT: forest, forest edge, secondary growth
SIZE: 7–9 in (19–23 cm)

A rather quiet, secretive bird, the Golden-olive Woodpecker feeds on tree-dwelling invertebrates, blackberries, and other fruits. Its foraging includes much peering and poking into bark crevices and the excavation of sub-surface insects. Occasionally, it will feed on the ground.

♂

race *cafer*

♂

race *auratus*

♀

NORTHERN FLICKER
Picidae *Colaptes auratus*
RANGE: North America S to Nicaragua
HABITAT: open forest, savanna, open areas with widely scattered trees
SIZE: 10–14 in (25.5–36 cm)

Although they occasionally take food from trees, Northern Flickers are perfectly at home on the ground, where they have become specialists in feeding on ants. They have a variety of calls and both sexes produce the characteristic woodpecker drumming sound with their bills.

race *campestroides*

♂

race *campestris*

CAMPO FLICKER
Picidae *Colaptes campestris*
RANGE: Suriname and lower Amazon Basin to E Bolivia, S Brazil, Paraguay, Uruguay, Argentina
HABITAT: grassland, savanna, forest edge
SIZE: 12 in (30 cm)

This species is an ant specialist and is not known to take other foods. Most food is taken from the ground, where the bird hops about in uneven terrain or walks on level turf. It often forages in small groups; foraging groups seem especially attracted to areas that have been recently burned.

CHESTNUT-COLORED WOODPECKER
Picidae *Celeus castaneus*
RANGE: Mexico to Panama
HABITAT: dense tropical evergreen forest and secondary growth
SIZE: 9–10 in (23–25 cm)

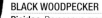

This woodpecker is difficult to see because of its dark plumage and shaded habitat; however, its constant tapping as it forages on large branches and tree trunks in the middle to upper layers of the forest makes it easy to locate. The call note is a low *kwar* or *keeyark*, sometimes followed by a lower, weaker *heh-heh-heh*.

PILEATED WOODPECKER
Picidae *Dryocopus pileatus*
RANGE: S Canada, E and NW USA
HABITAT: forest, especially moist forest
SIZE: 15–19 in (38–48 cm)

The female Pileated Woodpecker has a less extensive red cap than the male, the front of her crown being black, and she lacks the red on her "moustache" stripe. The call is a loud series of *kuk-kuk-kuk* notes. The bird carefully selects a drumming surface that will resonate very loudly across the forest.

race *viridis*

BLACK WOODPECKER
Picidae *Dryocopus martius*
RANGE: S Canada, E and NW USA
HABITAT: northern to warm-temperate hardwood and coniferous forest
SIZE: 18 in (45 cm)

This is a solitary species that is normally seen in pairs only during the breeding season. The Black Woodpecker feeds primarily on ants, termites, and the larvae of wood-boring beetles, but may occasionally eat the eggs and nestlings of other birds. It also eats some fruit in season.

GREEN WOODPECKER
Picidae *Ficus viridis*
RANGE: W Eurasia from S Scandinavia, Europe to mountains of N Africa, Turkey, Iran, Russia
HABITAT: deciduous and mixed forest edge, secondary growth, park-like habitats
SIZE: 12 in (30 cm)

This bird spends much of its time foraging on the ground. When it finds an anthill, the Green Woodpecker tears into it with a vigorous twisting of the head and probing of the beak. The female has an all-black "moustache," while juveniles have only a faint one and barred underparts.

IVORY-BILLED WOODPECKER
Picidae *Campephilus principalis*
RANGE: mountains of E Cuba (possibly also SE USA)
HABITAT: extensive, remote, mature forest
SIZE: 19½ in (50 cm)

Critically endangered and thought to be extinct until video footage of a single live Ivory-billed Woodpecker emerged in 2005, this is the third largest woodpecker in the world. It is intimately associated with virgin forests and its demise is tied to the loss of the forests and direct persecution by people.

OLIVE-BACKED WOODPECKER
Picidae *Dinopium rafflesii*
RANGE: Southeast Asia from Tenasserim through Malay Peninsula to Sumatra, Borneo
HABITAT: dense lowland forest
SIZE: 22 in (28 cm)

This species is sometimes known as the Olive-backed Three-toed Woodpecker. It forages alone or in pairs in the forest understorey by gleaning and probing for surface and sub-surface insects and spiders. The calls include a rapid, descending series of *kwee* notes.

GREATER FLAME-BACKED WOODPECKER
Picidae *Chrysocolaptes lucidus*
RANGE: S Asia from India to SW China, Greater Sundas, and the Philippines
HABITAT: forest, forest edge, mangroves
SIZE: 13 in (33 cm)

race *guttacristatus*

The Greater Flame-backed Woodpecker will tap along a branch to locate its insect prey, and then dig into the wood to reach them. It engages in distinctive and frequent bouts of drumming prior to nesting, often producing long, loud, rapid bursts that decrease in intensity.

GREAT SLATY WOODPECKER
Picidae *Mulleripicus pulverulentus*
RANGE: N India to SW China, Thailand, Vietnam, Malaysia, Indonesia
HABITAT: lowland forest and swamp forest
SIZE: 20 in (51 cm)

Although a bird of the virgin forest, the Great Slaty Woodpecker will also live in partially cleared areas with large trees if there is undisturbed forest nearby. Its primary food seems to be ants. The loudest, most distinctive call is a braying cackle. Other vocalizations include a *dit* note, a rattling series of *dits* and a flight call, rendered as *dwot*.

ORANGE-BACKED WOODPECKER
Picidae *Reinwardtipicus validus*
RANGE: S Myanmar, S Thailand, Malaysia, Sumatra, Java, Borneo
HABITAT: lowland forest, secondary growth, partially cleared areas with large trees
SIZE: 12 in (30 cm)

This is a noisy woodpecker that taps loudly, calls frequently, and forages from near ground level to the forest canopy. Occasionally, it scales bark from trees to reveal prey beneath. Its vocalizations all seem to be based on a metallic *pit* note, given singly, as a double note, or as a series of up to 9 notes.

Perching Birds

AFRICAN BROADBILL
Eurylaimidae *Smithornis capensis*
RANGE: Africa, from Ivory Coast and Kenya S to Natal and Angola
HABITAT: forest, secondary woodland, thickets
SIZE: 5 in (13 cm)

In its display flight, the African Broadbill flies in a tight circle around its perch, wings vibrating rapidly, generating a distinctive rattling trill that can be heard from several yards (meters) away. The performance usually occurs in a small clear space amid dense foliage and is rarely seen.

LESSER GREEN BROADBILL
Eurylaimidae *Calyptomena viridis*
RANGE: Lower Myanmar and peninsular Thailand to Sumatra and Borneo
HABITAT: forest and secondary woodland, up to 5,500 ft (1,700 m) in Borneo
SIZE: 8 in (20 cm)

The bill of this Asian broadbill is higher and more arched than those of other species, yet almost concealed by the elongated feathers that surround it, giving the bird's head a rounded, almost froglike appearance. With his shining grass-green plumage, the male blends in well with the rich greens of the tropical forest and can be surprisingly hard to see.

race *nigrirostris*

WEDGE-BILLED WOODCREEPER
Dendrocolaptidae *Glyphorhynchus spirurus*
RANGE: S Mexico to N Bolivia, Amazonia
HABITAT: humid tropical forest, secondary woodland
SIZE: 5½ in (14 cm)

The Wedge-billed Woodcreeper hunts by hitching its way up trees and along branches, using its stiffened tail feathers as a prop in much the same way as a woodpecker. As it climbs, it taps at the bark, searching for small insects and spiders.

LONG-BILLED WOODCREEPER
Dendrocolaptidae *Nasica longirostris*
RANGE: Venezuela to N Bolivia, Amazonia
HABITAT: humid tropical forest, seasonally flooded forest, swamps
SIZE: 14 in (36 cm)

The bill of this distinctive woodcreeper is ideally suited for probing the layered foliage of bromeliads and similar plants that grow on tropical forest trees. These plants often harbor a rich variety of insects, spiders, and other small animals.

race *radiolatus*

BARRED WOODCREEPER
Dendrocolaptidae *Dendrocolaptes certhia*
RANGE: Mexico to N Bolivia, Amazonia
HABITAT: humid tropical forest, secondary woodland
SIZE: 11 in (28 cm)

The strongly built Barred Woodcreeper is noted for its habit of following columns of army ants as they swarm over the forest floor. It ignores the ants themselves, preying instead on the insects that try to escape them.

RED-BILLED SCYTHEBILL
Dendrocolaptidae *Campylorhamphus trochilirostris*
RANGE: Panama, through N South America to Bolivia, Paraguay, N Argentina
HABITAT: humid tropical forest, swamps
SIZE: 12 in (30 cm)

Its downcurved bill allows this woodcreeper to penetrate the convoluted foliage of tree ferns, bromeliads, and other epiphytes in search of prey. It can also insert its bill into the smallest bark crevice to pick out insects that would be safe from almost any other bird.

COMMON MINER
Furnariidae *Geositta cunicularia*
RANGE: S South America, from Peru and Brazil to Tierra del Fuego
HABITAT: arid sandy plains, dunes, grassland, from coasts to mountaintops
SIZE: 6½–7½ in (17–19 cm)

The Common Miner takes its name from the 10 ft (3 m) nest-burrow that it excavates in a slope, earth bank, or sand dune. The birds forage for insects and seeds on the ground. After eating an insect, a Common Miner will often clean its bill by wiping both sides on a rock.

SCALE-THROATED EARTHCREEPER
Furnariidae *Upucerthia dumetaria*
RANGE: S South America
HABITAT: arid slopes and thorny brush
SIZE: 10 in (25 cm)

The Scale-throated Earthcreeper often lives in arid terrain where it searches for insects among the stones and boulders, or plunges its long bill into clumps of bunchgrass. If alarmed, it tends to run and hide rather than fly away; when it does fly, it rarely goes far.

RUFOUS HORNERO
Furnariidae *Furnarius rufus*
RANGE: E South America from Brazil to Argentina
HABITAT: groves of trees, open country
SIZE: 8 in (20 cm)

Hornero is Spanish for "baker"—a reference to the bird's nest, which is made of mud reinforced with straw and shaped like a traditional baker's oven. The nest has a low entrance hole and a spiral, ascending passageway leading to the nesting chamber. It may take months to complete, yet the birds build a new one each year. Abandoned nests are often adopted by other birds.

nest

DES MURS' WIRETAIL
Furnariidae *Sylviorthorhynchus desmursii*
RANGE: Chile and Argentina
HABITAT: humid forest, in thick understorey, especially bamboo thickets
SIZE: 9½ in (24 cm)

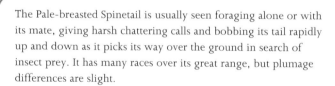

Des Murs' Wiretail, also known as Des Murs' Spinetail, is remarkable for its strange tail feathers. There are only 6 of them: the short outer pair is hidden among the tail coverts and the middle and inner pairs are very long—up to 3 times the length of the bird's body—but reduced to little more than fringed shafts. These often appear very worn, suggesting that they are used for some sort of abrasive purpose or for display.

PALE-BREASTED SPINETAIL
Furnariidae *Synallaxis albescens*
RANGE: SW Costa Rica to Argentina, E of Andes; Trinidad, Margarita Island
HABITAT: forest edge, plantations, mangroves, thickets, reedbeds, savanna, arid areas
SIZE: 6 in (16 cm)

The Pale-breasted Spinetail is usually seen foraging alone or with its mate, giving harsh chattering calls and bobbing its tail rapidly up and down as it picks its way over the ground in search of insect prey. It has many races over its great range, but plumage differences are slight.

STREAK-BACKED CANASTERO
Furnariidae *Thripophaga wyatti*
RANGE: NW Venezuela, NE Colombia, Ecuador to S Peru
HABITAT: mountain grassland with scattered bushes from the tree line to the snow line in the Andes
SIZE: 6 in (15 cm)

The Spanish word *canastero* means "basket maker," and refers to the large, domed basketlike nests of small twigs and grass built by this and the other 21 species of canastero. The Streak-backed Canastero has a patchy distribution on the open, rocky terrain just below the snow line on the Andes.

FIREWOOD-GATHERER
Furnariidae *Anumbius annumbi*
RANGE: Brazil, Uruguay, Paraguay, Argentina
HABITAT: open scrub and weedy areas
SIZE: 8 in (21 cm)

The nests of this bird look like piles of sticks ready for the fire. The birds often incorporate brightly colored rags, bones, and other debris into the main structure, and may add snakeskin, crab shells, and fragments of bark to the lining of the neatly arched tunnel leading to the main section. Each nest may last for several years.

BUFF-FRONTED FOLIAGE-GLEANER
Furnariidae *Philydor rufus*
RANGE: Costa Rica S to N Argentina
HABITAT: humid and wet mountain forest
SIZE: 7½ in (19 cm)

This bird lives up to its name by gleaning insects and spiders from tangled masses of vines growing up the trunks of forest trees. It frequently twists its body and sweeps its tail when looking for insects, perhaps to dislodge or frighten them from their hiding places.

PLAIN XENOPS
Furnariidae *Xenops minutus*
RANGE: SE Mexico to W Ecuador, and E of Andes
          S to N Argentina, Paraguay, S Brazil
HABITAT: humid forest and forest edge
SIZE: 5 in (12 cm)

There are several Xenops species and all but one have a distinctive white crescent on the cheek. They also share a characteristic foraging habit, hopping and sidling along branches, peering from side to side in search of insects, spiders, and other small creatures.

race *intermedius*

BARRED ANTSHRIKE
Formicariidae *Thamnophilus doliatus*
RANGE: Mexico to extreme N Argentina
HABITAT: lowland thickets and tangles
SIZE: 5½–6½ in (14–18 cm)

The song of the Barred Antshrike is a rolling rattle that ends in an emphatic nasal note. As it sings, the Barred Antshrike stretches its neck, raises its striking crest, and vibrates its slightly fanned tail. The amount of black barring on the underparts of the male varies between races.

BLUISH-SLATE ANTSHRIKE
Formicariidae *Thamnomanes schistogynus*
RANGE: SW Amazonia
HABITAT: lowland forest
SIZE: 5½ in (14 cm)

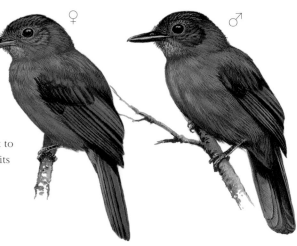

In the mixed-species flocks that sweep through the forest understorey, this species serves as a sentinel guarding against hawks and other predators. As the advancing flock disturbs insects from their hiding places, the Bluish-slate Antshrike sallies out to capture them in the air or on foliage. Sometimes it gives false alarm calls to freeze its flock mates, which gives it an advantage in capturing fleeing insects.

WHITE-FLANKED ANTWREN
Formicariidae *Myrmotherula axillaris*
RANGE: Central America to SE Brazil
HABITAT: humid lowland forest
SIZE: 4 in (10 cm)

White-flanked Antwrens are moderately specialized in foraging behavior, primarily finding insects on living leaves about 6–65 ft (2–20 m) off the ground. They typically move rapidly through branches, but also search by travelling up and down through the vines that encircle the tree trunks.

GRAY ANTBIRD
Formicariidae *Cercomacra cinerascens*
RANGE: Amazonia
HABITAT: forest
SIZE: 6 in (15 cm)

The Gray Antbird often contorts its long tail up, down, or sideways as it stretches to pick off prey. In display, the long tail wags back and forth while the head moves in the opposite direction, giving the bird the grotesque shape of the letter Z.

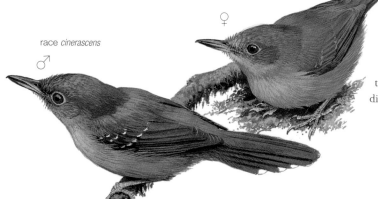

race *cinerascens*

BERTONI'S ANTWREN
Formicariidae *Drymophila rubricollis*
RANGE: SW Brazil, adjacent Paraguay, and Argentina
HABITAT: bamboo thickets
SIZE: 5½ in (14 cm)

Bertoni's Antwren is associated with bamboo, an extremely important element in the South American landscape. Hopping and fluttering among the highly flexible bamboo stalks, this sprightly little bird uses its long tail to help it retain its balance.

race *naevia*

♀

♂

SILVERED ANTBIRD
Formicariidae *Sclateria naevia*
RANGE: Amazonia
HABITAT: near water in wooded areas
SIZE: 5½–6 in (14–15 cm)

This bird is especially abundant where streams cut their way through areas of swampy forest. It works through the overhanging vegetation close to the water, picking off insects from the water surface, floating leaves, twigs, and branches. Its distinctive song begins with a single emphatic note and continues with a long, rapidly delivered staccato series of notes that rises slightly and then softly trails off.

♀

♂

CHESTNUT-TAILED ANTBIRD
Formicariidae *Myrmeciza hemimelaena*
RANGE: Amazonia, mostly S of River Amazon
HABITAT: forest undergrowth
SIZE: 5 in (12 cm)

The Chestnut-tailed Antbird is found close to the forest floor, perching on branches, vertical stems, and logs. It only occasionally jumps down to the leaf litter. The male utters a short series of loud clear whistles that accelerate and fall in pitch; the female answers with a slower, more evenly paced, downward series.

WHITE-PLUMED ANTBIRD
Formicariidae *Pithys albifrons*
RANGE: Amazonia, mostly N of River Amazon
HABITAT: forest undergrowth
SIZE: 4 in (11 cm)

♂

The White-plumed Antbird feeds almost entirely by snapping up cockroaches, katydids, and other insects fleeing formidable columns of army ants. To catch escaping insects, the White-plumed Antbird and other ant-following birds perch in the midst of the column of ants near the ground where the ants are thickest.

race *crissalis*

♂

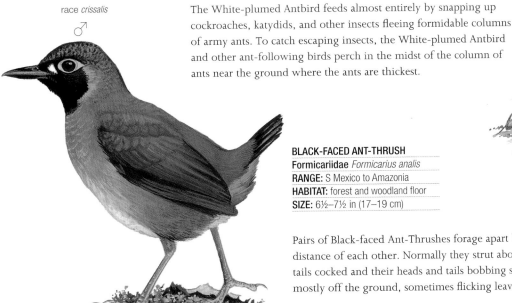

BLACK-FACED ANT-THRUSH
Formicariidae *Formicarius analis*
RANGE: S Mexico to Amazonia
HABITAT: forest and woodland floor
SIZE: 6½–7½ in (17–19 cm)

Pairs of Black-faced Ant-Thrushes forage apart but within easy calling distance of each other. Normally they strut about on the leaf litter, their tails cocked and their heads and tails bobbing slightly. They pick prey mostly off the ground, sometimes flicking leaves aside with their bills.

race *guatimalensis*

♂

SCALED ANTPITTA
Formicariidae *Grallaria guatimalensis*
RANGE: Mexico to Peru and Trinidad
HABITAT: mountains on damp ground near or in forest understorey
SIZE: 6–7½ in (16–19 cm)

Very shy and difficult to see, the Scaled Antpitta travels alone, taking springing hops across the ground, searching for beetles and other insects, as well as other invertebrates, such as millipedes.

♂

SLATE-CROWNED ANTPITTA
Formicariidae *Grallaricula nana*
RANGE: Andes and mountains of Colombia and Venezuela
HABITAT: thickets and understorey
SIZE: 4 in (11 cm)

Extremely secretive birds, Slate-crowned Antpittas flick their wings constantly as they jump and scurry about on fallen logs and on branches very close to the ground. Upon hearing the songs of rivals, Slate-crowned Antpittas crouch down, puff out their feathers until they resemble fuzzy balls, and quietly stare out with their oversized eyes to locate the intruders.

RUFOUS GNATEATER
Formicariidae *Conopophaga lineata*
RANGE: E and S Brazil, adjacent Paraguay and Argentina
HABITAT: forest understorey
SIZE: 5 in (13 cm)

♂

The characteristic white tuft of feathers behind the Rufous Gnateater's eye is normally folded into a thin line or obscured entirely. Females differ from males only in having this tuft of feathers gray rather than white.

BLACK-THROATED HUET-HUET
Rhinocryptidae *Pteroptochos tarnii*
RANGE: S Chile and adjacent Argentina
HABITAT: forest floor
SIZE: 9½ in (24 cm)

The Black-throated Huet-huet (named for the sound of its call) lives in thickets and heavy undergrowth in wooded areas. When pursued, it usually runs away but occasionally flies short distances before hiding in low trees.

SLATY BRISTLEFRONT

Rhinocryptidae *Merulaxis ater*
RANGE: SE Brazil
HABITAT: forest thickets
SIZE: 7½ in (19 cm)

The Slaty Bristlefront lives on mountain slopes in tangled vegetation often containing bamboo, epiphytes, or large vine-covered boulders. When it pauses to sing, it lifts its body diagonally and points its bill skyward. The long, vibrant song consists of rapidly delivered clear metallic notes that fall in pitch and volume, ending with a faster series of soft guttural notes.

UNICOLORED TAPACULO

Rhinocryptidae *Scytalopus unicolor*
RANGE: Andes S to N Bolivia
HABITAT: mountain forest thickets and undergrowth
SIZE: 5 in (13 cm)

The Unicolored Tapaculo inhabits high-altitude humid and wet forest containing low tangles of vegetation. Seeking insect prey, it hops on the ground or through fallen moss-covered limbs or bushy vegetation, often holding its tail upright.

BARRED FRUITEATER

Cotingidae *Pipreola arcuata*
RANGE: E and W slopes of the Andes, from W Venezuela
and N Colombia to C Bolivia
HABITAT: cloud forest, generally above 6,500 ft (2,000 m)
SIZE: 8½ in (22 cm)

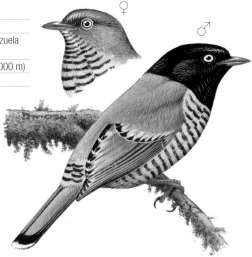

Fruiteaters pluck fruit and snatch insects by sallying out in short flights from a perch. Heavy-bodied birds, they take fruit from a perched position or in a clumsy hover. The Barred Fruiteater is the largest member of its genus and tends to occur at the highest altitudes.

KINGLET CALYPTURA

Cotingidae *Calyptura cristata*
RANGE: near Rio de Janeiro, Brazil
HABITAT: virgin forest, dense secondary growth
SIZE: 3 in (7.5 cm)

This critically endangered bird is by far the smallest of the cotingas, with a very restricted range. Its foraging behavior indicates a diminutive opportunist, poking into crevices for arthropods and snatching a ripe berry here and there. Its voice is reported to be loud for such a small bird.

SCREAMING PIHA
Cotingidae *Lipaugus vociferans*
RANGE: Amazonian South America, S Venezuela, Guianas, SE coastal Brazil
HABITAT: lowland forest
SIZE: 10–11 in (25–28 cm)

Male Screaming Pihas occupy large territories, which they defend by their loud voices. These territories may be arranged in groups, with several birds adjacent to one another. The territorial call begins with a series of 3–5 accelerating, increasingly loud whistled *weeoo* notes, and finishes with a piercing pair of *weeet weeoo* notes, dropping in pitch at the end. The males call frequently through the day, spending only a fraction of their time feeding.

LOVELY COTINGA
Cotingidae *Cotinga amabilis*
RANGE: S Mexico to N Costa Rica
HABITAT: tropical forest
SIZE: 8 in (20 cm)

The Lovely Cotinga occurs alone or in mixed-species flocks high in the forest canopy, where it feeds mostly on fruit. The nest is usually placed at least 100 ft (30 m) high in a large tree; the female may destroy it after the young fledge, possibly to reduce the chance of a predator discovering the nest site.

SNOWY COTINGA
Cotingidae *Carpodectes nitidus*
RANGE: Caribbean slopes of Honduras, Nicaragua, Costa Rica, W Panama
HABITAT: evergreen tropical forest
SIZE: 7½–8 in (19–21 cm)

The fruit-eating Snowy Cotinga lives much of the time in the tree canopy. Its white color and pigeonlike flight have earned it the local name of *Paloma del espiritu santo* or "Dove of the holy spirit."

AMAZONIAN UMBRELLABIRD
Cotingidae *Cephalopterus omatus*
RANGE: Amazonian South America, S Venezuela
HABITAT: open clearings, river edge or islands in lowland rain forest
SIZE: 20 in (51 cm)

Umbrellabirds take their name from their fluffy, platformlike crests. The Amazonian Umbrellabirds male advertisement call is a long, booming *boooo* note, which he utters in an elaborate display, leaning forward and down with his crest spread and throat-wattle dangling.

THREE-WATTLED BELLBIRD
Cotingidae *Procnias tricarunculata*
RANGE: Honduras to W Panama
HABITAT: breeds in forests above 5,000 ft (1,500 m);
migrates to lower tropical forests
SIZE: male 12 in (30 cm); female 10 in (25 cm)

This is one of 4 species of bellbird, renowned for their extremely loud, explosive calls, the striking differences in plumage between the sexes, and the variety of bizarre wattles that adorn the heads of the males. In the Three-wattled Bellbird, one of the wattles hangs from the base of the upper mandible while the other 2 hang from the edges of the bird's mouth.

GUIANAN COCK OF THE ROCK
Cotingidae *rupicola rupicola*
RANGE: S Venezuela, Guianas, N Brazil, E Colombia
HABITAT: lowland tropical forest with rocky outcrops
and boulders
SIZE: 12½ in (32 cm)

The brilliant-orange male Guianan Cock is remarkable for its group display "leks," where 5–25 males compete for the attention of the drabber, visiting females. The males are highly aggressive toward one another and perform ritualized threat displays, such as perching on vertical branches with the feathers of their wing and tail coverts fluffed up. They often utter a raucous *ka-rhaaow* call when flying in to the lek and a variety of squawking and cawing notes during their aggressive encounters. They also make a low, whistling sound with their wings.

THRUSHLIKE MANAKIN
Pipridae *Schiffornis turdinus*
RANGE: S Mexico to W Ecuador, Amazonia,
Venezuela, Guianas
HABITAT: tropical forest
SIZE: 6½ in (17 cm)

The song of the Thrushlike Manakin is a pure, syncopated, whistled series of 3–4 phrases, showing distinct variations across the bird's range. The male may mate with several females but he does not perform elaborate displays. Instead, he relies on persistent singing to defend his territory.

WHITE-BEARDED MANAKIN
Pipridae *Manacus manacus*
RANGE: tropical South America, NE Argentina; Trinidad
HABITAT: secondary growth woodland, riverside forest, forest edge
SIZE: 4 in (10 cm)

The White-bearded Manakin displays in a concentrated "lek." The display behavior includes a number of ritualized postures, movements, and wing noises. Females visit one or more leks, choose a mate, and perform all the nesting duties alone.

race *chrysopterus*

GOLDEN-WINGED MANAKIN
Pipridae *Masius chrysopterus*
RANGE: Andes from W Venezuela to Ecuador, E Andes in N Peru
HABITAT: humid cloud forest, from 4,000–7,500 ft (1,200–2,300 m);
down to 2,000 ft (600 m) in W Colombia and Ecuador
SIZE: 4 in (10 cm)

Male Golden-winged Manakin defend large territories with froglike *nurrt* calls. Their complex displays include flying down onto a mossy fallen log, rebounding, and turning right around in midair. On the log, they adopt motionless chin-down postures, with the tail pointed up, and side-to-side bowing displays, with the body plumage fluffed and the tail cocked at an angle.

LONG-TAILED MANAKIN
Pipridae *Chiroxiphia linearis*
RANGE: W Central America, from S Mexico to N Costa Rica
HABITAT: dry woodland, open secondary growth
SIZE: male 8–8½ in (20–22 cm); female 4 in (10 cm)

The male has wirelike, central tail feathers that are 4–5 in (10–12 cm) long and extend well beyond the rest of his tail. The females are dull olive-green, with only slightly elongated central tail feathers. Immature males are similar in plumage to the females, but molt gradually over 3–4 years into the brilliant full adult male regalia.

courtship display

RED-CAPPED MANAKIN
Pipridae *Pipra mentalis*
RANGE: S Mexico to W Colombia and W Ecuador
HABITAT: lowland tropical forest and secondary growth woodland
SIZE: 4 in (10 cm)

The center of the Red-capped Manakin's display activity is a main horizontal perch at least 13 ft (4 m) above the forest floor. Here he performs a variety of rituals, including the "backward slide," in which he lowers his foreparts, spreads his wings slightly, stretches his legs, exposing the yellow thighs, and slides backward along the perch with a series of extremely rapid steps.

WHITE-THROATED SPADEBILL
Tyrannidae *Platyrinchus mystaceus*
RANGE: S Mexico to Argentina and Bolivia; Trinidad and Tobago
HABITAT: humid forest undergrowth, forest edge, second growth,
open brush
SIZE: 4 in (10 cm)

This tiny flycatcher will perch silently for long periods, occasionally flitting its wings; but when it spies an insect creeping along the underside of a nearby leaf it makes a quick dash and scoops it up with its bill. The male usually has a concealed yellow crown stripe, which is much smaller or entirely lacking in the female.

ROYAL FLYCATCHER

Tyrannidae *Onychorhynchus coronatus*
RANGE: S Mexico to Guianas, Bolivia, Brazil
HABITAT: shaded lower levels of humid forest edge, often near streams
SIZE: 6½ in (16.5 cm)

In male Royal Flycatchers the crest feathers (which form a fan when erect) are vermilion tipped with blue, but in females the vermilion is replaced by orange in some races and yellow in others. Normally, the closed crest projecting backward and the long broad bill give this species a hammer-headed appearance.

ACADIAN FLYCATCHER

Tyrannidae *Empidonax virescens*
RANGE: breeds USA from Great Lakes region S to E Texas, Gulf coast, and C Florida; winters in Central and South America
HABITAT: moist, mature woodland
SIZE: 5½–6½ in (14–16.5 cm)

Typically found in wet woodland, the Acadian Flycatcher hunts beneath the canopy of tall trees, darting after flying insects and catching them on the wing. Its song is particularly memorable, since the explosive *peet-sa*, with the accent on the first syllable, sounds like a demand for pizza.

EASTERN PHOEBE

Tyrannidae *Sayornis phoebe*
RANGE: breeds N and E North America; winters SE and SC USA to Mexico
HABITAT: woods, farms, usually near water
SIZE: 7 in (18 cm)

Named for its pleasantly raspy *fee-bee* song, the Eastern Phoebe hunts in typical flycatcher fashion, sallying after insects from an exposed perch, and wagging its tail from side to side in a distinctive manner as it alights. It often uses man-made structures as breeding sites.

WHITE-FRONTED GROUND TYRANT

Tyrannidae *Muscisaxicola albifrons*
RANGE: Peru to NW Bolivia and N Chile
HABITAT: rocky hillsides with bushes, at 13,000–16,500 ft (4,000-5,000 m)
SIZE: 9 in (23 cm)

The rocks and scattered bushes of the White-fronted Ground Tyrant's open habitat provide commanding perches for spotting its invertebrate prey; when it does so, it makes a quick flight or a dash across the ground to snatch it.

VERMILION FLYCATCHER

Tyrannidae *Pyrocephalus rubinus*
RANGE: breeds SW USA to S Argentina; a few birds wander to California and Gulf coast in winter
HABITAT: semi-arid woodland near streams, ponds, and rivers
SIZE: 5½–6½ in (14–16.5 cm)

race *nanus*

As befits his dazzling coloration, the male is bold and aggressive in defense of the nest. He also puts on a fine courtship display, rising vertically in the air on vibrating wings with crest erect and tail lifted. Illustrated here are *P. r. mexicanus*, found from southwestern USA to Mexico, and the race *P. r. nanus*, which occurs only in the Galapagos Islands, apart from San Cristobal (Chatham) Island and has developed distinct plumage.

WHITE MONJITA

Tyrannidae *Xolmis irupero*
RANGE: E Brazil, Uruguay, Paraguay, E Bolivia, N Argentina
HABITAT: open country, brush, savanna
SIZE: 6½ in (17 cm)

This flycatcher will sit patiently on an exposed branch or fencepost, watching the ground intently and flying down to seize its prey. Its normal flight is swift and undulating, but the birds never seem to go far.

PIED WATER TYRANT

Tyrannidae *Fluvicola pica*
RANGE: Panama, N and C South America E of the Andes; Trinidad
HABITAT: river banks, ponds, and marshes
SIZE: 5–5½ in (12–14 cm)

These flycatchers feed by gleaning insects from foliage on or near the ground, or over the water. While waiting for their next meal they frequently flick their tails downward, sometimes giving a distinctive nasal, buzzing *zhreeo* call.

GREAT CRESTED FLYCATCHER

Tyrannidae *Myiarchus crinitus*
RANGE: breeds E North America from SC and E Canada to Texas and Gulf coast; winters S Florida to Mexico and South America
HABITAT: open woods, woodland edge
SIZE: 7–8 in (18–20 cm)

Great Crested Flycatchers and some other cavity-nesting flycatchers are well known for their habit of using cast snakeskins as nesting material. It was once thought that these somehow repelled marauding snakes, but the presence of various plastics in many nests suggests that the birds simply prefer such materials.

GREAT KISKADEE

Tyrannidae *Pitangus sulphuratus*
RANGE: S Texas to Argentina
HABITAT: semi-open areas, streamside thickets,
woodland edge, orchards
SIZE: 9–10 in (23–25 cm)

The Great Kiskadee dives for small fish or tadpoles from a perch, kingfisher-style, but after 3–4 such dives it has to dry out in the sun. At other times it will launch itself into the air to capture flying insects. It is named for its bawling *kis-ka-dee* calls, usually heard in the morning or evening.

BOAT-BILLED FLYCATCHER

Tyrannidae *Megarhynchus pitangua*
RANGE: C Mexico to NW Peru, S Brazil, and N Argentina
HABITAT: savanna, forest edge, clearings, plantations, usually near water
SIZE: 9 in (23 cm)

The massive, powerful bill of this large tyrant flycatcher reflects its varied diet, which includes not only insects, but also berries, catkins, and even the occasional frog, or other small vertebrate. It can be found along almost any forest edge, but it is most common along river banks.

juv

SCISSOR-TAILED FLYCATCHER

Tyrannidae *Tyrannus forficata*
RANGE: breeds SW USA, uncommonly E to Mississippi; wanders
N to Canada on migration; winters extreme S USA to
Mexico and Central America
HABITAT: open country with scattered trees and brush
SIZE: 12–15 in (30–38 cm)

The Scissor-tailed Flycatcher's courtship "sky dance" is famous, involving vertical and zigzag dives, tumbles, and somersaults, with the long tail feathers streaming and flicking like satin ribbons, all accented by rolling cackles. In true flycatcher manner it hunts from a perch, darting out after flying insects or dropping to the ground for grasshoppers or crickets.

EASTERN KINGBIRD

Tyrannidae *Tyrannus tyrannus*
RANGE: breeds S Canada through USA to the Gulf coast;
winters in Central and South America
HABITAT: open areas, woodland edge, streamsides, orchards
SIZE: 8–9 in (21–23 cm)

Celebrated for its dauntless defense of its breeding territory, the male Eastern Kingbird will attack anything that enters its airspace. At times this species will even land on its flying victim. Its noisy, blustering calls typify its temperament. At dusk it retreats to a communal roost, which may number hundreds or even thousands of birds.

race *albiventris*

♂ ♀

ROSE-THROATED BECARD
Tyrannidae *Pachyramphus aglaiae*
RANGE: S Texas and S Arizona to Costa Rica
HABITAT: open woodland and dry scrub
SIZE: 6 in (15 cm)

The Rose-throated Becard's nest is a large globular structure of sticks and other assorted vegetation, suspended from a branch some 20–70 ft (6–20 m) above a clearing. The clutch size of 5–6 eggs is large for a tropical bird and may be related to the protection provided by the walled, hanging nest.

MASKED TITYRA
Tyrannidae *Tityra semifasciata*
RANGE: S Mexico to W Ecuador, Guianas, and Amazonia
HABITAT: clearings in moist tropical forest, open woodland, and second growth
SIZE: 8 in (20 cm)

♀

♂

The Masked Tityra is frequently seen perched in the top of a tree near a clearing and often draws attention to itself with noisy croaks and low grunts. The birds form monogamous pairs that stay together throughout the year.

SLENDER-FOOTED TYRANNULET
Tyrannidae *Zimmerius gracilipes*
RANGE: Guianas, S Venezuela, E Colombia, S to N Bolivia and E Brazil
HABITAT: forest, savanna, secondary growth
SIZE: 4½ in (11.5 cm)

The Slender-footed Tyrannulet spends most of its time high in the outer canopy of tall trees, where its plumage and diminutive size make it very difficult to see against the foliage. Here it flutters about, gleaning insects from the leaves. The Slender-footed Tyrannulet's call is a sharp, unmelodious *what*.

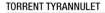

TORRENT TYRANNULET
Tyrannidae *Serpophaga cinerea*
RANGE: Costa Rica, W Panama, NW Venezuela, Colombia, N Bolivia
HABITAT: rocky streams in foothills and mountains
SIZE: 4 in (10 cm)

The Torrent Tyrannulet typically perches on a rock in mid-stream or on a bare branch hanging over water, where it nervously flicks its tail up and down as it watches for prey. The call note is a soft *tsip*, often repeated in a twittering manner.

race *rubrigastra*

MANY-COLORED RUSH TYRANT
Tyrannidae *Tachuris rubrigastra*
RANGE: parts of Peru, Bolivia, Paraguay,
S Brazil, Uruguay, E Argentina
HABITAT: tall cats'-tails and rushes of coastal
and freshwater marshes
SIZE: 4 in (10 cm)

The Many-colored Rush Tyrant is scattered in small populations where
suitably extensive habitat exists. It has relatively long legs, which it uses
to clamber about the stems of cats'-tails and rushes to glean insects in a
wrenlike fashion. It also makes short sallying flights into the air to catch
flying insects.

COMMON TODY FLYCATCHER
Tyrannidae *Todirostrum cinereum*
RANGE: S Mexico to NW Peru, Bolivia, SE Brazil
HABITAT: bushy areas, secondary growth, thickets,
gardens, overgrown clearings
SIZE: 3½–4 in (9–10 cm)

This tiny flycatcher forages by moving quickly among leaves to snatch insects, cocking its
tail slightly and jerking it from side to side. Its calls include low, but sharp, chipping notes
and a musical trill, which members of a pair use to keep in contact with each other.

SHORT-TAILED PYGMY TYRANT
Tyrannidae *Myiornis ecaudatus*
RANGE: Costa Rica S to N Bolivia, Amazonian
Brazil, Guianas, Trinidad
HABITAT: humid forest and forest edge
SIZE: 3 in (7 cm)

This tiny, virtually tailless bird is the smallest of all the tyrant flycatchers. From its perch it flies
up to snatch prey from foliage or out to capture flying insects. Its voice befits its size—a repeated
high-pitched *eek* that sounds remarkably like a tree frog or a cricket.

SHARPBILL
Oxyruncida *Oxyruncus cristatus*
RANGE: Costa Rica, Panama, SE Venezuela, Guyana,
Surinam, E Peru, E and SE Brazil, Paraguay
HABITAT: rain and cloud forest from 1,300–6,000 ft
(40–1,800 m), forest edge, secondary growth
SIZE: 6 in (15 cm)

race *frater*

The Sharpbill gleans insects and spiders from the foliage at the tips of branches
or from the bark of large limbs, and also eats ripe berries. To reach its food,
it often hangs upside down. Its song is a rough, slightly descending trill.
The long crest of brightly colored, silky feathers is usually concealed.

RUFOUS-TAILED PLANTCUTTER
Phytotomidae *Phytotoma rara*
RANGE: C and SC Chile, extreme W Argentina
HABITAT: open country with scattered bushes and thorn
        trees, wooded rivers, gardens, orchards
SIZE: 7½–8 in (19–20 cm)

As their name suggests, plantcutters use their thick, serrated bills for cutting or chewing off pieces of leaves, buds, and fruits. Because of this behavior, the birds are sometimes regarded as pests. This species is also known as the Chilean Plantcutter.

race *granatina*

race *ussheri*

GARNET PITTA
Pittidae *Pitta granatina*
RANGE: peninsular Myanmar, Sumatra, Borneo
HABITAT: swampy forest
SIZE: 6 in (15 cm)

The bright colors of the near-threatened Garnet Pitta conceal it in the contrasted shade of the forest floor. It eats fruit, seeds, and insects, foraging for them on the ground among leaf litter. It makes a prolonged whistling call that increases in volume and rises in pitch before stopping abruptly.

AFRICAN PITTA
Pittidae *Pitta angolensis*
RANGE: W Africa from Sierra Leone to Cameroon, then S to N Angola; also
        Uganda, E Democratic Republic of the Congo, Tanzania,
        E Zimbabwe, and Mozambique; non-breeders sometimes seen
        S as far as Cape Province
HABITAT: thick evergreen forest
SIZE: 8 in (20 cm)

The African Pitta prefers dense undergrowth, hopping along beneath the vegetation in search of slugs and insects, especially termites. If alarmed, it utters a short, soft call and usually runs away rapidly. It also has a threat display in which it crouches with feathers fluffed out, wings spread, and bill pointing skyward.

GURNEY'S PITTA
Pittidae *Pitta gurneyi*
RANGE: peninsular Thailand and Myanmar
HABITAT: lowland forest
SIZE: 8 in (21 cm)

This colorful, endangered pitta is most noisy in the morning and evening, uttering a sharp double note accompanied by flapping wings and a jerk of the tail.

RAINBOW PITTA

Pittidae *Pitta iris*
RANGE: N Australia
HABITAT: thick bush, monsoon forest
SIZE: 7 in (18 cm)

The Rainbow Pitta rarely flies, keeping to the ground where it is well concealed and difficult to locate despite its bright coloration. A loud, clear, whistling call (often rendered as *want a whip*) may give it away.

race *chloris*

RIFLEMAN

Xenicidae *Acanthisitta chloris*
RANGE: New Zealand
HABITAT: forest, ranging from mature stands to secondary growth scrubland
SIZE: 3 in (8 cm)

The Rifleman feeds by spiraling up tree trunks and probing for insects under the bark; its slightly upturned bill is well adapted for this task. It also gleans prey from foliage in the canopy. It remains in family groups for much of the year and is non-migratory. Breeding takes place from October to January, with some nesting pairs assisted by unmated males.

WATTLED FALSE SUNBIRD

Philepittidae *Neodrepanis coruscans*
RANGE: Madagascar
HABITAT: thick forest
SIZE: 4 in (10 cm)

In the forest, the Wattled False Sunbird may be found anywhere from the ground cover and leaf litter, through the middle layers to the high canopy. It visits long, showy flowers to feed, but, unlike the true sunbirds, its chief food is insects. The female lacks the blue wattle around the eye of the male and is duller and greener above.

SUPERB LYREBIRD

Menuridae *Menura novaehollandiae*
RANGE: SE Australia, introduced to Tasmania
HABITAT: eucalypt and rain forest
SIZE: male 31½–38½ in (80–98 cm); female 29–33 in (74–84 cm)

The Superb Lyrebird is renowned for the male's 20–24 in (50–60 cm) long lyre-shaped tail. From midwinter, male Superb Lyrebirds scratch up display mounds and sing. The song contains rich and powerful elements, along with a great variety of mimicked sounds from other birds.

courtship display

RUFOUS SCRUB-BIRD
Atrichornithidae *Atrichornis rufescens*
RANGE: CE Australia
HABITAT: forest margins
SIZE: 6½–7 in (16.5–18 cm)

The endangered Rufous Scrub-bird is restricted to isolated upland regions in northeastern New South Wales and extreme southeastern Queensland. It inhabits cool temperate rain forest where this adjoins eucalypt forest, or subtropical rain forest where the canopy is fairly open. Difficult to spot, Rufous Scrub-birds are usually detected only by the male's loud chipping song.

SKY LARK
Alaudidae *Alauda arvensis*
RANGE: Europe, extreme N Africa, Middle East, NC and E Asia, Japan; introduced to Vancouver Island (Canada), Hawaii, Australia, and New Zealand
HABITAT: open areas, arable fields
SIZE: 7 in (18 cm)

The Sky Lark is renowned for its varied, prolonged song, which is almost exclusively given in flight as the bird rapidly climbs, hovers, and gradually descends. This species is now one of the most typical farmland birds in Europe. It feeds on the ground.

PURPLE MARTIN
Hirundinidae *Progne subis*
RANGE: breeds North America; winters in Amazon Basin, and sometimes as far N as Florida
HABITAT: open areas, often near water
SIZE: 7 in (18 cm)

The Native Americans of southeastern USA provided calabash gourds for Purple Martins to use as nest sites. In return, the birds mobbed crows and other animals that fed on crops or on meat hung out to dry. Early European settlers continued the tradition of providing homes for the birds. In western North America, the birds still nest in natural sites, usually dead trees with woodpecker holes.

BARN SWALLOW
Hirundinidae *Hirundo rustica*
RANGE: parts of E and S Africa
HABITAT: open areas, often near water
SIZE: 7 in (18 cm)

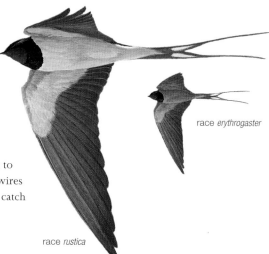

race *erythrogaster*

race *rustica*

Over much of its nesting range, the Barn Swallow attaches its mud nest to the rough walls of barns and other human structures, and depends on wires for use as perches. Barn Swallows prey on small flying insects that they catch mainly during low flights over water or moist vegetation.

BLUE SWALLOW
Hirundinidae *Hirundo atrocaerulea*
RANGE: parts of E and S Africa
HABITAT: mountain grassland near streams
SIZE: 8 in (20 cm)

The Blue Swallow, regarded as vulnerable because of widespread disturbance to its habitat, is migratory, but keeps within the tropics, breeding in the southern part of its range and wintering in Uganda. It shows marked sexual differences: the male has a long, forked tail while the female's tail is short. It nests alone rather than in colonies.

HOUSE MARTIN
Hirundinidae *Delichon urbica*
RANGE: breeds Europe, Asia (except far N, S), N Africa, irregularly S Africa; winters sub-Saharan Africa, Southeast Asia
HABITAT: open areas, particularly near water and human habitation
SIZE: 5 in (13 cm)

House Martins feed primarily on flying insects, especially flies and aphids. Outside the nesting season they feed and roost in very large flocks. They have a soft, twittering song and their calls include shrill, high-pitched contact and alarm calls.

FANTEE SAW-WING
Hirundinidae *Psalidoprocne obscura*
RANGE: Sierra Leone to Cameroon
HABITAT: savanna, forest edge, grassland, flooded areas
SIZE: 6½ in (17 cm)

The name saw-wing (or rough-wing) refers to the series of barbs on the outer web of the outer primary wing feathers of the male. Their function is unknown, but they may produce the noise made by the bird's wings during courtship.

FOREST WAGTAIL
Motacillidae *Dendronanthus indicus*
RANGE: breeds Manchuria, Korea, parts of China and Siberia, winters Southeast Asia, Indonesia
HABITAT: open areas in moist, often evergreen forest
SIZE: 6 in (15 cm)

This species belongs to a separate genus from most wagtails, and its tail-wagging action is unique in that the whole body sways from side to side, rather than up and down. It also differs from most members of its family in its preference for trees rather than open country and often occurs along wooded streams.

YELLOW WAGTAIL

Motacillidae *Motacilla flava*

RANGE: breeds Europe E across Asia to coastal Alaska; winters Africa, S Asia

HABITAT: marshes, lowland grassland, some arable crops

SIZE: 6½ in (17 cm)

Some 18 races of this bird have been described, in which the head pattern of the breeding male varies. Females are generally indistinguishable racially. The Yellow Wagtail occurs in flocks that run gracefully through the ground vegetation foraging for invertebrates.

race *flavissima*
♀

race *flavissima*
"Yellow Wagtail"
♂

race *feldegg*
"Black-headed Wagtail"
♂

race *leucocephala*
"White-headed Wagtail"
♂

race *flava*
"Blue-headed Wagtail"
♂

PIED WAGTAIL

Motacillidae *Motacilla alba*

RANGE: breeds most of Eurasia, except tropics; N birds winter S to Africa N of Equator, Arabia, India, and Southeast Asia

HABITAT: open ground, often near water

SIZE: 7 in (18 cm)

race *yarrellii juv*

race *yarrellii*
♂

race *alba*
"White Wagtail"
♂

This striking bird's plumage varies across its extensive range. It is fond of water and often paddles into shallows and puddles as it searches for aquatic insects. It often uses communal roosts outside the breeding season.

GOLDEN PIPIT

Motacillidae *Tmetothylacus tenellus*

RANGE: Horn of Africa S to Tanzania

HABITAT: dry open country

SIZE: 5½ in (14 cm)

A sedentary bird, the Golden Pipit is often very local in occurrence, even where apparently suitable habitat is extensive. It performs its simple song during parachutelike glides from the tops of bushes to the ground, with its wings held in a V above its back.

♂

♀

♂

CAPE LONGCLAW

Motacillidae *Macronyx capensis*

RANGE: South Africa, C Zimbabwe

HABITAT: open damp grassland

SIZE: 7½ in (19 cm)

The Cape Longclaw is generally seen doggedly foraging in small parties through short grassland. It quickly chases or pounces on any food item that is startled from cover and will often beat large insects on the ground before swallowing them. It utters whistling and piping calls as well as a catlike *meeoo* of alarm.

RICHARD'S PIPIT
Motacillidae *Anthus novaeseelandiae*
RANGE: sub-Saharan Africa, much of C, E, and S Asia, New
Guinea, Australia, New Zealand; N populations
migrate to S of breeding range
HABITAT: open country
SIZE: 7 in (18 cm)

Richard's Pipit, sometimes called the New Zealand Pipit, exhibits considerable
variation in plumage, with the upperparts of many races quite darkly marked.
It hunts for invertebrates on the ground and will sometimes pursue insects in the air.
It gives chirruping and trilling calls and sings in flight.

BUFF-BELLIED PIPIT
Motacillidae *Anthus rubescens*
RANGE: breeds NE Siberia, N North America, W Greenland;
winters S to Southeast Asia and Central America
HABITAT: breeds on mountains and tundra; winters on
beaches, fields
SIZE: 6½ in (17 cm)

The Buff-bellied Pipit nests on the tundra in the north of its range
but is a mountain bird farther south. It is sometimes known as
the American Pipit. Where its range meets that of the Water Pipit in
Siberia. The Water Pipit tends to breed on open ground and the
Buff-bellied Pipit on more rocky areas.

ROCK PIPIT
Motacillidae *Anthus petrosus*
RANGE: breeds NW France, British Isles, Scandinavia, Faroe
Islands; some N populations winter in NW and S Europe
HABITAT: seashore
SIZE: 6½ in (17 cm)

The Rock Pipit gains most of its food by foraging
among beach debris, searching for invertebrates
such as insects and their larvae, molluscs, and
small crustaceans. The birds nest either on sea
cliffs or in a bank, or under dense vegetation
close to the shore.

WATER PIPIT
Motacillidae *Anthus spinoletta*
RANGE: S European mountains E across Asia to Lake Baikal;
C and E Asian races winter S to Southeast Asia and Japan
HABITAT: breeds in mountains; winters in open country at lower elevations
SIZE: 6½ in (17 cm)

The Water Pipit breeds above the tree line in high mountain
areas, usually siting its nest close to rushing streams. In some
regions it occurs close to glaciers and even nests above the
snow line. In winter, it is driven down to lower altitudes, to
such habitats as flooded or damp meadows.

BLACK-FACED CUCKOO-SHRIKE

Campephagidae *Coracina novaehollandiae*
RANGE: breeds India, Southeast Asia, New Guinea, Australia; many SE Australian and Tasmanian birds winter in N Australia and New Guinea
HABITAT: woodland and forests
SIZE: 13 in (33 cm)

Black-faced Cuckoo-Shrikes have an undulating flight and when they land they shuffle their wings in a distinctive manner. The rather metallic voice of this bird includes a rolling *churrrink* contact call and a higher, trilling *chereer-chereer-chereer*, often given in display.

BLUE CUCKOO-SHRIKE

Campephagidae *Coracina azurea*
RANGE: Sierra Leone to the Democratic Republic of the Congo
HABITAT: primary and secondary forest
SIZE: 8½ in (22 cm)

The Blue Cuckoo-Shrike is an unobtrusive bird that frequents the tops of tall trees. Although often solitary, it may be seen in small parties that hunt diligently through the foliage for beetles, grasshoppers, and caterpillars. The calls range from grating noises to more pleasant musical notes.

WHITE-WINGED TRILLER

Campephagidae *Lalage sueurii*
RANGE: Sulawesi, Lesser Sundas, Java, SE New Guinea, Australia
HABITAT: open woodland and shrubland
SIZE: 7 in (18 cm)

Outside the breeding season, the male resembles the grayish-brown and buff female. An alternative name for the trillers is "caterpillar-eaters," and, indeed, they do take many larvae, which they glean or snatch from foliage. Nectar and fruit are also sometimes eaten.

eclipse plumage

LONG-TAILED MINIVET

Campephagidae *Pericrotus ethologus*
RANGE: breeds E Afghanistan through Himalayas to Southeast Asia and China, N to Manchuria
HABITAT: open forest, sparsely wooded hills, mainly 3,300–8,000 ft (1,000–2,500 m)
SIZE: 7 in (18 cm)

Highly gregarious, Long-tailed Minivets are always on the move, hovering and fluttering in search of insects, buds, and fruit. Individuals in a group keep in contact with sweet, twittering calls. This species is migratory in some areas and many birds move to lower altitudes in winter.

CRESTED FINCHBILL
Pycnonotidae *Spizixos canifrons*
RANGE: Assam, W Myanmar
HABITAT: forest, clearings, mountain
scrub to 8,000 ft (2,500 m)
SIZE: 8 in (20 cm)

Finchbills have short, stout bills, used (like those of finches) for cracking seeds. Adult Crested Finchbills have yellowish bills that look white in the field and are very distinctive. The 2-note alarm call is musical but strident, increasing to 5 syllables when the bird is really excited.

STRIATED GREEN BULBUL
Pycnonotidae *Pycnonotus striatus*
RANGE: E Himalayas, W Myanmar
HABITAT: evergreen forest, rhododendron forest,
bushes, to 10,000 ft (3,000 m)
SIZE: 8 in (20 cm)

This bulbul is a resident of hill forests but moves down to lower levels in winter. It prefers jungle and bushy forest that is not too dense or too high; flocks of up to 15 birds straggle loosely from bush to bush in search of fruit, each bird giving almost continuous sharp *tyiwut* calls.

race *monticola*

WHITE-CHEEKED BULBUL
Pycnonotidae *Pycnonotus leucogenys*
RANGE: Himalayas, NW India to S Iran
HABITAT: scrub jungle, bushy hillsides, villages
SIZE: 8 in (20 cm)

race *leucogenys*

RED-WHISKERED BULBUL
Pycnonotidae *Pycnonotus jocosus*
RANGE: China, Assam, Nepal, India
HABITAT: open humid jungle, gardens
SIZE: 8 in (20 cm)

Red-whiskered Bulbuls are familiar in gardens, even in the noisiest cities, where they live in pairs or gather in loose flocks. Each pair tends to remain in its territory all year, eating fruits and buds or dropping to the ground to feed on ants. Their calls are typically noisy, full-throated, and cheerful.

Sprightly and active, The White-cheeked Bulbul is common up to 7,000 ft (2,100 m) in the dry Himalayas, but in wetter east Nepal it occurs only in the lower, drier valleys. The Himalayan race *P. l. leucogenys* is a long-crested form; *P. l leucotis* is a crestless race with a much wider range farther west.

race *leucotis*

GARDEN BULBUL

Pycnonotidae *Pycnonotus barbatus*
RANGE: N Africa S to Tanzania
HABITAT: open forest, gardens, town parks
SIZE: 7 in (18 cm)

race *barbatus*

race *leucogenys*

The Garden, or Common, Bulbul will thrive almost anywhere where there are fruits, buds, and berries, although it does not like dense forest. The northern race *P. b. barbatus* is white under the tail, but the southern race *P. b. tricolor* has a splash of yellow in the same place.

HONEYGUIDE GREENBUL

Pycnonotidae *Baeopogon indicator*
RANGE: W Africa from Sierra Leone to the Congo
HABITAT: forest clearings and secondary growth
SIZE: 8 in (20 cm)

This heavily built bulbul has conspicuous white outer tail feathers like those of a honeyguide. It also behaves a little like a honeyguide, keeping to the tops of tall trees, but its calls are quite distinctive, and its fluty, jumbled song resembles that of a thrush.

SPOTTED GREENBUL

Pycnonotidae *Ixonotus guttatus*
RANGE: Ghana and Gabon to C Democratic Republic of the Congo
HABITAT: primary and secondary tropical forest
SIZE: 6 in (15 cm)

Easily recognized by the amount of white in its plumage, the Spotted Greenbul lives in loose groups that draw attention to themselves by repeated cheerful calls and restless behavior in the treetops. Like some other bulbuls, it will often raise one wing over its back while it perches.

race *flavicollis*

YELLOW-THROATED LEAFLOVE

Pycnonotidae *Chlorocichla flavicollis*
RANGE: W Africa from Senegal to Cameroon, Central African Republic, and the Republic of the Congo
HABITAT: forest edge and thorny thickets
SIZE: 7 in (18 cm)

The Yellow-throated Leaflove is a bird of the dense thickets where the savanna blends into the forest and is rarely seen among the tall forest trees. Some races, such as *C.f. flavicollis,* have the yellow throat referred to in the name, but others, such as *C.f. soror* of the Central African Republic, the Republic of the Congo, and Sudan, are white-throated and duller.

race *flavostriatus*

YELLOW-STREAKED GREENBUL
Pycnonotidae *Phyllastrephus flavostriatus*
RANGE: Nigeria and Cameroon E and S to South Africa
HABITAT: mountain forest
SIZE: 8 in (20 cm)

This large bulbul is easily identified by its plumage and its liking for thick forests high in the mountains, where it keeps to trees and thick bush, often in the highest branches. It has a habit of raising one wing over its back, lowering it, and then raising the other.

race
chloronotus

race *notata*

race eximia

GREEN-TAILED BRISTLE-BILL
Pycnonotidae *Bleda eximia*
RANGE: W Africa, from Sierra Leone to Central African Republic and the Republic of the Congo
HABITAT: tall tropical forest
SIZE: 8 in (20 cm)

race *barbatus*

BEARDED GREENBUL
Pycnonotidae *Criniger barbatus*
RANGE: Sierra Leone to Gabon and Central African Republic
HABITAT: rain forest
SIZE: 8 in (20 cm)

The most remarkable feature of the Bearded Greenbul is its beautiful, arresting whistle; it also sometimes utters a loud, throaty babbling. The eastern race *C. b. chloronotus* has distinctive white throat feathers, whereas the race *C. b. barbatus*, found from Sierra Leone to Togo, has a yellow throat.

Although this bulbul is always found among tall trees, it spends most of its time on or near the ground, picking ants out of the huge columns of these insects that march across the leaf litter. The western race *B. e. notata* has a conspicuous yellow spot on its face, absent in the eastern race *B. e. eximia*.

WESTERN NICATOR
Pycnonotidae *Nicator chloris*
RANGE: Senegal to Gabon and the Republic of the Congo, the Democratic Republic of the Congo, and Uganda
HABITAT: thick forest
SIZE: 8½ in (22 cm)

The Western Nicator lives in the tops of smaller trees or among the lower canopy of forest giants. The only time it comes close to the ground is when nesting, for it builds its frail, flat nest in a fork 3–6 ft (1–2 m) from the forest floor.

LONG-BILLED BULBUL
Pycnonotidae *Setornis criniger*
RANGE: Borneo, Sumatra, Bangka Islands
HABITAT: lowland primary forest
SIZE: 7 in (18 cm)

The striking Long-billed Bulbul's white-tipped outer tail feathers help identify it in the dense woodland it prefers. Its varied diet is typical of bulbuls and includes dragonfly nymphs, beetles, and other insects, and a wide range of fruits and berries.

CHESTNUT-EARED BULBUL
Pycnonotidae *Hypsipetes amaurotis*
RANGE: Japan, Taiwan, S China
HABITAT: forested slopes, gardens, parks
SIZE: 10½ in (27 cm)

Chestnut-eared Bulbuls that breed in the north move
south in winter, often roaming in sizable flocks that
communicate with continual loud, fluty, rhythmic
calls. In summer this species is very common in
forests on lower mountain slopes.

BLACK BULBUL
Pycnonotidae *Hypsipetes madagascariensis*
RANGE: SW India, Nepal E to Vietnam, Thailand, China
HABITAT: oak, pine, rhododendron forest
SIZE: 9 in (23 cm)

race
sinensis

race
leucothorax

race *psaroides*

Of the Black Bulbuls illustrated here, *H.m. sinensis*
is from southwest China, Thailand, and Laos;
H.m. psaroides is found along the Himalayas; and the
white-headed *H.m. leucothorax* is from western China
and northern Vietnam. The Black Bulbul is a summer
visitor to the higher parts of its range, but elsewhere it
is mainly resident.

BLACK-COLLARED BULBUL
Pycnonotidae *Neolestes torquatus*
RANGE: Gabon, Republic and Democratic Republics of the Congo, Angola
HABITAT: grassy woodland, savanna
SIZE: 6 in (15 cm)

The small Black-collared Bulbul keeps to more open areas than most bulbuls
and has a unique display flight, ascending to 100 ft (30 m) or more and
hovering in one spot for 2–3 minutes, emitting a continuous stream of
twittering calls. It moves around in small parties and feeds on fruit.

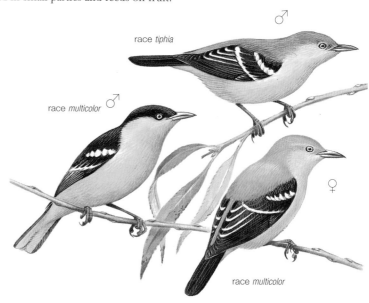

race *tiphia*

♂

race *multicolor* ♂

♀

race *multicolor*

COMMON IORA
Chloropseidae *Aegithina tiphia*
RANGE: India, Sri Lanka to Southeast Asia, Java, Borneo
HABITAT: forest, groves, cultivated land
SIZE: 5½ in (14 cm)

The Common Iora is remarkable for its display: the courting male
fluffs out his rump and his long white flank feathers and jumps into
the air, gliding down again to his perch like a feathered ball. Of the
races illustrated, *A. t. tiphia* ranges from the Himalayas to Myanmar,
while *A. t. multicolor* occurs in southern India and Sri Lanka.

race *frontalis*

race *auritrons*

GOLDEN-FRONTED LEAFBIRD
Chloropseidae *Chloropsis aurifrons*
RANGE: Sri Lanka, India, Himalayas to Southeast Asia, Sumatra
HABITAT: forest, open woodland, scrub
SIZE: 7½ in (19 cm)

There are several races of this bird, including the blue-throated *C. a. aurifrons* of Bangladesh and India, and the black-throated *C. a. frontalis* of central and southern India. A great mimic, this leafbird is often to be seen foraging in flowering or fruiting trees; it is partial to both figs and mistletoe.

BLUE-BACKED FAIRY BLUEBIRD
Irenidae *Irena puella*
RANGE: W India, Nepal to Southeast Asia, Philippines
HABITAT: heavy deciduous or evergreen forest
SIZE: 10½ in (27 cm)

A fruiting fig tree is a magnet for Blue-backed Fairy Bluebirds. They are always on the move in the forest, usually working their way through the canopy or the middle layers of vegetation, and they seldom descend to the ground.

BRUBRU SHRIKE
Laniidae *Nilaus afer*
RANGE: tropical Africa
HABITAT: savanna woodland; occasionally forest edge
SIZE: 6 in (15 cm)

This bird takes its name from the male's repeated *bruuu-bruuu* call with which he proclaims his territory and keeps in close contact with the female. It occurs mainly in the tree canopy, where it gleans insects from the foliage, occasionally catching food on the wing.

courtship display

PUFFBACK
Laniidae *Dryoscopus gambensis*
RANGE: W, C, and E Africa
HABITAT: savanna woodland; also thickets, forest clearings, mangroves, and gardens
SIZE: 7 in (18 cm)

The species' name reflects the male's ability to fluff up the long, gray-white feathers of the lower back. The Puffbird spends most of its time in the tree canopy, rarely descending to ground level. It is a vocal bird, with a wide variety of calls, including a chattering alarm note.

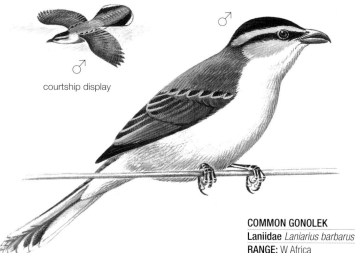

courtship display

BLACK-HEADED TCHAGRA
Laniidae *Tchagra senegala*
RANGE: sub-Saharan Africa, NW Africa, SW Arabia
HABITAT: open savanna woodland with bushes and
long grass, margins of cultivated land
SIZE: 8½ in (22 cm)

During courtship song-flights, male Black-headed Tchagras ascend noisily into the air and whistle as they glide back down to cover. Duetting is well developed, the female adding a drawn-out trill to the male's song; she often joins him in his song-flight.

COMMON GONOLEK
Laniidae *Laniarius barbarus*
RANGE: W Africa
HABITAT: thorny acacia, dense shrub and woodland in
savannas; also mangroves and riverside thickets
SIZE: 8½ in (22 cm)

The Common Gonolek hops nimbly through thickets and makes brief flights from cover to cover using rapid, shallow wing beats followed by long glides. The male has a variety of calls, the most common being a repeated *whee-u* note. The birds are highly sensitive to disturbance and will readily abandon, or even destroy, their nests.

FOUR-COLORED BUSH-SHRIKE
Laniidae *Telophorus quadricolor*
RANGE: coastal regions of E and S Africa
HABITAT: dense tangled bush; also forest edge
SIZE: 8 in (20.5 cm)

The female shares the multihued appearance of the male but her tail is a lighter green, her throat is more orange-yellow, and there are no red tinges on her underparts. An alternative name is Gorgeous Bush-Shrike.

FIERY-BREASTED BUSH-SHRIKE
Laniidae *Malaconotus cruentus*
RANGE: W and C Africa
HABITAT: lowland rain forest
SIZE: 10 in (25 cm)

This beautiful bush-shrike usually occurs in pairs in the tangled foliage of the rain forest canopy and middle layer. It searches among the leaves for beetles, grasshoppers, caterpillars, and other invertebrates. Seeds and the remains of frogs have also been found in its stomach.

YELLOW-BILLED SHRIKE
Laniidae *Corvinella corvina*
RANGE: W and C Africa, E to W Kenya
HABITAT: savanna woodland, suburban gardens
SIZE: 12 in (30 cm)

Although its plumage is fairly drab, this shrike is conspicuous because of its noisy habits, its large size, and its tapering, 7 in (18 cm) tail. An alternative name is Western Long-tailed Shrike. The sexes differ in the central flank feathers that are exposed when the birds preen or display—rufous in the male, but cinnamon or maroon in the female.

race *tricolor*

LONG-TAILED SHRIKE
Laniidae *Lanius schach*
RANGE: Iran and C Asia to China, Southeast Asia,
Philippines, Indonesia, New Guinea
HABITAT: open country, scrub, farmland
SIZE: 10 in (25 cm)

race *erythronotus*

This species shows marked variation in plumage across its geographical range. The Rufous-backed Shrike *L. s. erythronotus* of central Asia and western India has a gray head, for instance, while the Black-headed Shrike *L. s. tricolor* of the Himalayas, Myanmar, and northern Indochina has a black head. Only the northerly populations migrate; other populations are sedentary.

RED-BACKED SHRIKE
Laniidae *Lanius collurio*
RANGE: Europe, W Siberia, W Asia; winters mainly E and S Africa
HABITAT: breeds in bushes, thickets, and hedgerows; winters in savanna woodland
SIZE: 6½ in (17 cm)

Like many other northern shrikes, the Red-backed Shrike has the habit of impaling its prey on thorns or barbed wire fences and keeping "larders" of stored food. The species is widespread across western Eurasia. It winters in Africa, taking a southward route several hundred miles to the west of its return journey.

LOGGERHEAD SHRIKE
Laniidae *Lanius ludovicianus*
RANGE: S Canada to Mexico and Florida
HABITAT: open country with thickets, hedgerows and farmland
SIZE: 8–9 in (21–23 cm)

race *ludovicianus*

juv

The Loggerhead Shrike occurs over much of North America, with the more northerly populations retreating southward in winter. It prefers open, thinly wooded country, where it feeds largely on insects, often impaling its prey on thorns. Habitat destruction and pesticides have caused its numbers to decline steadily.

race *collaris* ♂

♀

race *subcoronatus*

FISCAL SHRIKE
Laniidae *Lanius collaris*
RANGE: sub-Saharan Africa
HABITAT: open woodland savanna; also parks and forest clearings
SIZE: 8½ in (20 cm)

This widespread shrike has several races; in all but one, the females differ from the males in having chestnut flanks. This is an aggressive, solitary species that readily attacks and kills other birds. It maintains its territorial boundaries with both visual and vocal displays.

♂

BORNEAN BRISTLEHEAD
Pityriasididae *Pityriasis gymnocephala*
RANGE: Borneo
HABITAT: lowland forest
SIZE: 10 in (25 cm)

The Bornean Bristlehead, now near threatened, spends most of its time in the forest canopy, where it hunts for a variety of insects and their larvae. The female shares the heavy build, massive hooked beak, and general coloration of the male, but differs in having red spots on the flanks.

CORAL-BILLED NUTHATCH
Vangidae *Hypositta corallirostris*
RANGE: E Madagascar
HABITAT: evergreen forest from sea level to 6,000 ft (1,800 m)
SIZE: 5–6 in (13–15 cm)

♂

HELMET BIRD
Vangidae *Euryceros prevostii*
RANGE: NE Madagascar
HABITAT: primary, dense evergreen forest from sea level to 6,000 ft (1,800 m)
SIZE: 10½–12 in (27–31 cm)

Its large, heavy bill distinguishes the Helmet Bird from all other members of the family. It is also known as the Helmeted Vanga. Although this odd species is difficult to observe, its tremulous, prolonged whistle is easy to identify, particularly at dusk.

This small vanga is usually found in mixed feeding flocks in the middle layer of the forest. The female and juvenile differ from the male in having dark slate-gray underparts and dark brown crowns.

LONG-CRESTED HELMET SHRIKE
Prionopidae *Prionops plumata*
RANGE: sub-Saharan Africa, except arid areas, and S South Africa and Namibia
HABITAT: open deciduous woodland, orchard bush, and cultivated areas with scattered trees
SIZE: 8 in (21 cm)

Long-crested Helmet Shrikes chatter noisily as they leapfrog along the same foraging route in their territory each day. A wide range of loud, rolling, ringing calls is used to maintain contact and structure. This species is also known as the Straight-crested Helmet Shrike, White Helmet Shrike, or Common Helmet Shrike.

PHAINOPEPLA
Bombycillidae *Phainopepla nitens*
RANGE: breeds SW USA, S to Baja California and C Mexico; winters in S
HABITAT: brushland, river banks, and chaparral in wetter areas
SIZE: 8 in (20 cm)

The flight of this species is buoyant and fluttery, but direct and often very high. Its call note is a querulous whistled warp and its brief warbling song is seldom heard. The Phainopepla is particularly fond of mistletoe berries and also takes winged insects in flycatcher like style.

juv

BOHEMIAN WAXWING
Bombycillidae *Bombycilla garrulus*
RANGE: breeds N Eurasia and North America; irregular winter migrant to temperate areas S to 35°N
HABITAT: breeds in dense coniferous or mixed forest; occasionally found in town parks and gardens in winter
SIZE: 8 in (20 cm)

The beautiful pinkish-buff plumage of the Bohemian Waxwing is offset by yellow tips to the tail feathers, and waxlike red blobs at the tips of the secondary wing feathers, from which the common name of this species is derived.

GRAY HYPOCOLIUS
Bombyceillidae *Hypocolius ampelinus*
RANGE: breeds SW Asia and Middle East; occasional migrant to Himalayan foothills, N India, and Pakistan
HABITAT: fields, scrub, and gardens in semi-arid climates
SIZE: 8½ in (22 cm)

These sociable birds communicate with squeaking calls. Outside the breeding season, small groups of them feed together on fruits, berries, and the occasional insect. Both male and female build the bulky and untidy nest, generally well concealed among the leaves of a palm tree.

juv

PALMCHAT
Dulidae *Dulus dominicus*
RANGE: Hispaniola, Gonave (West Indies)
HABITAT: open woodland, palms, pines
SIZE: 8 in (18 cm)

Palmchats are sociable birds that live in large communal nests woven around the trunk and base of the fronds of a royal palm tree. Some nests have housed as many as 30 pairs, each with a separate entrance burrow leading into its own compartment.

juv

race *gularis*

WHITE-THROATED DIPPER
Cinclidae *Cinclus cinclus*
RANGE: Europe and C Asia
HABITAT: fast-flowing upland streams
SIZE: 7–8 in (18–21 cm)

The White-throated Dipper has a rich diet of insect larvae, fish fry and fish eggs, freshwater shrimps, and molluscs. Male and female both build the dome-shaped nest of moss, grass, and leaves, with an entrance directly over running water. The birds generally roost communally during the winter.

juv

NORTH AMERICAN DIPPER
Cinclidae *Cinclus mexicanus*
RANGE: Alaska to S Mexico
HABITAT: fast-flowing upland streams from
    2,000 ft (600 m) up to the tree line
SIZE: 7–8 in (18–21 cm)

Like other dippers, the North American Dipper has a well-developed whitish nictitating membrane that protects its eyes from spray and when it is submerged. It uses this membrane in a blinking action to signal alarm, excitement, or aggression, combining it with the bobbing, or "dipping," of its body.

BLACK-CAPPED DONACOBIUS
Troglodytidae *Donacobius atricapillus*
RANGE: E Panama to Bolivia, N Argentina
HABITAT: marsh vegetation, swampy river
    bank scrub, wet meadows
SIZE: 9 in (23 cm)

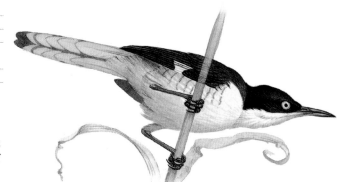

The Black-capped Donacobius is the largest of all species of wren. When disturbed from cover, it typically flies to an open perch on marsh grasses where it scolds. During displays, pair members perch together and each bobs its head and wags its tail. Orange patches of skin on the neck are often exposed and the pair calls antiphonally.

BICOLORED WREN
Troglodytidae *Campylorhynchus griseus*
RANGE: Colombia, Venezuela, N Brazil, Guyana
HABITAT: semi-arid to arid savanna, cactus scrub, open woods,
　　　　　　some habitats near human habitations
SIZE: 8½ in (22 cm)

This large, bold, and conspicuous wren is usually found on or close to the ground, poking and peering into crevices in search of insects and their eggs. Its song is less guttural and scratchy than those of its close relatives.

ROCK WREN
Troglodytidae *Salpinctes obsoletus*
RANGE: breeds W Canada and NW USA to Costa Rica;
　　　　　　winters in N breeding areas
HABITAT: arid and semi-arid rocky barrens
SIZE: 6 in (15 cm)

The Rock Wren is distinguished from other wrens by its cinnamon rump and the buff tips of its outer tail feathers. It survives in a harsh rock-strewn environment, with little or no vegetation, by eating a variety of small insects and worms.

SEDGE WREN
Troglodytidae *Cistothorus platensis*
RANGE: breeds S Canada to E and C USA, C Mexico S to
　　　　　　W Panama; winters in SE USA, E Mexico
HABITAT: wet, grassy meadows, drier bogs,, and marshes
　　　　　　dominated by sedges
SIZE: 4 in (11 cm)

The Sedge Wren's song is a weak, staccato chattering trill, often delivered at night. Its call note, a robust chip, is often doubled. As with other wrens, the male constructs dummy nests, from which the female selects one for egg laying.

ZAPATA WREN
Troglodytidae *Ferminia cerverai*
RANGE: Zapata Swamp (Cuba)
HABITAT: sawgrass and woody hummocks in
　　　　　　drier parts of the swamp
SIZE: 6 in (16 cm)

The endangered Zapata Wren is the only wren native to the Greater Antilles. Almost flightless, this species was only discovered in 1926, and by 1974 it had become extremely rare.

NORTHERN WREN

Troglodytidae *Troglodytes troglodytes*
RANGE: breeds C and S Canada, Alaska, coastal W USA, parts of E USA,
⠀⠀⠀⠀⠀Europe, Asia E to Japan, N Africa; N populations winter to S
HABITAT: woodland, gardens, cultivated land, moors, heaths, rocky islands
SIZE: 3 in (8 cm)

race zetlandicus

race indigenus

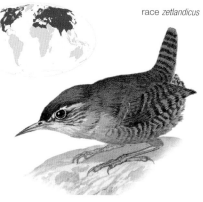

The tiny, cock-tailed Northern Wren, the only wren that occurs in the Old World, is equally at home in a damp, broad-leaved wood, in the gorse and bracken of an upland moor, or on the cliffs of a windswept Atlantic or Pacific island. There are nearly 40 races.

FLUTIST WREN

Troglodytidae *Microcerculus ustulatus*
RANGE: S Venezuela, Guyana, N Brazil
HABITAT: humid mountain forest
SIZE: 5 in (12 cm)

As its name suggests, the song of this wren has a flutelike character. It can start with 3–4 single notes and end with a long ascending whistle, or consist of a descending series of high-pitched whistles, and may last up to 30 seconds. It lives in dense and humid cloud forest at altitudes of 2,800–7,000 ft (850–2,100 m).

GRAY CATBIRD

Mimidae *Dumetella carolinensis*
RANGE: breeds S Canada, USA; winters Central America, West Indies
HABITAT: dense vegetation in woodland edge; readily adapts to
⠀⠀⠀⠀⠀human settlements
SIZE: 8 in (20 cm)

Known for the catlike cries that give it its name, the Gray Catbird is a nocturnal migrant that often arrives in the southern USA in spring in large waves; since it can survive on fruit alone, it can winter occasionally in some northern areas.

juv

NORTHERN MOCKINGBIRD

Mimidae *Mimus polyglottos*
RANGE: S Canada, USA, Mexico, Caribbean islands; introduced
⠀⠀⠀⠀⠀to Bermuda, Hawaiian islands
HABITAT: open areas in cities, suburbs, countryside, deserts
SIZE: 9–11 in (23–28 cm)

The Northern Mockingbird is sometimes called the American Nightingale because of its habit of singing on moonlit nights. Its habit of wing flashing—pausing as it runs along the ground and deliberately raising and partially opening its wings—is a common but, as yet, poorly explained form of behavior. Some ornithologists believe it may be a way of startling potential prey out of hiding.

BROWN THRASHER
Mimidae *Toxostoma rufum*
RANGE: E USA and S Canada to the foothills of the Rocky Mountains
HABITAT: woodland, forest edge, hedgerows, scrubland, pastures, gardens
SIZE: 10 in (25 cm)

This well-known species is most commonly observed skulking along the ground in search of food, or singing on an exposed perch. It typically forages by poking through leaves and other ground cover with its bill, occasionally pausing to pick up leaves and toss them aside. Fruits and acorns also contribute to its diet, especially in winter.

BROWN TREMBLER
Mimidae *Cinclocerthia ruficauda*
RANGE: Lesser Antilles
HABITAT: rain forest; also secondary forest
SIZE: 9–10 in (23–25 cm)

This uncommon species—named for its strange and unexplained habit of violently shaking—moves about chiefly by hopping on the ground and through vegetation and by making short, direct flights. It has also been observed flapping upward in trees, hanging upside down, and clinging vertically like a woodpecker.

juv

ALPINE ACCENTOR
Prunellidae *Prunella collaris*
RANGE: from Iberia and NW Africa E through S and E Asia to Japan
HABITAT: breeds in rocky areas and alpine meadows from about 5,000 ft (1,500 m) to at least 16,500 ft (3,300 m); usually winters lower down
SIZE: 7 in (18 cm)

The Alpine Accentor has a huge range, but normally occurs only at high altitudes, where it is well adapted to survive the harsh conditions. It is a larger and stouter bird than any other accentor, with quite colorful plumage. It has rippling, larklike calls and a larklike song.

DUNNOCK
Prunellidae *Prunella modularis*
RANGE: Europe S to C Spain and Italy and E to the Urals, Lebanon, Turkey, N Iran, Caucasus
HABITAT: scrub, heathland, mixed woodland, young coniferous forest, farmland hedgerows, parks, gardens, vacant urban land, scrubby coastal cliffs, and dunes
SIZE: 5½ in (14 cm)

This unobtrusive little bird spends much of its time in cover among shrubs and hedgerows, but also forages on the open ground for its food with a curious, shuffling, jerky, rather mouselike gait. At one time it was known in the British Isles as the Hedge Sparrow.

juv

BLUE SHORTWING
Turdidae *Brachypteryx montana*
RANGE: E Nepal to W and S China,Taiwan, Philippines,
Borneo, Sumatra, Java
HABITAT: upland forest thickets of rhododendron and oak
SIZE: 6 in (15 cm)

race *cruralis*

The 6 species of shortwing breed mainly in Southeast Asia and the islands of Indonesia. The Blue, or White-browed, Shortwing is typical of the group in its preference for dense undergrowth in evergreen forests. There are some 13 races, differing mainly in plumage details.

RUFOUS SCRUB-ROBIN
Turdidae *Erythropygia galactotes*
RANGE: Mediterranean, SW Asia E to Pakistan, C Asia
HABITAT: open grassland, scrub, stony country, oases, parks, gardens
SIZE: 6 in (15 cm)

The Rufous Scrub-Robin is intermediate in form between the thrushes and the warblers. It stands high off the ground on its long pinkish-gray legs and can cock its long rufous tail up over its back to create a U shape. The male's song is rich and flutelike and is often uttered during the display flight.

juv

EUROPEAN ROBIN
Turdidae *Erithacus rubecula*
RANGE: Europe and N Africa E to W Siberia and N Iran
HABITAT: woodland and forest; also gardens, parks in Britain
SIZE: 5½ in (14 cm)

The European Robin has an upright, bold stance on the ground, regularly flicking its wings and tail. It is largely monogamous and both sexes defend winter territories. Although they are very aggressive birds, they rarely make physical contact during fights. When they do, one may peck the other to death.

NIGHTINGALE
Turdidae *Luscinia megarhynchos*
RANGE: NW Africa, Eurasia S to Caucasus, E to Altai range; winters
Nigeria E to Kenya, Tanzania
HABITAT: woodland, dense hedges, thickets near water, shrubland
SIZE: 6½ in (16.5 cm)

juv

The sombrely colored Nightingale is richly praised for its fine song, which consists of deep, plaintive notes, trills, and slurred *jug-jugs*. It sings both at night and in the daytime. It forages on the ground and in the dense vegetation under the shrub layer, searching for insects such as ants and beetles.

BLUETHROAT

Turdidae *Luscinia svecica*
RANGE: Eurasia, W Alaska
HABITAT: wooded tundra, alpine meadows, dry, stony
slopes, shrubby wetlands
SIZE: 5½ in (14 cm)

The Bluethroat has a more upright stance on the ground
than the European Robin, but, like that species, frequently
flicks its tail. The song is more tinkling than that of the
Nightingale. It may be uttered in the air or from a perch
and often dominates the sounds of the Arctic tundra.

RED-CAPPED ROBIN-CHAT

Turdidae *Cossypha natalensis*
RANGE: South Africa N to Somalia, SW Ethiopia, W to Cameroon
HABITAT: dense evergreen forest and undergrowth
SIZE: 8 in (20 cm)

Although its plumage is striking, the Red-capped, or Natal, Robin-Chat is a shy
bird and could be overlooked were it not for its loud, warbling songs, which often
mimic other birds. It has extended its choice of habitat to include deciduous as well
as evergreen forests.

FIRE-CRESTED ALETHE

Turdidae *Alethe castanea*
RANGE: C Africa
HABITAT: tropical forest
SIZE: 6–6½ in (16–17 cm)

The Fire-crested Alethe often associates with parties of safari ants: the
advancing ants disturb insects in their path, which the birds wait to snap up.
It is active and pugnacious, erecting its tawny orange crest and spreading its
tail when excited or threatened.

ASIAN MAGPIE-ROBIN

Turdidae *Copsychus saularis*
RANGE: India, S China, Southeast Asia,
Indonesia, Philippines
HABITAT: up to 6,500 ft (2,000 m) in scrub, around
cultivation, gardens; also coastal mangroves
SIZE: 8 in (20 cm)

The magpie-robins are sometimes known as shamas and tend to range in
color from bluish to black. They are fine singers; the Asian Magpie-Robin's
loud, varied, and melodious song is interspersed with some discordant
notes and imitations of other birds' calls.

WHITE-THROATED ROBIN
Turdidae *Irania gutturalis*
RANGE: Turkey to Afghanistan; winters S through Arabia and Iran to Kenya, Tanzania, Zimbabwe
HABITAT: stony slopes with shrubs, oak steppes up to altitudes of 9,500 ft (2,850 m); dense scrub along dry riverbeds in winter
SIZE: 7 in (17.5 cm)

The male White-throated Robin resembles a Nightingale *Luscinia megarhynchos* in its gait, moving across the ground with hops and drooping wings. In flight it reveals its long wings and tail. The male has a loud, fluid, and melodious song.

COMMON REDSTART
Turdidae *Phoenicurus phoenicurus*
RANGE: Europe, Asia S to Iran and E to Lake Baikal; winters S to Arabia and W and E Africa
HABITAT: forests with clearings, heaths, moors with scattered trees, parks, orchards; winters on savanna and woodland
SIZE: 5½ in (14 cm)

The Common Redstart's diet consists mainly of insects and the male's aerial flycatching technique, as well as his prominent display flight, demand open spaces in its woodland habitat. The female feeds mainly on the ground. Both sexes supplement their diet with small snails, berries, and fruit.

PHILIPPINE WATER REDSTART
Turdidae *Rhyacornis bicolor*
RANGE: Luzon Island (Philippines)
HABITAT: mountain streams
SIZE: 5½ in (14 cm)

The Philippine Water Redstart lives along clear mountain streams and rivers. It often occurs in rocky gorges and other inaccessible terrain. It feeds mainly on insects, which it gleans from boulders among the torrents. Habitat destruction has rendered it vulnerable.

HODGSON'S GRANDALA
Turdidae *Grandala coelicolor*
RANGE: Himalayas, mountains of SE Tibet and W China
HABITAT: boulder-strewn alpine meadows, rocky slopes, scree and cliffs above scrub zone
SIZE: 8½ in (22 cm)

Hodgson's Grandala is a bird of the high mountains of Asia, foraging in scrub and on the open slopes up to 14,800 ft (4,500 m) above sea level for insects, seeds, and berries. When perched, it looks rather like a rock thrush, but in flight it more closely resembles a starling.

EASTERN BLUEBIRD

Turdidae *Sialia sialis*
RANGE: E North America and Central America
HABITAT: open woodland, roadsides, farms, orchards, gardens, parks
SIZE: 5½–7½ in (14–19 cm)

juv

Eastern Bluebirds typically they have a hunched appearance when perching. They often fly down from their perch to catch insects on the ground. Multiple broods are common, with 2 chicks often produced in a single season in northern areas, and up to 4 in southeastern USA.

WHITE-CROWNED FORKTAIL

Turdidae *Enicurus leschenaulti*
RANGE: Himalayas, S to Malaysia, Indochina, Sumatra, Java, and Borneo
HABITAT: rocky streams, forest rivers, swamps
SIZE: 8–11 in (20–28 cm)

This is the largest and darkest of the 7 species of forktail, all of which have black-and-white plumage. It lives close to mountain torrents, where it forages for insects on the surface of the water or along rocky banks. Its penetrating alarm call is a high-pitched screech.

GREEN COCHOA

Turdidae *Cochoa viridis*
RANGE: Himalayas and mountains of N Southeast Asia
HABITAT: undergrowth, often near streams in dense evergreen forest
SIZE: 11–12 in (28–30 cm)

One of 3 species of cochoa, this bird haunts forested mountain slopes, usually 3,300–5,000 ft (1,000–1,500 m) above sea level. It lives singly or in pairs, and searches through the undergrowth for insects and other invertebrates and berries.

race *hibernans*

STONECHAT

Turdidae *Saxicola torquata*
RANGE: much of Eurasia and Africa
HABITAT: grassland, heaths, plantations, coastal gorse
SIZE: 5 in (12.5 cm)

The Stonechat uses low exposed perches to spot its invertebrate prey, which it usually catches after a glide or hop to the ground. In spring the perch is usually about 3 ft (1 m) above the ground, but in summer, when the vegetation is taller, the preferred height is about 5 ft (1.6 m).

♂
♀

race *homochroa*
♂

♀

♂

♀

ARNOT'S CHAT
Turdidae *Myrmecocichla arnoti*
RANGE: C, E, and S Africa
HABITAT: open woodland, margins of cultivated land
SIZE: 7 in (18 cm)

Sometimes known as the White-headed Black Chat, this species has a loud, whistled song, which first rises then falls in pitch, often combined with mimicry of other bird calls. It forages at low level for spiders and insects, particularly ants.

DESERT WHEATEAR
Turdidae *Oenanthe deserti*
RANGE: N Africa, Middle East, C Asia, Mongolia
HABITAT: heaths, coasts, dunes, rocky mountain passes; N and high-altitude
S breeders move to lower altitudes or migrate S in winter
SIZE: 5½–6 in (14–15 cm)

The Desert Wheatear occurs in a variety of dry, open habitats where there are sandy or stony soils. It perches freely on low shrubs, mounds, and stones from which it can watch the ground for prey. In the breeding season, the male performs a song-flight up to 25–30 ft (8–10 m) into the air and utters a few mournful notes.

ROCK THRUSH
Turdidae *Monticola saxatilis*
RANGE: breeds NW Africa, S and C Europe E to Lake
Baikal and China; winters in W Africa
HABITAT: rocky, shrubby terrain, vineyards; savanna,
stony gullies, gardens in winter
SIZE: 7 in (18.5 cm)

The male Rock Thrush has a far-carrying, mellow song. He begins singing from a perch, then climbs steeply into the air with slow, powerful wing beats. His song reaches a peak at the top of his ascent, then he flutters his wings quickly, and mimics song phrases of other birds before parachuting silently down to earth.

RUFOUS-THROATED SOLITAIRE
Turdidae *Myadestes genibarbis*
RANGE: West Indies
HABITAT: mountain forest
SIZE: 7½ in (19 cm)

The Rufous-throated Solitaire is a tropical forest bird, with a diet consisting mainly of fruit but also including insects and other invertebrates. It obtains much of its food from a perched position, although it will dart out from a perch to catch flying beetles and moths on the wing. Its song is a series of flutelike whistling notes.

BLUE WHISTLING THRUSH

Turdidae *Myiophoneus caeruleus*
RANGE: C Asia, India, W China, Southeast Asia, Java, Sumatra
HABITAT: edges of mountain and forest streams; also limestone
rock faces
SIZE: 12–12½ in (30–32 cm)

Sometimes known as the Whistling Schoolboy, this is one of about 6 semi-aquatic species within the thrush family. Its rich songs can be heard ringing out over the roar of tumbling waters as it forages on and around the wet rocks, damp moss, and water surface for insects, snails, and crustaceans.

WHITE'S THRUSH

Turdidae *Zoothera dauma*
RANGE: E Europe E to China and Japan, Southeast Asia, Indonesia,
New Guinea, E and S Australia; N populations migrate S
HABITAT: woodland and forest
SIZE: 10–11 in (26–28 cm)

race *dauma*

This large thrush feeds on the forest floor, turning over dead leaves with its bill in search of earthworms, snails, and insects. It suddenly opens its wings and tail to panic insects into movement, and apparently also raises itself up on its toes and vibrates its whole body rapidly for several seconds to bring worms to the surface.

♂

♀

VARIED THRUSH

Turdidae *Ixoreus naevius*
RANGE: W coast of North America, from NC Alaska
S to N California
HABITAT: moist coniferous forest
SIZE: 8–10 in (20–25 cm)

The Varied Thrush often forages on the ground, taking a variety of insects, snails, earthworms, seeds, and fruit. The song is a long, vibrating whistle, followed by a pause and then a series of rapidly trilled notes at different pitches. Juveniles resemble the females, but they have an incomplete breast band and speckling on the breast.

ORANGE-BILLED NIGHTINGALE-THRUSH

Turdidae *Catharus aurantiirostris*
RANGE: Mexico, Central America, Venezuela, Colombia
HABITAT: low rain forest and cloud forest, forest edge,
dense thickets, coffee plantations
SIZE: 6½ in (17 cm)

The Orange-billed Nightingale-Thrush has a poor voice compared with most other nightingale-thrushes, its simple song consisting of short, jumbled warbles with a rather squeaky tone. It also has a nasal *waa-a-a-a* call.

HERMIT THRUSH
Turdidae *Catharus guttatus*
RANGE: North and Central America
HABITAT: coniferous, deciduous, or mixed
woodland, forest edge, thickets
SIZE: 6–8 in (15–20 cm)

The Hermit Thrush has one of the most beautiful of all bird songs. The song has a clear, flutelike introductory note followed by a series of rising and falling phrases of different pitches. This bird slowly raises and drops its tail several times a minute while perched; this is usually accompanied by a low *chuck* call.

WOOD THRUSH
Turdidae *Hylocichla mustelina*
RANGE: E North and Central America,
from S Canada to Panama
HABITAT: vwoodland, wooded slopes,
parks, often near streams
SIZE: 7½–8½ in (19–22 cm)

Male Wood Thrushes first appear in the southern USA in March or April. They then move north and begin singing when they arrive in their nesting territories. The song consists of loud, flutelike phrases with 3–5 notes, each differing in pitch and ending with a soft, guttural trill.

BLACKBIRD
Turdidae *Turdus merula*
RANGE: breeds NW Africa, Europe E to India, S China; N and some E populations winter
S to Egypt, SW Asia, Southeast Asia; introduced to Australia, New Zealand
HABITAT: diverse, including forest, farmland, moors, scrub, gardens, parks, inner city
SIZE: 9½–10 in (24–25 cm)

Blackbirds prise earthworms from the soil all year round and, by avidly turning over leaf litter, they catch a variety of insects and other invertebrates. They have a mixed diet and at certain times of the year the fruits of hawthorn, holly, elder, and yew provide an important source of food.

ISLAND THRUSH
Turdidae *Turdus poliocephalus*
RANGE: Christmas Island, Taiwan, Indonesia through
Melanesia to Samoa and Fiji
HABITAT: dense rain forest and clearings
SIZE: 9½–10 in (24–25 cm)

race *niveiceps*

race *layardi*

race *papuensis*

There are about 50 races of this species, reflecting its wide geographical range. Many are restricted to single islands or groups of islands. Island Thrushes are basically ground-feeding birds, with a diet that includes worms and snails. They build their nests on rocky ledges.

FIELDFARE

Turdidae *Turdus pilaris*
RANGE: breeds N Eurasia E to C Siberia, Greenland;
winters widely in Europe, SW Asia
HABITAT: subarctic scrub, light coniferous and birch
woodland, parks, gardens, towns; winters in
open country, woodland edges, fields
SIZE: 10 in (26 cm)

juv

The Fieldfare is essentially a migratory species that breeds in northern latitudes and usually only winters in the southern part of its range. It eats many kinds of invertebrates, as well as plant food such as seeds and fruit.

RED-LEGGED THRUSH

Turdidae *Turdus plumbeus*
RANGE: West Indies
HABITAT: forest areas in mountains and lowlands, gardens, city lawns
SIZE: 10–11 in (25–28 cm)

This striking bird's plumage varies among the islands, the chin and throat ranging from white to black, and the belly from reddish-yellow to gray and white. Its song is rather weak and melancholy and, when disturbed, the bird utters a loud *wet-wet* call, sometimes repeatedly.

AUSTRAL THRUSH

Turdidae *Turdus falcklandii*
RANGE: Chile, Argentina, Falkland Islands, Juan Fernandez Islands
HABITAT: farmland with some trees, groves of willows, forest borders
SIZE: 10–10½ in (25–27 cm)

The Austral Thrush frequently feeds on the ground, hopping about on grassy areas and cocking its head from side to side to look for earthworm burrows. The territorial song, which is made up of repeated whistled phrases such as *tee-yoo, churr,* and *tee,* is delivered from a conspicuous perch.

CLAY-COLORED THRUSH

Turdidae *Turdus grayi*
RANGE: SE Mexico, Central America, coastal Colombia
HABITAT: open woodland, woodland edge and clearings,
usually near streams
SIZE: 9–9½ in (23–24 cm)

The Clay-colored Thrush is one of the best known tropical American songsters, with a musical, carolling song. A generalist in feeding habits, it spends much of its time on the ground searching for insects, earthworms, slugs, and lizards. Fruit also forms part of its diet.

AMERICAN ROBIN
Turdidae *Turdus migratorius*
RANGE: North America
HABITAT: forest borders, woodland, parks, lawns, suburbs
SIZE: 9–11 in (23–28 cm)

juv

This is the largest of the North American thrushes. It occurs in almost any environment with cover, from city suburbs to western mountainsides 12,000 ft (3,600 m) high. American Robins usually feed on grassy ground, cocking their heads to search for earthworm burrows. Experiments have shown that the birds locate earthworms by sight rather than sound, as was previously believed.

EASTERN WHIPBIRD
Orthonychidae *Psophodes olivaceus*
RANGE: E coast of Australia from N Queensland to Victoria
HABITAT: thick shrubbery in wet forest, dense heath
SIZE: 10–12 in (25–30 cm)

The Eastern Whipbird takes its name from the contact call uttered while pairs forage out of sight of each other in thick cover. The male gives a long whistle ending in a sharp whip-crack and this is answered by 2 or 3 chirrups from the female.

MID-MOUNTAIN RAIL-BABBLER
Orthonychidae *Ptilorrhoa castanonota*
RANGE: New Guinea, Batanta Island, Yapen Island
HABITAT: lower mountain forest
SIZE: 9 in (23 cm)

♀

race *pulcher*

♂

race *castanonota*

The Mid-mountain Rail-Babbler, also known as the Chestnut-backed Jewel Babbler, has a beautiful song of clear, bell-like whistles. Pairs or small groups of this species often occur together, walking on the ground and foraging in the leaf litter or probing in the earth on the forest floor.

PALE-BREASTED THRUSH-BABBLER
Timaliidae *Illadopsis rufipennis*
RANGE: W Africa E to Kenya and Tanzania
HABITAT: forests
SIZE: 5½ in (14 cm)

A sedentary species of thick forest, the Pale-breasted Thrush-Babbler spends its life either on or close to the forest floor. There is some evidence that it is most active at dawn and dusk, when it seems to forage more widely for insects and small molluscs.

race *temporalis*

race *rubeculus*

GRAY-CROWNED BABBLER
Timaliidae *Pomatostomus temporalis*
RANGE: N and E Australia
HABITAT: open woodland
SIZE: 10 in (25 cm)

The Gray-crowned Babbler lives in family groups of up to 12 individuals, which defend communal territories. Each group usually consists of a pair or trio and their offspring from previous years. These all forage together, bounding along the ground or along branches, and making short, weak, fluttering and gliding flights.

LARGE WREN-BABBLER
Timaliidae *Napothera macrodactyla*
RANGE: Malay Peninsula, Java, Sumatra
HABITAT: forests
SIZE: 7½ in (19 cm)

The Large Wren-Babbler occurs in lowland rather than hill forest, and is therefore under greater threat from logging operations than some of its highland relatives. Its song is a series of repeated whistles.

WHITE-NECKED TREE-BABBLER
Timaliidae *Stachyris leucotis*
RANGE: S Thailand to Sumatra, Borneo
HABITAT: forests
SIZE: 6 in (15 cm)

The White-necked Tree-Babbler haunts tall, mature forest in the lowlands and foothills of its range. A sedentary bird, it keeps close to ground level. It has a rather heavy bill and strong feet, and appears to feed on beetles and caterpillars.

race *fasciata*

WREN-TIT
Timaliidae *Chamaea fasciata*
RANGE: USA from W Oregon S to N Baja, California
HABITAT: chaparral, coniferous brushland
SIZE: 6 in (15 cm)

The Wren-Tit dwells secretively in dense chaparral and low tangles, which it seldom leaves except to make short, weak, tail-pumping flights from bush to bush. The male's loud song begins with a series of accelerating staccato notes and runs together in a descending trill at the end *pit-pit-pit-r-r-r.* The female sings a similar, but trill-less version.

COMMON BABBLER
Timaliidae *Turdoides caudatus*
RANGE: S Iraq and Indian peninsula E to Bangladesh
HABITAT: dry scrub and bushes in open country
SIZE: 9 in (23 cm)

race *caudatus*

This species scuttles and hops below the bushes or along a hedgerow in an almost ratlike manner, jerking its long tail spasmodically. It is a reluctant flier. A noisy bird, especially when alarmed, flocks constantly utter musical whistling calls to keep in contact as they move through the undergrowth.

race *leucolophus*

WHITE-CRESTED LAUGHING-THRUSH
Timaliidae *Garrulax leucolophus*
RANGE: Himalayas through Southeast Asia to Sumatra
HABITAT: undergrowth, scrub, and bamboo thickets
SIZE: 11 in (28 cm)

race *bicolor*

As these birds forage, there is a constant subdued chuckling and chirruping. Every now and then, these sounds erupt into bursts of wild, cackling laughter, from which the birds take their name. White-crested Laughing-Thrushes typically bounce over the ground or follow one another in short glides over gulleys or ravines.

CHESTNUT-TAILED MINLA
Timaliidae *Minla strigula*
RANGE: Himalayas and Southeast Asia
HABITAT: deciduous or evergreen forest and rhododendron groves
SIZE: 6 in (16 cm)

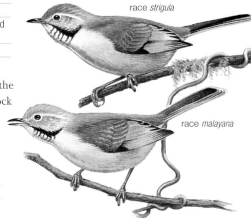

race *strigula*

race *malayana*

This is a bird of the middle storey of the forest, where it moves quite acrobatically among the small twigs. Small parties of Chestnut-tailed Minlas keep up a constant chirruping as the flock moves onward. Insects provide the bulk of its food, but it also eats seeds and berries.

RED-BILLED LEIOTHRIX
Timaliidae *Leiothrix lutea*
RANGE: Himalayas, Myanmar, S China
HABITAT: undergrowth in forests
SIZE: 5 in (13 cm)

This bird's loud, melodious, warbling song is often uttered from the cover of dense undergrowth in a shady ravine, where the bird's bright colors are difficult to detect. Outside the breeding season, it often occurs in small parties that forage through bamboo, grass, or scrub, keeping in touch with a constant, low, piping note.

CHESTNUT-HEADED FULVETTA
Timaliidae *Alcippe castaneceps*
RANGE: Himalayas and Southeast Asia
HABITAT: thick undergrowth and scrub, forest edge and clearings
SIZE: 4 in (10 cm)

This tiny, titlike babbler is a bird of high altitudes, ranging up to 13,000 ft (4,000 m) above sea level. Every branch, patch of moss, or clump of fern is searched carefully as the birds swing on the slender stems or flutter upside down. They will also launch briefly into the air after a passing insect.

young in nest

WHITE-NECKED ROCKFOWL
Timaliidae *Picathartes gymnocephalus*
RANGE: W Africa from Guinea and Sierra Leone to Togo
HABITAT: rock outcrops with caves in primary forest
SIZE: 16 in (40 cm)

The function of the brightly colored bare skin on the rockfowls' heads is unknown, since the birds spend much of their time in dark caves and dense forest. Their dependence on caves for nesting is unusual among birds. They construct mud nests on the smooth cave ceilings, possibly using existing wasps' nests as foundations

race *flavicollis*

race *alibicollis*

WHISKERED YUHINA
Timaliidae *Yuhina flavicollis*
RANGE: Himalayas E to Myanmar and Laos
HABITAT: secondary forest and scrub, clearings and forest edge
SIZE: 5 in (13 cm))

The erect crest gives this babbler a perky appearance as it swings through the twigs, or clings briefly to a tree trunk, like a tit, while inspecting the bark for insects or grubs. Its diet also includes many varieties of berry and seed. It is highly vocal, keeping up a continual "chipping" note.

BEARDED REEDLING
Paradoxornithidae *Panurus biarmicus*
RANGE: W Europe, Turkey, Iran across Asia to E Manchuria
HABITAT: reedbeds
SIZE: 6 in (15 cm)

Delightfully active and acrobatic, the Bearded Reedling is adept at straddling 2 reeds with its feet turned outward to grip each stem. Pairs often roost together on reed stems, the male distinguished by his blue-gray head and jaunty black moustaches.

race *webbianus*

race *bulomachus*

VINOUS-THROATED PARROTBILL
Paradoxornithidae *Paradoxornis webbianus*
RANGE: Manchuria, S through China and Korea to Myanmar
HABITAT: bamboo groves, scrub, tea plantations, and reedbeds
SIZE: 5 in (12 cm)

Outside the breeding season Vinous-throated Parrotbills often move through the undergrowth in large flocks in search of seeds and insects, keeping in touch with one another with a constant sharp, chirruping call. The plumage varies with race. All races have a strong bill that is used for tearing bamboo and reed stems to expose the insects within.

HALF-COLLARED GNATWREN
Sylviidae *Microbates cinereiventris*
RANGE: Central and South America from Nicaragua to Colombia, Ecuador, and Peru
HABITAT: lowland forest
SIZE: 4½ in (11.5 cm)

Gnatwrens are found in the lower levels of woodland and forest. The Half-collared, or Tawny-faced, Gnatwren forages actively for insects, either making excursions from a perch down to the ground or flitting among the foliage. It will often hover to pick its prey off a twig or leaf.

BLUE-GRAY GNATCATCHER
Sylviidae *Polioptila caerulea*
RANGE: North America from S Canada to Guatemala and Cuba; winters S of South Carolina along Atlantic coast, and S of S Mississippi and S Texas
HABITAT: forest, timbered swamps, thorny chaparral, wooded areas of towns
SIZE: 4½–5 in (11.5–13 cm)

The Blue-gray Gnatcatcher is a tiny, restless bird, often pugnacious, that forages among the leaves and twigs of trees for insects. The nest is a beautifully constructed cup made of plant down, bound together with spider and insect silk and covered with pieces of lichen.

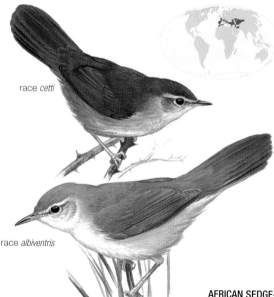

race *cetti*

race *albiventris*

CETTI'S WARBLER
Sylviidae *Cettia cetti*
RANGE: Mediterranean E to Iran and Turkestan; currently spreading N
HABITAT: swamps, scrub alongside reedbeds, dense bushes and hedges with brambles and tamarisks, edges of cornfields
SIZE: 5½ in (14 cm)

Skulking and secretive, Cetti's Warbler spends most of its time in dense cover but it occasionally shows itself on top of a bush or hedge. The position of the male is often given away by his brief, explosive song.

AFRICAN SEDGE-WARBLER
Sylviidae *Bradypterus baboecalus*
RANGE: S Africa (except dry W) N to Chad and Ethiopia
HABITAT: reedbeds, swamps, sewage works
SIZE: 6–7½ in (15–19 cm)

Shy by nature, the African Sedge-Warbler rarely emerges from among the sedges and rushes where it forages close to the ground for insects, but it can be located by its call, a series of sharp, staccato notes.

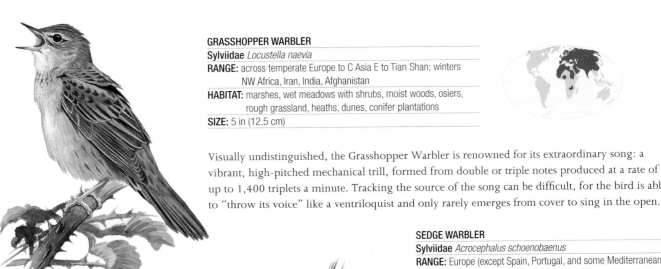

GRASSHOPPER WARBLER
Sylviidae *Locustella naevia*
RANGE: across temperate Europe to C Asia E to Tian Shan; winters NW Africa, Iran, India, Afghanistan
HABITAT: marshes, wet meadows with shrubs, moist woods, osiers, rough grassland, heaths, dunes, conifer plantations
SIZE: 5 in (12.5 cm)

Visually undistinguished, the Grasshopper Warbler is renowned for its extraordinary song: a vibrant, high-pitched mechanical trill, formed from double or triple notes produced at a rate of up to 1,400 triplets a minute. Tracking the source of the song can be difficult, for the bird is able to "throw its voice" like a ventriloquist and only rarely emerges from cover to sing in the open.

SEDGE WARBLER
Sylviidae *Acrocephalus schoenobaenus*
RANGE: Europe (except Spain, Portugal, and some Mediterranean coasts) E to Siberia and SE to Iran; winters Africa S of Sahara and E of Nigeria
HABITAT: osiers, marsh ditches, lakes, sewage works, gravel pits, conifer plantations, cereal and rape fields
SIZE: 5 in (12.5 cm)

Essentially marsh-dwelling birds, Sedge Warblers feed mainly on slow-moving insects, which they pick out of low vegetation. They nest in hedges, among osiers, reeds, or coarse grass, or even among standing crops of beans, rape, or cereals, binding the cup-shaped nest securely to the stems.

CLAMOROUS REED-WARBLER
Sylviidae *Acrocephalus stentoreus*
RANGE: NE Africa, across S Asia to Australia
HABITAT: swampy vegetation, especially reedbeds
SIZE: 6 in (16 cm)

race *australis*

race *stentoreus*

The Clamorous Reed-Warbler is a denizen of thick reedbeds but it will often venture into other swampy habitats. It feeds on insects gleaned from vegetation and, sometimes, by flycatching. The nest is skilfully woven from reed sheaths and decayed water plants and is attached to several reed stems.

SEYCHELLES BRUSH-WARBLER
Sylviidae *Bebrornis sechellensis*
RANGE: Aride, Cousine, Denis, and Fregate islands, Seychelles
HABITAT: dense scrub and swamp
SIZE: 5 in (13 cm)

Once threatened with extinction, despite a successful conservation program, this species is still classed as vulnerable. A distinctive warbler with a weak and fluttering flight, its favored haunts are the dense bushy growth alongside old coconut plantations, mangroves, and coastal scrub. It pursues flying insects and forages for caterpillars among the branches of small trees and bushes.

ICTERINE WARBLER
Sylviidae *Hippolais icterina*
RANGE: N and E Europe S to Alps, Asia Minor, and Caucasus, Asia E
to Altai Mountains; winters E and tropical Africa
HABITAT: open broad-leaved woods, parks, riversides, farmland,
orchards and large gardens
SIZE: 5 in (13 cm)

The Icterine Warbler is more conspicuous than many tree warblers as it moves about the tree canopy in search of insects and their larvae. Built in the fork of a tree, its nest is made of stems or grasses held together with wool and spiders' silk; some nests incorporate bark, paper, or even rags.

BARRED WARBLER
Sylviidae *Sylvia nisoria*
RANGE: C and E Europe, Asia E to Tian Shan
HABITAT: thorny scrub, wet fields with trees, broad-leaved woods,
parks, peat bogs; winters on thorn savanna
SIZE: 6 in (15 cm)

The Barred Warbler is shy and secretive with a preference for thick cover, where it searches through the foliage for ants, young locusts, beetles, and a variety of bugs. When startled, it utters a harsh chattering alarm note but its song is rich and melodious, resembling that of the Nightingale.

BLACKCAP
Sylviidae *Sylvia atricapilla*
RANGE: Eurasia E to River Irtysh in Siberia and N Iran, NW Africa, and
Atlantic islands; winters Mediterranean and Africa S to Tanzania
HABITAT: broad-leaved and conifer woods, overgrown hedges, scrub
with tall trees
SIZE: 5½ in (14 cm)

The glossy black cap of the male and the reddish-brown cap of the female are distinctive. The male has a wavy or rippling song full of rich, pure notes; he is also an accomplished mimic.

CYPRUS WARBLER
Sylviidae *Sylvia melanothorax*
RANGE: Cyprus, but may wander to nearby coasts of E Mediterranean
HABITAT: hill scrub and orange groves up to 6,500 ft (2,000 m)
SIZE: 5 in (13.5 cm)

The Cyprus Warbler is usually heard rather than seen as it forages for food among the hillside orange groves or maquis scrub of its native island. It tends to hold its tail up at right angles to its body and usually keeps to cover, betraying its presence with a harsh single-note alarm call.

DARTFORD WARBLER

Sylviidae *Sylvia undata*
RANGE: S England, W France, S Europe E to Italy and Sicily, N Africa E to Tunisia
HABITAT: in N, lowland heath with dense heather or gorse; in S, spiny maquis
SIZE: 5 in (12.5 cm)

Dartford Warblers are generally skulking, furtive birds that keep to the bushes, but on sunny mornings the males will propel themselves some 7 ft (2 m) into the air in dancing song-flights. They feed almost exclusively on insects in summer, but often eat small fruits during winter.

WILLOW WARBLER

Sylviidae *Phylloscopus trochilus*
RANGE: Scandinavia and NW Europe to E Siberia and Alaska; winters tropical and S Africa
HABITAT: open woods, scrub, conifer plantations, moorland with shrubs, hedges
SIZE: 4 in (10.5 cm)

The Willow Warbler will thrive in any type of open woodland. It feeds on insects taken on the wing or picked off the foliage with delicate precision. In winter, when the insect supply fails in the north, it flies south to Africa.

PALLAS'S LEAF-WARBLER

Sylviidae *Phylloscopus proregulus*
RANGE: Himalayas, mountains from Altai to Sakhalin; vagrants often reported to W; winters N India and S China
HABITAT: pine or birch forest; winters in light woodland, mixed forest, or scrub
SIZE: 3½ in (9 cm)

This diminutive leaf warbler has a distinctive yellow crown stripe, double wing bar, and rump. It often feeds by hovering among the leaves, and it will also hawk after flying insects. Its nest is domed, with a hair or feather lining, and is built on the branch of a moss-covered tree.

race *chloronotus*

race *proregulus*

YELLOW-BREASTED FLYCATCHER-WARBLER

Sylviidae *Seicercus montis*
RANGE: Malaysia, Sumatra to Borneo, Palawan, and Timor, usually above 6,500 ft (2,000 m)
HABITAT: mountain forest
SIZE: 4 in (10 cm)

The Yellow-breasted Flycatcher-Warbler is generally seen in mountain gullies and among the scrub and undergrowth in forest clearings. The male has an attractive trilling song. Like all the flycatcher-warblers, it builds a dome-shaped nest, locating it in a crevice beneath an overhanging bank.

RUBY-CROWNED KINGLET

Sylviidae *Regulus calendula*
RANGE: North America, from NW Alaska S to Arizona, also E Canada to Nova Scotia; winters S to N Mexico
HABITAT: mixed woods, spruce bogs, fir woods
SIZE: 4–4½ in (9.5–11.5 cm)

This tiny, short-tailed American species habitually flits its wings with sudden, jerking movements—a useful recognition point, since the characteristic scarlet patch on the crown is often concealed. It hunts assiduously for insects among the twigs and leaves and may also dart after any that fly past.

GOLDCREST

Sylviidae *Regulus regulus*
RANGE: discontinuous, from Azores and NW Europe and Scandinavia to E Asia
HABITAT: conifer woods to 14,700 ft (4,500 m), also some broad-leaved woods
SIZE: 3½ in (9 cm)

The crest is orange in the male and yellow in the female. Small groups of Goldcrests can often be seen flying from tree to tree in coniferous forest, drawing attention to themselves by their soft but extremely shrill *zee* calls. They feed mainly on small insects, but have also been seen sipping tree sap.

SEVERTZOV'S TIT-WARBLER

Sylviidae *Leptopoecile sophiae*
RANGE: Pakistan, NW India, Nepal, Sikkim, and China, from Tian Shan to Sichuan
HABITAT: rhododendron and juniper scrub above the tree line
SIZE: 4 in (11 cm)

Severtzov's Tit-Warbler is restricted to mountain habitats where it feeds on insects gathered in the scrub belt from 8,000–13,000 ft (2,500–4,000 m). It spends much of its time in dense undergrowth; occasionally it will perch on the top of a bush with its tail cocked, uttering loud, high-pitched calls.

non-breeding

TINK-TINK CISTICOLA

Sylviidae *Cisticola textrix*
RANGE: The Democratic Republic of the Congo, S Angola, Zambia, and South Africa in S and on highveld N to Transvaal
HABITAT: short grassland with bare patches between tufts; flat marshland in the Cape
SIZE: 3½–4 in (9–10 cm)

The Tink-tink Cisticola, also known as the Pinc-pinc, or Cloud, Cisticola, is a grassland species that feeds on the ground on insects, especially grasshoppers. The male has a rattling song produced during a display flight that often takes the bird high in the air, well beyond the range of human vision.

race *saharae*

race *buryi*

STREAKED SCRUB-WARBLER
Sylviidae *Scotocerca inquieta*
RANGE: N Africa from Morocco to Red Sea, Iran, and Afghanistan
HABITAT: rocky desert and semi-desert with sparse bushes, dry hillsides, wadis
SIZE: 4 in (10 cm)

The Streaked Scrub-Warbler feeds on insects, small snails, and seeds, tending to stay in cover. It may hop about on the ground or among low vegetation with its long tail cocked up and waving up and down or from side to side.

ZITTING CISTICOLA
Sylviidae *Cisticola juncidis*
RANGE: discontinuous around Mediterranean, W France, sub-Saharan Africa, India, Sri Lanka, Southeast Asia, Indonesia, N Australia
HABITAT: grassland, marshy savanna, paddy fields, brush in open areas
SIZE: 4 in (10 cm)

song-flight

♂

Also know as the Fan-tailed Warbler, this bird is best known for its song—a series of high, rasping dzeep notes separated by very short intervals uttered by the male during a jerky, high, aerial song-flight. The Zitting Cisticola is essentially a lowland bird, spending most of its time foraging in the grass, and rarely flies unless disturbed.

KAROO PRINIA
Sylviidae *Prinia maculosa*
RANGE: S Namibia, S and E South Africa
HABITAT: Karoo veld, valleys and mountain slopes, farmland, and coastal scrub
SIZE: 5–6 in (13–15 cm)

The Karoo Prinia can be hard to spot as it hunts for insects through the bushes and tall grasses, but when alarmed it may perch atop a tall plant, flicking its wings and uttering its harsh chirping calls. If approached closely, it often dives into thick vegetation and hides.

winter

ASHY PRINIA
Sylviidae *Prinia socialis*
RANGE: Indian subcontinent and W Myanmar
HABITAT: scrub, grassland, grain fields, open forest, reedbeds, stream banks, mangroves
SIZE: 5 in (12.5 cm)

This nervous, long-tailed bird can be found on hills up to 4,000 ft (1,200 m). It feeds on insects gleaned from low vegetation and also takes nectar from flowers. There is a marked difference between summer and winter plumages and the tail is longer in winter.

BLACK-COLLARED APALIS

Sylviidae *Apalis pulchra*
RANGE: Africa, from Cameroon to Sudan and Kenya
HABITAT: undergrowth in highland forest
SIZE: 5 in (12.5 cm)

The Black-collared Apalis is a noisy, lively resident of mountain and upland forests, feeding mainly on insects picked out of the ground vegetation. This species occasionally adopts the nests of other birds but, if it has to, it will build a purse-shaped nest of its own.

LONG-TAILED TAILORBIRD

Sylviidae *Orthotomus sutorius*
RANGE: Indian subcontinent, Southeast Asia to Java, S China; up to 5, 250 ft (1,600 m) in Southeast Asia
HABITAT: thickets, scrub, bamboo, gardens
SIZE: 5 in (12 cm); breeding male 6 in (15.5 cm)

The Long-tailed Tailorbird's name is derived from its astonishing nestbuilding technique. Taking 1 or 2 large leaves on a low bush or branch, it uses its bill as a needle to perforate the edges and sew them together using individual stitches of cottony plant material or the silk from spiders' webs or insect cocoons. The nest itself—made of soft plant fibers—is formed inside this pocket.

at nest

MOUSTACHED GRASS-WARBLER

Sylviidae *Melocichla mentalis*
RANGE: From W Africa to Ethiopia in the N, down to Angola and across to Zambezi River in the S
HABITAT: edges of mountain evergreen forest with coarse grass and scattered trees, marshy land along streams
SIZE: 7–8 in (18–20 cm)

Only the male sports the black cheek stripe that gives the species its name. Its alarm note is a rasping call, but the male has an attractive, thrushlike song and will sometimes sing or sunbathe on top of a tuft of grass.

BLEATING CAMAROPTERA

Sylviidae *Camaroptera brachyura*
RANGE: sub-Saharan Africa
HABITAT: woodland thickets, forest edge, riverine bush, parks, gardens
SIZE: 5 in (12.5 cm)

race *brevicaudata*
"Gray-backed Camaroptera"

race *brevicaudata*
"Green-backed Camaroptera"

The alarm call of these birds is quite distinctive, like the bleating of a lamb. Another equally curious call sounds like stones being tapped together. The soft, downy nest is made within a frame formed from the broad leaves of a single twig or spray, with more leaves added to make a roof.

YELLOW-BELLIED EREMOMELA

Sylviidae *Eremomela icteropygialis*
RANGE: Africa from Sudan, Ethiopia, and Somalia S through Kenya and Tanzania to Zimbabwe and Transvaal
HABITAT: woodland, bushveld, scrub
SIZE: 4–4½ in (10–11 cm)

This pert, short-tailed warbler is usually seen in pairs or family parties, busily seeking insects among the twigs and branches of trees, especially acacias. The nest is a thin-walled cup of dry grass, bound together with spiders' silk and sited in a bush.

NORTHERN CROMBEC
Sylviidae *Sylvietta brachyura*
RANGE: widespread across the S Sahel zone from Senegal in the W to Somalia in the E; thence through Uganda and Kenya to Tanzania
HABITAT: acacia woodland, dry scrub, coastal bush
SIZE: 3½ in (9 cm)

race *brachyura*

race *carnapai*

The Northern Crombec's habit of running along branches and climbing through the foliage of thorn trees in search of insects has earned it the alternative name of Nuthatch Warbler. There are about 6 races. *S. b. camapi* of Cameroon and Central African Republic has distinctive chestnut underparts.

SOUTHERN TIT-WARBLER
Sylviidae *Parisoma subcaeruleum*
RANGE: S Africa N to Angola and S Zambia
HABITAT: thornveld, semi-arid scrub, dry hillsides, savanna thickets, riverine bush
SIZE: 5½–6 in (14–16 cm)

The Southern Tit-Warbler is commonly seen alone or in pairs hopping restlessly through the foliage in search of insects, spiders, and fruit, or taking short, low flights from tree to tree. The male has a piping, bubbling song that often includes mimicry of other species.

GRAY LONGBILL
Sylviidae *Macrosphenus concolor*
RANGE: W and C Africa from Sierra Leone to Uganda
HABITAT: undergrowth, vines and creepers, canopy of dense forest
SIZE: 5 in (13 cm)

The Gray Longbill is a secretive bird, with a long, thin, hook-tipped bill and loose-feathered flanks, that frequents dense vegetation and feeds largely on a diet of insects. Longbills are a poorly studied group, and the facts about their breeding are hazy.

LITTLE MARSHBIRD
Sylviidae *Megalurus gramineus*
RANGE: E and SW Australia, Tasmania
HABITAT: grassy swamps and marshes
SIZE: 5 in (13 cm)

The Little Marshbird, or Little Grassbird, lives in swamp vegetation, where it feeds on a variety of small insects and spiders gleaned from the foliage. It rarely flies, but when it does, it flutters its wings continuously, moving slowly and keeping low down, with its tail trailing downward.

race *punctatus*

FERNBIRD
Sylviidae *Megalurus punctatus*
RANGE: New Zealand
HABITAT: reed mace swamps, marshy scrub with ferns, bracken
SIZE: 7 in (18 cm)

The Fembird usually feeds on or near the ground. It is reluctant to take flight and will travel only short distances on the wing, flying clumsily with its tail hanging down. The race illustrated, *M. p. punctatus*, occurs on the main (North and South) islands; other races, differing in plumage, occur on small offshore islands.

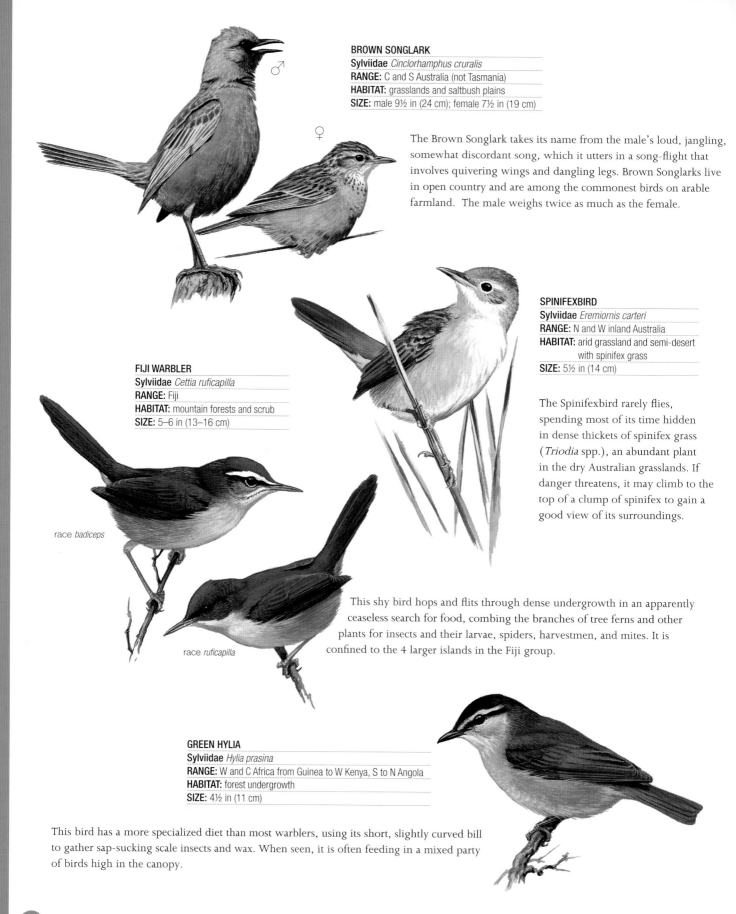

BROWN SONGLARK
Sylviidae *Cinclorhamphus cruralis*
RANGE: C and S Australia (not Tasmania)
HABITAT: grasslands and saltbush plains
SIZE: male 9½ in (24 cm); female 7½ in (19 cm)

♂

♀

The Brown Songlark takes its name from the male's loud, jangling, somewhat discordant song, which it utters in a song-flight that involves quivering wings and dangling legs. Brown Songlarks live in open country and are among the commonest birds on arable farmland. The male weighs twice as much as the female.

SPINIFEXBIRD
Sylviidae *Eremiornis carteri*
RANGE: N and W inland Australia
HABITAT: arid grassland and semi-desert with spinifex grass
SIZE: 5½ in (14 cm)

FIJI WARBLER
Sylviidae *Cettia ruficapilla*
RANGE: Fiji
HABITAT: mountain forests and scrub
SIZE: 5–6 in (13–16 cm)

The Spinifexbird rarely flies, spending most of its time hidden in dense thickets of spinifex grass (*Triodia* spp.), an abundant plant in the dry Australian grasslands. If danger threatens, it may climb to the top of a clump of spinifex to gain a good view of its surroundings.

race *badiceps*

race *ruficapilla*

This shy bird hops and flits through dense undergrowth in an apparently ceaseless search for food, combing the branches of tree ferns and other plants for insects and their larvae, spiders, harvestmen, and mites. It is confined to the 4 larger islands in the Fiji group.

GREEN HYLIA
Sylviidae *Hylia prasina*
RANGE: W and C Africa from Guinea to W Kenya, S to N Angola
HABITAT: forest undergrowth
SIZE: 4½ in (11 cm)

This bird has a more specialized diet than most warblers, using its short, slightly curved bill to gather sap-sucking scale insects and wax. When seen, it is often feeding in a mixed party of birds high in the canopy.

SPOTTED FLYCATCHER
Muscicapidae *Muscicapa striata*
RANGE: Eurasia N to N Russian Federation and W Siberia, E to N Mongolia,
S to NW Africa and Himalayas; winters C and S Africa, Arabia, NW India
HABITAT: open woods and scrub, parks, gardens; winters in acacia woods and thorn bush
SIZE: 5½ in (14 cm)

The Spotted Flycatcher sits on a bare branch or other exposed perch, from which it makes short aerial sallies after insects, often returning to the same spot. Its flying style is erratic, with many swerves and twists; it flicks its wings or tail when at rest.

PIED FLYCATCHER
Muscicapidae *Ficedula hypoleuca*
RANGE: much of Europe, W Asia to River Yenisey, NW Africa; winters
in tropical Africa S to Tanzania
HABITAT: ancient broad-leaved woodland (especially in uplands),
coniferous forest, well-timbered parks, orchards, gardens
SIZE: 5 in (13 cm)

The Pied Flycatcher often flicks its wings and moves its tail up and down. It sallies out from a perch after insects and usually returns to a different one. Besides insects, these birds will take earthworms and berries in the fall.

race *cyanomelana*

BLUE-AND-WHITE FLYCATCHER
Muscicapidae *Cyanoptila cyanomelana*
RANGE: breeds in NE and E Asia, including Manchuria,
W China, and Japan; migrates through E and S China
to winter in Southeast Asia, S to Greater Sundas
HABITAT: mountain forest and wooded regions
SIZE: 7 in (18 cm)

This flycatcher of the eastern Palearctic region lives in forested areas, and on migration and in its winter quarters it can be found up to heights of 6,500 ft (2,000 m). The face, throat, and breast of the Japanese race *C. c. cyanomelana* are black, while those of the race *C. c. cumatilis* are greenish-blue.

RUFOUS-BELLIED NILTAVA
Muscicapidae *Niltava sundara*
RANGE: Himalayas to W China, Myanmar
HABITAT: forest undergrowth and scrub
SIZE: 7 in (18 cm)

The male Rufous-bellied Niltava has a shining blue neck patch and a black throat with a straight lower edge. The female has a white gorget on her lower throat. Immatures have brown upper-parts with rusty buff spots, and buff-brown underparts with blackish scales.

JACKY WINTER
Muscicapidae *Microeca leucophaea*
RANGE: most of Australia, except the deserts, Tasmania, and extreme NE; also S New Guinea
HABITAT: open forest, woodland, and eucalypt scrub
SIZE: 5 in (13 cm)

juv

The male and female Jacky Winter, or Australian Brown Flycatcher, are similar in appearance; the juvenile is spotted brown and white. It is most often found in partly cleared country or on the edge of woodland and farmland. Its song is a loud *peter peter*, also sometimes described as *jacky winter*.

♂ ♀

FLAME ROBIN
Muscicapidae *Petroica phoenicea*
RANGE: SE Australia and Tasmania
HABITAT: breeds in upland eucalypt forest and woodland; winters in more open habitat
SIZE: 5½ in (14 cm)

Flame Robins are most common in open woodland near to the tree line in the Great Dividing Range. In the fall, they migrate to lower altitudes and often westward into drier, more open country. The female and immatures are much duller than the male.

CHIN-SPOT PUFF-BACK FLYCATCHER
Monarchidae *Batis molitor*
RANGE: S Sudan, Kenya (except coast), SW Africa, Mozambique, and E Cape Province
HABITAT: open acacia woodland, forests and their edges, cultivated areas, gardens
SIZE: 4½ in (11.5 cm)

♀ ♂

The Chin-spot Puff-back Flycatcher is a restless bird, hawking after insects like a true flycatcher and hovering in the air while searching leaves. It will also forage in lower branches like a tit. The wings produce a rattle in flight.

♀ ♂

BROWN-THROATED WATTLE-EYE
Monarchidae *Platysteira cyanea*
RANGE: W, C, and E Africa, including Sudan, Uganda, and Kenya
HABITAT: forest strips and secondary growth
SIZE: 5 in (13 cm)

This species is markedly black and white with bright scarlet eye-wattles. It occurs in pairs or noisy little flocks. It feeds restlessly among the foliage and flicks its wings audibly in flight.

BLUE FLYCATCHER
Monarchidae *Elminia longicauda*
RANGE: W Africa, E to Kenya, S to Angola
HABITAT: woodland and forest, gardens, farmland
SIZE: 5½ in (14 cm)

imm

♂

Beautifully colored and elegant in shape, this flycatcher is typically alert, upright, and full of nervous energy, frequently fanning its rather long, graduated tail. It has a brief, twittering song, which is somewhat insignificant but reminiscent of the songs of several of the sunbirds.

♂

chestnut phase

♀

white phase

race *azurea*

AFRICAN PARADISE FLYCATCHER
Monarchidae *Terpsiphone viridis*
RANGE: sub-Saharan Africa
HABITAT: forest and riverside woodland with mature trees
SIZE: 16 in (40 cm)

In flight, this bird gives a sudden flash of color and a glimpse of a long, trailing tail. Its call is a distinctive, sharp double or treble note. The nest is a splendidly neat, surprisingly small construction of fibers and fine roots, bound and camouflaged with spiders' webs and lichens.

♂

♀

BLACK-NAPED BLUE MONARCH
Monarchidae *Hypothymis azurea*
RANGE: Indonesia, Philippines, China, W to India
HABITAT: mixed primary or secondary forest, farmland,
                plantations, bamboo
SIZE: 6 in (16 cm)

Black-naped Blue Monarchs are always active, with flicking wings and cocked, fanned tails. They catch insects in agile twisting and looping sallies from a perch. Insect prey is taken back to a perch and held under one foot as it is broken into pieces in a shrikelike manner. The species has no real song.

race *sandwichenis*

race *sclateri*

♂

ELEPAIO
Monarchidae *Chasiempis sandwichensis*
RANGE: Hawaiian islands
HABITAT: high-altitude native and exotic forests and volcanic areas
SIZE: 5½ in (14 cm)

The 5 races of the Elepaio are found only on the Hawaiian islands. All adults have 2 white wing bars, a white rump, and a white-tipped tail. Hawaiian immatures are dull brown and those on Kauai and Oahu are rusty brown. The song is a loudly whistled *chee-whee-o* or *e-le-pai-o*.

imm

BLACK-FACED MONARCH
Monarchidae *Monarcha melanopsis*
RANGE: E Australia and New Guinea
HABITAT: rain forest and wet eucalypt forest
SIZE: 7 in (18 cm)

The black face of this lovely bird gives it its usual Australian name; an alternative name is the Pearly-winged Monarch. Females are very similar to males, whereas immatures lack the black face. The birds have a loud whistling song and various harsher notes.

♂

♀

YELLOW-BREASTED BOATBILL
Monarchidae *Machaerirhynchus flaviventer*
RANGE: NE Queensland, New Guinea
HABITAT: rain forest
SIZE: 4–5 in (11–12 cm)

The broad, flat bill with its strongly hooked tip is this bird's most unusual feature. Boatbills feed by flycatching, or by gleaning from foliage, apparently only taking small, soft-bodied insects. They tend to keep to the canopy of rain forest.

SILKTAIL
Monarchidae *Lamprolia victoriae*
RANGE: Fiji Islands
HABITAT: rain forest
SIZE: 5 in (13 cm)

The Silktail's white rump and tail are conspicuous in the dim forest interior as the bird flits about on its large, rounded wings. Its courtship displays involve bowing and raising the tail, or flicking the wings and fanning the tail. Both postures produce a dramatic flash of white.

WHITE-BROWED FANTAIL
Monarchidae *Rhipidura aureola*
RANGE: Sri Lanka, India, Pakistan, Bangladesh
HABITAT: forests, gardens, scrub
SIZE: 6½ in (17 cm)

race *aureola*

The sexes are similar in appearance, but females are generally a little paler on the head than the males. The tail is often fanned and held up high, with the wings drooped. The species is thought to use its flicking wings and tail to disturb insects from crevices in old bark.

RUFOUS FANTAIL
Monarchidae *Rhipidura rufifrons*
RANGE: New Guinea, Pacific and Indonesian
islands, N and E Australia
HABITAT: eucalypt forests, rain forests,
and mangroves
SIZE: 6–6½ in (15–16.5 cm)

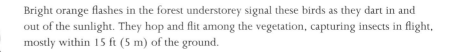

race *rufifrons*

Bright orange flashes in the forest understorey signal these birds as they dart in and out of the sunlight. They hop and flit among the vegetation, capturing insects in flight, mostly within 15 ft (5 m) of the ground.

WILLIE WAGTAIL
Monarchidae *Rhipidura leucophrys*
RANGE: throughout Australia; rare in Tasmania,
New Guinea, Soloman Islands, Bismarck
Archipelago, and Moluccas
HABITAT: open woodland, scrub, grassland
SIZE: 8 in (20 cm)

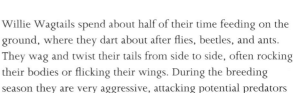

Willie Wagtails spend about half of their time feeding on the ground, where they dart about after flies, beetles, and ants. They wag and twist their tails from side to side, often rocking their bodies or flicking their wings. During the breeding season they are very aggressive, attacking potential predators up to the size of an eagle.

SUPERB FAIRY-WREN
Maluridae *Malurus cyaneus*
RANGE: SE Australia, including Tasmania
HABITAT: eucalypt woodland and forest with patches of dense cover
SIZE: 5 in (13 cm)

The Superb Fairy-Wren, or Blue Wren, feeds on centipedes and other arthropods on the ground, usually in open grassy areas, but rarely far from dense cover to which it retreats if danger threatens. The breeding male closely guards the female during her fertile periods.

STRIATED GRASSWREN
Maluridae *Amytornis striatus*
RANGE: inland Australia
HABITAT: sandy desert and scrub
SIZE: 5½–6½ in (14–16.5 cm)

The Striated, or Striped, Grasswren's favorite habitat is sand plains with prickly porcupine grass (*Triodia*). They feed on the ground, usually in dense cover, eating invertebrates, as well as small seeds. They seldom fly, but run through the undergrowth like mice and hop vigorously.

RUFOUS-CROWNED EMU-WREN
Maluridae *Stipiturus ruficeps*
RANGE: C Australia
HABITAT: grassland, desert, and scrubland
SIZE: 5½ in (14 cm)

Emu-Wrens have central tail feathers that are nearly twice as long as the body of the bird and lack barbicels—the tiny hooks that interlock with one another to keep a feather smooth and neat. This gives them the open and loose appearance of an Emu's feathers. The birds inhabit remote areas of desert, which are usually covered with dense hummocks of porcupine grass (*Triodia*) or other grasses and low shrubs.

RUFOUS BRISTLEBIRD
Acanthizidae *Dasyornis broadbenti*
RANGE: restricted to a small area of SE Australia
HABITAT: dense scrub and thickets
SIZE: 10½ in (27 cm)

race *broadbenti*

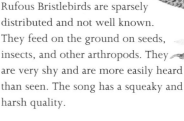

FERNWREN
Acanthizidae *Crateroscelis gutturalis*
RANGE: NE Australia
HABITAT: mountain rain forest above 2,000 ft (650 m)
SIZE: 5–5½ in (12–14 cm)

The Fernwren lives almost entirely on the ground. Moving alone or in pairs, they throw leaf litter into the air when searching for small invertebrates such as snails. They may also take insects disturbed by the foraging activities of larger birds.

Rufous Bristlebirds are sparsely distributed and not well known. They feed on the ground on seeds, insects, and other arthropods. They are very shy and are more easily heard than seen. The song has a squeaky and harsh quality.

ORIGMA
Acanthizidae *Origma solitaria*
RANGE: C coastal New South Wales
HABITAT: forest and heathland with rocky outcrops
SIZE: 5½ in (14 cm)

The Origma, or Rock Warbler, feeds mostly on bare rock surfaces and may climb almost vertically like a treecreeper. They eat insects and spiders. Their nesting behaviour is unusual as the nest is almost invariably placed in the dark, in a cave, a deep cleft in the rock, or even behind a waterfall. They sometimes take advantage of human structures, nesting in mineshafts and buildings. The nest is spherical and is usually suspended by spiders' webs from the ceiling of a cave or building.

♂

race *laegivaster*

race *humilis*

♂

WHITE-BROWED SCRUBWREN
Acanthizidae *Sericornis frontalis*
RANGE: W, S, and E Australia, Tasmania
HABITAT: understorey of forest, heathland
SIZE: 5 in (12 cm)

White-browed Scrubwrens feed on the ground in dense cover or in low bushes on insects and seeds. Birds in the far northwest of the range experience very high temperatures that restrict their feeding. They are able to drink weak salt solutions and can also concentrate their urine to conserve water.

race *frontalis*

♂

race *apicalis*

INLAND THORNBILL
Acanthizidae *Acanthiza apicalis*
RANGE: S and C Australia
HABITAT: arid woodland and eucalypt scrub; forests,
coastal scrub, heaths in SW; also mangroves
SIZE: 4 in (10 cm)

The Inland Thornbill carries its tail cocked and is a perky, conspicuous bird. It forages within shrubs for insects and sometimes seeds, working through one bush and then flying jerkily to the next. It also feeds at flowers, inserting its bill into the flower head.

WEEBILL
Acanthizidae *Smicrornis brevirostris*
RANGE: almost throughout Australia
HABITAT: eucalypt woodland and forest; acacia woodland
SIZE: 3–3½ in (8–9 cm)

The Weebill has a pale iris and eyebrow and a very short, stubby beak. The song is quite loud for such a tiny bird and resembles *I'm a weebill*. Weebills glean insects from the outer foliage of eucalypts and other trees, often hovering on the edge of the canopy.

WHITE-THROATED GERYGONE
Acanthizidae *Gerygone olivacea*
RANGE: N and E Australia; migrates as far as SE Australia;
also SE New Guinea
HABITAT: eucalypt woodland
SIZE: 4 in (11 cm)

White-throated Gerygones have a lively, high-pitched song, which has earned them the name of bush-canary. The pendant nest hangs from a low eucalypt branch and has a long tail and a side entrance with a small veranda. Nests may be infested with ants or wasps, which may protect the birds from predators.

NEW ZEALAND CREEPER
Acanthizidae *Finschia novaeseelandiae*
RANGE: South Island, Stewart Island, and neighboring islands (New Zealand)
HABITAT: mature forest and scrubland
SIZE: 5 in (13 cm)

The New Zealand Creeper, or Brown Creeper, lives in family groups throughout the year. They are easily detected by song and calls, but remain in the canopy and are difficult to see. The Maori name for the bird, Pipipi, is imitative of its calls.

♀

race *frontatus*
"Eastern Shrike-tit"

♂

CRESTED SHRIKE-TIT
Pachycephalidae *Falcunculus frontatus*
RANGE: SE, SW, and NW Australia
HABITAT: eucalypt forests and woods
SIZE: 7 in (18 cm)

The Crested Shrike-Tit uses its powerful, hooked, shrikelike beak to noisily prise and shred loose bark from eucalypt trees in search of larvae and beetles. It also picks scale insects off twigs and rips open caterpillar cocoons and galls to prey on the animals within.

race *pectoralis*
♀

♂

GOLDEN WHISTLER
Pachycephalidae *Pachycephala pectoralis*
RANGE: E and S Australia, Tasmania, New Guinea, Indonesia, and Pacific islands
HABITAT: rain forest, eucalypt forest
SIZE: 6 in (16 cm)

♂

The male Golden Whistler is the most variable bird in the world, with at least 73 island races showing variations in plumage and bill pattern. The females of all races and males of some of the island races have dull olive plumage.

race *torquata*

♂

race *littayei*

race *pallidus*   race *aruensis*

VARIABLE PITOHUI
Pachycephalidae *Pitohui kirhocephalus*
RANGE: New Guinea, adjacent islands to W
HABITAT: lowland forest and forest edge
SIZE: 9 in (23 cm)

There are 7 species of pitohui, all restricted to the New Guinea area. The Variable Pitohui is remarkable for the striking geographic variation in its plumage: the largely black race *P. k. aruensis* of the Aru Islands and the gray-hooded race *P.k. pallidus* of the far western mainland and Waigeo and Batanta islands are extreme examples.

BLACK-CAPPED CHICKADEE
Paridae *Parus atricapillus*
RANGE: Alaska, Canada, S to C USA
HABITAT: coniferous and broad-leaved forest
SIZE: 5 in (13 cm)

The Black-capped Chickadee is a familiar garden visitor in winter, when small parties of 6 or so birds regularly descend on feeding stations, but in spring these parties split up into nesting pairs that spend the summer feeding in the forest.

race *britannicus*

COAL TIT
Paridae *Parus ater*
RANGE: Eurasia from Britain to Japan, N Africa
HABITAT: forests, mainly coniferous
SIZE: 4½ in (11.5 cm)

In general, Coal Tits favor conifer forests although some, such as those in Ireland, are found mainly in broad-leaved woodland. Coal Tits do not excavate their own nest-holes; they prefer to nest in vacant holes in trees, but they will sometimes use abandoned rodent burrows in the ground.

race *aemodius*

CRESTED TIT
Paridae *Parus cristatus*
RANGE: Europe and Scandinavia E to Urals
HABITAT: mature conifer forest
SIZE: 4½ in (11.5 cm)

The Crested Tit lives almost exclusively among mature conifer trees, particularly spruce and pine, and as a result it is patchily distributed throughout its range. Easily recognized by its speckled crest, it feeds mainly on insects, which it picks out of crevices in the bark with its short bill, and pine seeds.

SOUTHERN BLACK TIT
Paridae *Parus niger*
RANGE: SE Africa, N to Tanzania
HABITAT: woods, woodland edge, lightly wooded country
SIZE: 6 in (16 cm)

Found in a wide variety of woodland, ranging from dense evergreen forest to scattered trees, the Southern Black Tit breeds in family groups consisting of 3–4 birds; the "helpers" are generally the breeding pair's male offspring from the previous year's brood.

race *cinereus*

race *major*

GREAT TIT
Paridae *Parus major*
RANGE: Eurasia, from Britain through Eastern Europe and S Asia to Japan
HABITAT: forests, mountain scrub, parks and gardens, mangroves
SIZE: 5½ in (14 cm)

There are about 30 distinct races of Great Tit. Many of these are yellow-bellied, green-backed birds, like *P. m. major* of Europe and central Asia, but several eastern races, including *P. m. cinereus* of Java and the Lesser Sunda Islands, have a gray back and a whitish belly.

CHINESE YELLOW TIT
Paridae *Parus spilonotus*
RANGE: Nepal, Myanmar, Thailand, S China
HABITAT: mountain forests
SIZE: 5½ in (14 cm)

The Chinese Yellow Tit lives in all types of forest, ranging from subtropical jungle to mountain pinewoods. It forages for food high in the trees and rarely descends to ground level.

BLUE TIT
Paridae *Parus caeruleus*
RANGE: Europe E to Volga, Asia Minor, N Africa
HABITAT: woods, parks, gardens
SIZE: 4 in (11 cm)

The Blue Tit lays the largest clutch of any bird in the world (excluding some ducks and gamebirds, which do not feed their young). In good habitats, 11 eggs are common, while clutches of as many as 14–15 are by no means rare.

race *atricristatus*

race *bicolor*

TUFTED TITMOUSE
Paridae *Parus bicolor*
RANGE: E North America, S to Texas, and currently extending N to Ontario
HABITAT: broad-leaved forest, open woods
SIZE: 6½ in (17 cm)

The Tufted Titmouse's stout bill enables it to hammer open nuts that would be too tough for most other tits to crack. The race *P. b. bicolor* is from eastern, central, and southeastern USA. At the other end of its range, in Texas, *P. b. atricristatus* has a longer, black crest.

race *sultanea*

race *gayeti*

SULTAN TIT
Paridae *Melanochlora sultanea*
RANGE: E Nepal to S China and Southeast Asia
HABITAT: chiefly in lowland forest
SIZE: 8½ in (22 cm)

This giant among tits is so unlike the other members of its family that it has been classified in a genus of its own. Most races, such as *M.s. sultanea* of the eastern Himalayas, sport a flamboyant yellow crest, but an Indo-Chinese race *M. s. gayeti* has a black crest.

race *melanotis*
"Black-eared Bushtit"

BUSHTIT
Aegithalidae *Psaltriparus minimus*
RANGE: W North America, from British Columbia to Guatemala
HABITAT: open woods, chaparral scrub
SIZE: 4 in (11 cm)

race *minimus*

The Bushtit is the only North American long-tailed tit. It is a common and familiar bird that often feeds in gardens. Its finely woven nest is suspended from branches rather than attached at the bottom like that of the Long-tailed Tit.

race *caudatus*

LONG-TAILED TIT
Aegithalidae *Aegithalos caudatus*
RANGE: continuous from Europe through C Asia to Japan
HABITAT: woods, woodland edge, scrub
SIZE: 5½ in (14 cm)

race *roseceus*

These tiny birds, whose tails are more than half their body length, lose heat easily; on winter nights they huddle together in family groups to keep warm. The British race *A. c. rosaceus* has a distinctive broad black stripe above the eye, in contrast to the white-headed northern race *A. c. caudatus*.

PENDULINE TIT
Remizidae *Remiz pendulinus*
RANGE: S and E Europe, W Siberia, Asia Minor, C Asia, E to NW India, N China, and Korea
HABITAT: reedbeds
SIZE: 4 in (11 cm)

race *pendulinus*

race *macronyx*

The penduline tits are celebrated for their superbly made suspended purselike nests, which appear to be woven from woolly felt and have elaborate spoutlike entrances. There are several races. They are all restricted to reedbeds, where they feed on the seeds of reed mace (cat's-tail) and nest in marsh-edge trees such as willow and tamarisk.

VERDIN
Remizidae *Auriparus flaviceps*
RANGE: SW USA and N Mexico
HABITAT: semi-desert scrub
SIZE: 11 in (4 cm)

This common desert bird lives and nests among thorny bushes and cactus plants, weaving a rather untidy nest out of thorn twigs and siting it within the protection of the plant's spines.

race caesia

♂

♂

race *europaea*

EURASIAN NUTHATCH
Sittidae *Sitta europaea*
RANGE: W Europe E to Japan and Kamchatka (Russia, Far East)
HABITAT: woodland with large trees
SIZE: 4–5 in (11–13 cm)

This widespread species depends on woodland trees, both for food and for the old tree holes to use as nest sites. It often wedges large items in crevices and hammers them vigorously with its sharp bill to break them open.

KABYLIE NUTHATCH
Sittidae *Sitta ledanti*
RANGE: E Algeria
HABITAT: mixed woodland above 5,000 ft (1,500 m)
SIZE: 5 in (12 cm)

Discovered only as recently as 1975, the endangered Kabylie, or Algerian, Nuthatch is one of the world's rarest birds. During the summer, it feeds mainly among oak trees, where insects are most abundant; in winter, seeds form its staple diet.

♂

♂

RED-BREASTED NUTHATCH
Sittidae *Sitta canadensis*
RANGE: S Canada to Mexico
HABITAT: coniferous forest
SIZE: 4–5 in (11–13 cm)

The Red-breasted Nuthatch smears the rim of its tree hole with pine resin. This may keep ants and larger creatures out of the nest, but means that the parents have to perform deft twists and turns in the air if they are to avoid becoming stuck fast themselves.

WALLCREEPER
Sittidae *Tichodroma muraria*
RANGE: N Spain E to the Himalayas
HABITAT: rocky gorges, cliffs, mountainsides
SIZE: 6 in (15 cm)

The Wallcreeper is an excellent rock climber, using its wings for support when climbing up sheer walls, and is nimble enough to walk beneath overhangs and jump across gaps. The colorful wings and its graceful, buoyant flight have earned it the nickname "butterfly bird."

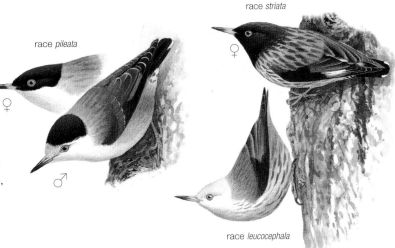

race *pileata*

race *striata*

race *leucocephala*

VARIED SITTELLA
Sittidae *Neositta chrysoptera*
RANGE: Australia
HABITAT: eucalypt woodland and forest; mallee scrub in more arid areas
SIZE: 11 in (4 cm)

Sittellas comb the branches of large trees, prising into the rough bark for insects. Like many Australian birds, they live in groups all year in which birds other than the breeding pair bring food to the young.

COMMON TREECREEPER
Certhiidae *Certhia familiaris*
RANGE: W Europe to Japan
HABITAT: woodland, especially coniferous
SIZE: 5 in (12.5 cm)

The feeding behavior of the treecreepers is similar to that of the nuthatches, but a treecreeper cannot move down a tree trunk and must use its stiff tail as support during its spiral ascent. It takes generally smaller food items, including tiny insect eggs, and is exclusively insectivorous.

SPOTTED GRAY CREEPER
Certhiidae *Salpornis spilonotus*
RANGE: sub-Saharan Africa, India
HABITAT: open bush and savanna
SIZE: 5 in (13 cm)

The Spotted Gray Creeper runs rapidly over tree bark, its progress quite unlike the jerky movements of a treecreeper. Its tail is not stiffened and, like a nuthatch, it can run down, as well as up, trees.

PLAIN-HEADED CREEPER
Rhabdornithidae *Rhabdornis inornatus*
RANGE: Samar Island (Philippines)
HABITAT: deep forests, among large trees
SIZE: 6 in (15 cm)

The Plain-headed Creeper feeds mainly in the outer canopy of the trees, gleaning insects from leaves and twigs. It also uses its brush-tipped tongue to take advantage of the year-round supply of flower nectar in its tropical forest home and occasionally eats small fruits.

RED-BROWED TREECREEPER
Climacteridae *Climacteris erythrops*
RANGE: SE Australia
HABITAT: tall eucalypt forests in mountains; less often near coast
SIZE: 5½–6 in (14–16 cm)

The female Red-browed Treecreeper differs slightly from the male in that her upper breast is streaked with rufous. The immature bird has a gray rather than reddish face and few streaks on the underparts.

FAN-TAILED BERRYPECKER
Dicaeidae *Melanocharis versteri*
RANGE: New Guinea
HABITAT: understorey shrubs and trees of upland rain forest over 4,000 ft (1,200 m)
SIZE: 4 in (10 cm)

At 4–5 in (10–12 cm) in diameter, the nest is large for the size of the bird and is constructed from stems, bark, and spiders' webs placed astride a large branch. Unusually among passerines, the female is heavier than the male.

MISTLETOEBIRD
Dicaeidae *Dicaeum hirundinaceum*
RANGE: Australia, Aru Islands
HABITAT: varied, from dry scrub to wet forest
SIZE: 4 in (10 cm)

Flowerpeckers generally have a reduced stomach, but in the Mistletoebird the stomach has almost completely degenerated. The mistletoe berries pass very rapidly through the intestine, where most of the sweet flesh is stripped from the husk, but the seeds are left intact. Seeds may be defecated just 30 minutes after the berries are swallowed.

CRIMSON-BREASTED FLOWERPECKER

Dicaeidae *Prionochilus percussus*
RANGE: Malay Peninsula, Sumatra, Java, Borneo, Philippines
HABITAT: lowland rain forest; also mangroves and overgrown plantations
SIZE: 3–3 ½ in (8–9 cm)

This is a lively, noisy bird, aggressive toward other birds even though it is one of the region's smallest species. It spends much time among flowers, either catching spiders and insects or drinking nectar with its long, tubular tongue. However, the principal food is berries, especially those of mistletoes.

SCARLET-BACKED FLOWERPECKER

Dicaeidae *Dicaeum cruentatum*
RANGE: India to S China, Southeast Asia, Indonesia
HABITAT: coastal lowland plains, open forest, scrub, gardens
SIZE: 4 in (10 cm)

This tiny bird is noticeable even at a distance because of its constant twittering while feeding, its frequent staccato calls, and its erratic, dipping flight. It builds a purse-shaped nest of cotton down and spiders' webs, suspended from a branch, that has a side entrance impossible for most predators to reach, although snakes may be able to penetrate the defenses.

CRESTED BERRYPECKER

Dicaeidae *Paramythia montium*
RANGE: C and SE New Guinea
HABITAT: moss forest from 6,500 ft (2,000 m) to tree line
SIZE: 8 in (20 cm)

race *olivaceum*

race *montium*

The Crested Berrypecker has the bizarre habit of plucking certain large flowers and rubbing its plumage with the crushed petals. It feeds on berries and insects. The larger-crested race *P. m. olivaceum* has less white on its head.

race *melanocephalus*

race *ornatus*

STRIATED PARDALOTE

Pardalotidae *Pardalotus striatus*
RANGE: Australia
HABITAT: forest, woodland, parks with eucalypts
SIZE: 4 in (10 cm)

The pardalotes are small birds that comb the foliage for insects and other food. They feed heavily on "lerps"—sugary secretions exuded by the sap-sucking larvae of psyllid scale insects. There are 2 main groups of Striated Pardalote: black-crowned and stripe-crowned races.

PYGMY SUNBIRD
Nectariniidae *Anthreptes platurus*
RANGE: Senegal to Egypt, Ethiopia, NW Kenya
HABITAT: savanna, parks, gardens
SIZE: 6–7 in (16–18 cm)

During summer the males have long tail spikes and metallic upper plumage, but in winter they have short tails and dull plumage, like the females. This rather dull, non-breeding eclipse plumage is a characteristic of many sunbirds.

SAO THOMÉ GIANT SUNBIRD
Nectariniidaé *Nectarinia thomensis*
RANGE: Sao Thome Island (W Africa)
HABITAT: thick forest on W slopes
SIZE: 9 in (23 cm)

The largest sunbird of all, this species uses its strong, hooked bill to probe into the bark of trees for insects, rather like a nuthatch. Its plumage looks black from a distance, for the steely-blue feather edges show up only at close range.

SCARLET-CHESTED SUNBIRD
Nectariniidae *Nectarinia senegalensis*
RANGE: W and E Africa from Senegal to Kenya and S to Zimbabwe
HABITAT: woodland, parks, riverside scrub
SIZE: 6 in (15 cm)

This is a large species, with marked plumage variations depending on age, sex, and time of year. An adult male in his breeding condition looks intensely black, except for the magnificent, eyecatching splash of red across his breast, but out of season his eclipse plumage is like that of the dull, mottled female or juvenile.

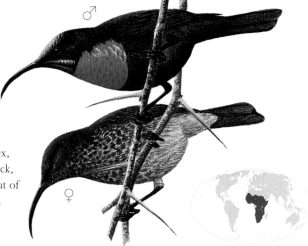

PURPLE-RUMPED SUNBIRD
Nectariniidae *Nectarinia zeylonica*
RANGE: peninsular India, Bangladesh, Sri Lanka
HABITAT: jungle and dry cultivated plains with deciduous trees
SIZE: 4 in (10 cm)

Purple-rumped Sunbirds use their short bills to pierce large flowers neatly at the base of the petals to reach the nectar. Males and females differ in appearance; although young males look like rather yellow females, the adult males keep their metallic plumage all year round.

YELLOW-BELLIED SUNBIRD
Nectariniidae *Nectarinia jugularis*
RANGE: Southeast Asia, from Indonesia to Solomon Islands, NE Australia
HABITAT: coastal rain forest, mangroves, and gardens
SIZE: 4–5 in (10–12 cm)

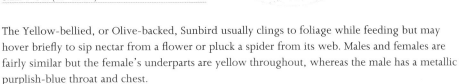

The Yellow-bellied, or Olive-backed, Sunbird usually clings to foliage while feeding but may hover briefly to sip nectar from a flower or pluck a spider from its web. Males and females are fairly similar but the female's underparts are yellow throughout, whereas the male has a metallic purplish-blue throat and chest.

PURPLE SUNBIRD
Nectariniidae *Nectarinia asiatica*
RANGE: Iran, India, Sri Lanka, Indochina
HABITAT: thorny riverbeds, forest edge, scrub
SIZE: 4 in (10 cm)

The Purple Sunbird is always found around flowering trees, which it raids for nectar, and it is an important pollinator. Single birds often catch insects on the wing. Outside the breeding season, the male has a much less dramatic eclipse plumage.

REGAL SUNBIRD
Nectariniidae *Nectarinia regia*
RANGE: W Uganda, W Tanzania
HABITAT: mountain forest up to 12,000 ft (3,650 m)
SIZE: 4 in (11 cm)

The Regal Sunbird exhibits the sexual differences typical of sunbirds, with splendid, metallic males and rather dowdy females. Young birds are duller and somewhat darker than the adult female. It has a rapid trilling or warbling song with little precise pattern.

NORTHERN ORANGE-TUFTED SUNBIRD
Nectariniidae *Nectarinia osea*
RANGE: Syria, Israel, W and S edge of Arabian peninsula
HABITAT: woods, orchards, gardens
SIZE: 4 in (11 cm)

From July to November the mature males look like dull females, but they often have a few traces of their breeding colors on the wings or throat. The small orange tufts flanking the breast are visible only in display.

RED-TUFTED MALACHITE SUNBIRD

Nectariniidae *Nectarinia johnstoni*
RANGE: Kenya and Uganda, S to Tanzania
HABITAT: alpine moorlands with giant lobelia and proteaceous flowers
SIZE: 10–12 in (25–30 cm)

Unusually, the male Red-tufted Malachite Sunbird retains its long tail feathers even in its dull eclipse plumage. It is found only on high alpine slopes with distinctive vegetation types on remote, bleak uplands such as Mount Kenya, the Ruwenzori Mountains, and Mount Kilimanjaro.

SUPERB SUNBIRD

Nectariniidae *Nectarinia superba*
RANGE: Sierra Leone E to Central African Republic, S to Republic of the Congo
HABITAT: forest edge and clearings
SIZE: 6 in (15 cm)

In poor light the male Superb Sunbird looks almost black, but in full sunshine his metallic plumage dazzles the eye with its breathtakingly beautiful coloration. These birds are usually found in sunny places at the edges of forests.

GOLDEN-WINGED SUNBIRD

Nectariniidae *Nectarinia reichenowi*
RANGE: Uganda, Kenya, W Tanzania
HABITAT: highland moors, scrub, forest edge above 5,000 ft (1,500 m)
SIZE: 9 in (23 cm)

The Golden-winged Sunbird is a highland specialist, found on bleak moorland and mountain scrub, apparently unlikely surroundings for a nectar-feeder. But as the sun warms the landscape each day, many of the upland plants such as the orange mint *Leonotis nepetifolia* unfurl large, showy flowers that are rich in nectar, which the Golden-winged Sunbird extracts with its powerful, strongly-hooked bill.

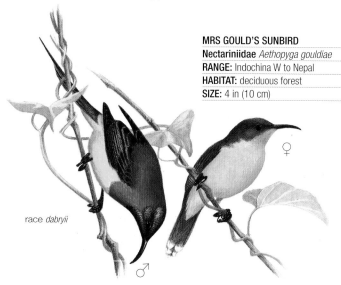

race *dabryii*

MRS GOULD'S SUNBIRD

Nectariniidae *Aethopyga gouldiae*
RANGE: Indochina W to Nepal
HABITAT: deciduous forest
SIZE: 4 in (10 cm)

This tiny sunbird inhabits some demanding places: in Nepal it breeds at altitudes of up to 12,000 ft (3,600 m) and may remain at 9,000 ft (2,700 m) even in winter, although most descend lower. A scarlet-breasted race *A.g. dabryii* is found in the east of the species' range. Other races are yellow-breasted.

YELLOW-BACKED SUNBIRD
Nectariniidae *Aethopyga siparaja*
RANGE: Sumatra, Borneo, Malaysia, W to India
HABITAT: gardens, orchards, pine forest
SIZE: 4 in (10 cm)

Unlike many sunbirds, the male Yellow-backed, or Crimson, Sunbird retains his bright plumage throughout the year. The bird adapts its feeding technique to suit the flower, piercing larger blooms to reach the nectar through the base of the petals, but drinking from tubular flowers by hovering before them and inserting its tubular tongue.

LONG-BILLED SPIDERHUNTER
Nectariniidae *Arachnothera robusta*
RANGE: Malaysia, Sumatra, Borneo
HABITAT: moist, dense forest
SIZE: 6 in (15 cm)

Spiderhunters resemble large, long-billed female sunbirds. The sexes are similar, although the male has a small orange-yellow tuft on each flank. They have fast, sharp, metallic calls. They take spiders from their webs while hovering on long, whirring wings, but they also drink nectar.

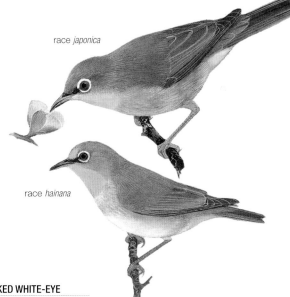

race *japonica*

race *hainana*

JAPANESE WHITE-EYE
Zosteropidae *Zosterops japonica*
RANGE: China, Indochina, Japan
HABITAT: low hill forest, parks, and gardens
SIZE: 4 in (11 cm)

In summer, the Japanese White-eye uses its brush-tipped tongue to soak up nectar from large blooms, but its main diet consists of insects and spiders, which it gleans from tree foliage and picks out of bark crevices with its short, fine-pointed bill.

CHESTNUT-FLANKED WHITE-EYE
Zosteropidae *Zosterops erythropleura*
RANGE: Manchuria, N Korea, China
HABITAT: forest, open woodland
SIZE: 4 in (11 cm)

Chestnut-flanked White-eyes are generally seen foraging in flocks, diligently searching through the foliage for insects and their larvae and occasionally feeding on fruit. Males and females form stable pairs, often for life, and build their nests in tree forks in well-protected positions.

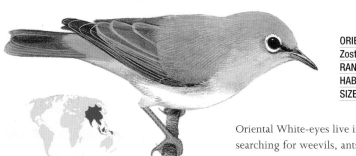

ORIENTAL WHITE-EYE
Zosteropidae *Zosterops palpebrosa*
RANGE: Afghanistan E to China, Malaysia, Indonesia
HABITAT: hill forest, mangroves, gardens
SIZE: 4 in (10 cm)

Oriental White-eyes live in small groups that spend much of their time in the trees, searching for weevils, ants, and other insects, and their eggs. They set up a high, querulous chorus of calls as they feed, repeating the song over and over with no variation.

GRAY-BACKED WHITE-EYE
Zosteropidae *Zosterops lateralis*
RANGE: Australia, Tasmania, SW Pacific islands
HABITAT: practically every type of vegetation, from rain forest, mangroves, woods, and heaths to urban parks and gardens
SIZE: 4–5 in (11–13 cm)

race *lateralis*

race *gouldii*

race *chlorocephala*

Also known as the Gray-breasted Silvereye, the Gray-backed White-eye exhibits a huge range of plumage variation, with 14 races distributed across the islands of the southwest Pacific. The female is usually paler than the male within a given pair, but may be brighter than other females.

PALE WHITE-EYE
Zosteropidae *Zosterops citrinella*
RANGE: islands of Lesser Sundas and Torres Strait; isolated islands off N Australia
HABITAT: forest, monsoon scrub, mangroves, grassland with low shrubs
SIZE: 4–5 in (10–12 cm)

The Pale White-eye is restricted to remote, isolated islands in northern Australasia. Little is known about its biology, but it is regularly seen foraging at all levels in the forest, gleaning insects from leaves and flowers and feeding on berries and nectar when these foods are available.

AFRICAN YELLOW WHITE-EYE
Zosteropidae *Zosterops senegalensis*
RANGE: sub-Saharan Africa
HABITAT: open thornbush, dry woods, gardens
SIZE: 4 in (10 cm)

Small parties of African Yellow White-eyes flit through the canopy and down into lower bushes in a constant search for the insects that make up most of their diet. The birds maintain contact with one another by means of weak, twittering calls and piping notes as they fly from tree to tree.

WOODFORD'S WHITE-EYE
Zosteropidae *Woodfordia superciliosa*
RANGE: Rennell Island (Solomon Islands)
HABITAT: woodland, bushes
SIZE: 5½ in (14 cm)

Woodford's White-eye has a rather long bill for a white-eye and its facial patch and eye ring are of bare skin, not small white or silver feathers as in most of the family. It lays its clutch of 2 eggs in a delicate nest.

RUFOUS-THROATED WHITE-EYE
Zosteropidae *Madanga ruficollis*
RANGE: NW Buru Island (Indonesia)
HABITAT: forests
SIZE: 5–5½ in (13–14 cm)

The endangered Rufous-throated White-eye was first described in 1923, from just 4 specimens that were collected from the mountain forests of Buru Island. It is not closely related to any other white-eye. It has been recorded at between 2,500 and 5,300 ft (820 and 1,750 m), but little is known of its behavior.

TRUK WHITE-EYE
Zosteropidae *Rukia ruki*
RANGE: Faichuk Islands, Micronesia
HABITAT: dense mountain forest
SIZE: 5½ in (14 cm)

The endangered Truk White-eye is found on four tiny islands in the Faichuk Islands of Micronesia. Here it keeps to the outer branches of the canopy, probing among the tangled vines and other creepers to find its insect prey. It lacks the greenish plumage of the true white-eyes and has only a small white mark beneath its eye instead of a complete ring.

CRESTED WHITE-EYE
Zosteropidae *Lophozosterops dohertyi*
RANGE: Sumbawa and Flores islands (Indonesia)
HABITAT: forests
SIZE: 5 in (12 cm)

race *subcristatus*

race *dohertyi*

On Flores Island the race *L.d. subcristatus* is found in light rain forest, at altitudes of 1,000–3,500 ft (300–1,100 m); it has a pale grayish crown with a very slight crest. The race found on Sumbawa, *L. d. dohertyi*, has a darker, browner crown, with each feather sharply spotted white, and a much more obvious crest.

PYGMY WHITE-EYE
Zosteropidae *Oculocincta squamifrons*
RANGE: Borneo
HABITAT: damp moss forest, clearings
SIZE: 4 in (10 cm)

This tiny white-eye is found along the mountain chain that forms the backbone of Borneo, at altitudes of 600–4,000 ft (180–1,200 m). It is known for its habit of approaching humans and cattle very closely in dense scrub—possibly to snap up the insects they disturb. Despite this, its main food appears to be berries and seeds.

OLIVE BLACK-EYE
Zosteropidae *Chlorocharis emiliae*
RANGE: Borneo
HABITAT: low-growing mountain heath, mossy areas, rhododendron thickets
SIZE: 4½ in (11.5 cm)

race *emiliae*

Many isolated island white-eyes have developed distinctive plumage variations of their own, but most have retained at least part of the white eye ring characteristic of the family. The Olive Black-eye is a unique exception to the rule. There are 4 races: the race illustrated is *C.e. emiliae*, found only on Mount Kinabalu in northern Borneo.

CINNAMON WHITE-EYE
Zosteropidae *Hypocryptadius cinnamomeus*
RANGE: Mindanao Island (Philippines)
HABITAT: mountain forest, at 3,000–6,000 ft (900–1,800 m)
SIZE: 5 in (13 cm)

The Cinnamon White-eye is restricted to the mountain forests of Mount Apo on the Philippine island of Mindanao. Its plumage is markedly different from that of other white-eyes. It feeds mainly on insects, picking them off leaves and tangled vegetation with its sharp-pointed bill. Very little is known about its behavior.

race *lugubris*

race *melanocephalus*

BLACK-CAPPED SPEIROPS
Zosteropidae *Speirops lugubris*
RANGE: Cameroon, Sao Thomé Island (Gulf of Guinea)
HABITAT: mountain forest clearings
SIZE: 5 in (13 cm)

On Sao Thomé the race *S.l. lugubris* feeds in trees, in typical white-eye fashion, but the white-throated race *S.l. melanocephalus*, found in the mountain forests of Cameroon, prefers bushy places and clearings. Little is known about the nesting behavior of either race.

CARDINAL HONEYEATER
Meliphagidae *Myzomela cardinalis*
RANGE: islands of Vanuatu, Samoa, Santa Cruz, and Solomons
HABITAT: coastal scrub, secondary forest, woodland, gardens
SIZE: 5 in (13 cm)

In most honeyeaters the sexes are similar; in the Cardinal Honeyeater the female is dull olive-gray with small red patches, whereas the male has bright scarlet and black plumage. His flamboyant appearance is matched by his noisy, aggressive territorial behavior.

MIMIC MELIPHAGA
Meliphagidae *Meliphaga analoga*
RANGE: New Guinea, Aru, and Geelvink islands
HABITAT: rain forest, forest edge, scrub
SIZE: 6–6½ in (15–17 cm)

The Mimic Meliphaga spends most of its time among the smaller trees, but often ventures out into nearby scrub or enters gardens to feed on fruit and insects and take advantage of nectar-bearing flowers.

race *lunatus*

race *chloropsis*

WHITE-NAPED HONEYEATER
Meliphagidae *Melithreptus lunatus*
RANGE: E and SW Australia (not Tasmania)
HABITAT: eucalypt forest and woodland
SIZE: 5–6 in (13–15 cm)

The White-naped Honeyeater is one of several short-beaked species with generally olive-green upper plumage and black heads. The small patch of skin, or wattle, above the eye is red in the eastern race *M. l. lunatus* and chalky white in the western *M. l. chloropsis*.

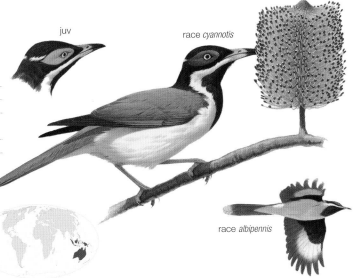

juv

race *cyannotis*

BLUE-FACED HONEYEATER
Meliphagidae *Entomyzon cyanotis*
RANGE: S New Guinea, N and E Australia
HABITAT: eucalypt and paperbark woodland, plantations, parks, gardens; occasionally mangroves
SIZE: 9½–12 in (24–30 cm)

The Blue-faced Honeyeater is well known for its pugnacious, inquisitive character. The northwestern race *E. c. albipennis* has white wing patches which are conspicuous in flight. The eastern race *E. c. cyanotis* has only a small buff patch on its wings.

race *albipennis*

STITCHBIRD
Meliphagidae *Notiomystis cincta*
RANGE: Little Barrier Island (New Zealand); introduced to Kapiti and Tiritiri Matangi islands
HABITAT: mature forest
SIZE: 7–7½ in (18–19 cm)

Little Barrier Island is the last natural population of this bird, though translocated populations exist. Usually detected by its sharp, high-pitched call, it moves rapidly through the vegetation with its tail cocked, feeding on fruit, nectar, and insects. Unusually for a honeyeater, it nests in a hole in a tree trunk or branch, 10–60 ft (3–18 m) above the ground.

NOISY FRIARBIRD
Meliphagidae *Philemon corniculatus*
RANGE: S New Guinea, E Australia
HABITAT: open forest, woodland and lowland savanna
SIZE: 12–13 in (30–34 cm)

This large honeyeater is also known as the Knobby-nosed Leatherhead because of the black naked skin on its head and the small knob at the base of its upper mandible. It often gathers in groups at flowering trees, squabbling raucously over the spoils.

NEW HOLLAND HONEYEATER
Meliphagidae *Phylidonyris novaehollandiae*
RANGE: SW and E Australia, Tasmania
HABITAT: heathland, mallee heath, woods, and forests with shrubs
SIZE: 6½–7 ½ in (17–19 cm)

LONG-BEARDED MELIDECTES
Meliphagidae *Melidectes princeps*
RANGE: New Guinea, on E highlands of Central Range
HABITAT: mossy woodland, alpine scrub and grassland above tree line
SIZE: 10½ in (27 cm)

Unlike most other honeyeaters, the Long-bearded Melidectes spends much of its time on the ground, sifting through leaf litter to find fruit, berries, sedge seeds, and insects. Its nesting behavior is little known.

New Holland, or Yellow-winged, Honeyeaters are aggressive birds but their aggression varies with the abundance of nectar and nesting resources. They catch insects for their protein content but rely on honeydew and nectar to supply energy.

WESTERN SPINEBILL
Meliphagidae *Acanthorhynchus superciliosus*
RANGE: SW comer of Australia
HABITAT: heathland, eucalypt woodland with shrubs
SIZE: 6 in (15 cm)

Being small, the Western Spinebill is usually displaced from rich nectar sources by larger honeyeaters, but its size enables it to forage efficiently at a wide range of less productive blooms that would not support bigger birds.

NOISY MINER
Meliphagidae *Manorina melanocephala*
RANGE: E Australia, Tasmania
HABITAT: open forest, woodland, and partly cleared land
SIZE: 10–11½ in (25–29 cm)

Noisy Miners have a complex social system, with territorial groups of 6–30 birds gathering together into large colonies. The group members cooperate to mob predators and they will aggressively exclude most other bird species from the nesting area.

imm

YELLOW WATTLEBIRD
Meliphagidae *Anthochaera paradoxa*
RANGE: E Tasmania and King Island
HABITAT: dry eucalypt forest and woodland, occasionally orchards and gardens
SIZE: 17–19 in (44–48 cm)

The Yellow Wattlebird is the largest of the honeyeaters. Outside the breeding season it often lives in flocks of 10–12 birds, foraging through the canopy for insects, gleaning them from the leaves, branches and bark. In addition, the birds eat nectar and fruit.

TUI
Meliphagidae *Prosthemadura novaeseelandiae*
RANGE: New Zealand
HABITAT: forests, suburban areas
SIZE: 12 in (31 cm)

Tui often congregate in large numbers around rich food sources. They are wider-ranging than the other 2 New Zealand honeyeaters (the Stitch-bird and the Billbird) and take more nectar in their diet. Their song is complex, involving both harsh and tuneful elements and even some notes inaudible to the human ear.

CAPE SUGARBIRD
Promeropidae *Promerops cafer*
RANGE: S tip of South Africa
HABITAT: mountain slopes with protea blooms
SIZE: male 14½–17 in (37–44 cm);
female 9½–11½ in (24–29 cm)

The Cape Sugarbird's chief food is insects, often caught in midair, but they also roam around in groups in search of protea flowers, from which they drink nectar with their long bills. The male's tail is 8½–12½ in. (22–32 cm) whereas the female's is only 4–6 in (11–15.5 cm) long.

CRIMSON CHAT
Ephthianuridae *Ephthianura tricolor*
RANGE: inland and W Australia
HABITAT: acacia scrub, savanna, succulent
shrub-steppe, often near salt lakes
SIZE: 4–5 in (11–12 cm)

Closely related to the honeyeaters, the Crimson Chat is a nomad of the arid zone. After the young fledge each year, Crimson Chats gather in flocks, sometimes with several hundred birds, and move across the country picking insects off the ground and sipping nectar from flowers.

REED BUNTING
Emberizidae (subfamily **Emberizinae**) *Emberiza schoeniclus*
RANGE: Eurasia S to Iberia and S Russian Federation and E to NE Asia and Manchuria;
N and E populations winter S as far as N Africa, Iran, and Japan
HABITAT: lowland marshes, reedbeds, and, increasingly, drier habitats
SIZE: 6–6½ in (15.5–16.5 cm)

The Reed Bunting constantly flicks and half spreads its tail so that its bold white outer tail feathers serve as a conspicuous signal to others of its kind in the dense reedbeds and marshes. The shape of the bill varies geographically to a striking extent, from very small, slight and pointed to thick and almost parrot-shaped; this is related to the birds' habitat and winter diet.

LAPLAND BUNTING
Emberizidae (subfamily **Emberizinae**) *Calcarius lapponicus*
RANGE: circumpolar in Arctic region; winters S to NE France and S Russian
Federation in Eurasia, and S to New Mexico and Texas in USA
HABITAT: Arctic tundra and high mountains; winters on moors, grassy fields,
grain stubble, and shores
SIZE: 6–6½ in (15.5–16.5 cm)

This bunting prefers to breed in areas of tundra with some shrubs or dwarf trees. The male, in his handsome, bright, breeding plumage, utters a brief, tinkling, larklike song in a display flight or from a prominent perch on a rock or stunted tree. Lapland Buntings often nest in small colonies.

SNOW BUNTING
Emberizidae (subfamily **Emberizinae**) *Plectrophenax nivalis*
RANGE: circumpolar in Arctic region; winters S to N France and S Russian Federation in Eurasia, and S to NW California, C Kansas, and Virginia in the USA
HABITAT: Arctic stony tundra and rocky shores, rock outcrops in glaciers and snowfields, and on a few high mountains; winters on sandy shores, salt marshes, in fields, and on grassy moorland
SIZE: 6½ in (16.5 cm)

The Snow Bunting is the world's northernmost breeding land bird, nesting as far north as the northern tip of Greenland. To escape the intense cold, these plump little birds sometimes burrow in the snow. Their nests are hidden deep in a crack or beneath a large stone among fragmented rocks and boulders.

race *saltonis*

race *maxima*

SONG SPARROW
Emberizidae (subfamily **Emberizinae**) *Melospiza melodia*
RANGE: S Alaska, C Canada S to N Mexico
HABITAT: brushy, grassy areas, often near water; also hedgerows, thickets, gardens
SIZE: 5½ in (14 cm)

Different races of this bird show great variation in size and color. Those illustrated are the largest race *M. m. maxima* of the Aleutian Islands and the pale desert race *M. m. saltonis* of southwestern USA. Songs also vary among populations, so much so that researchers can identify birds by their "dialect."

race *costaricensis*

RUFOUS-COLLARED SPARROW EMBERIZIDAE
Emberizidae (subfamily **Emberizinae**) *Zonotrichia capensis*
RANGE: S Mexico S to Tierra del Fuego, Hispaniola, Netherlands Antilles
HABITAT: open and semi-open natural and disturbed habitats, including cities
SIZE: 5½–6 in (14–15 cm)

Although the song of this species varies considerably over the bird's wide range, the basic pattern is easily recognizable, consisting of 1–2 slurred whistles followed by a trill. There are many races, which differ chiefly in the darkness and pattern on their heads: the one illustrated, *Z. c. costaricensis*, is from Costa Rica, Panama, Venezuela, and Colombia.

race *caniceps*
"Gray-headed Junco"

race *hyemalis*
"Slate-colored Junco"

DARK-EYED JUNCO EMBERIZIDAE
Emberizidae (subfamily **Emberizinae**) *Junco hyemalis*
RANGE: breeds Canada, N and C USA; N populations migrate S as far as Mexico
HABITAT: forests of conifers, birch, aspen; various on migration and in winter
SIZE: 6 in (16 cm)

There are 5 recognizable forms of the Dark-eyed Junco. Although they vary considerably in plumage, they all have white outer tail feathers, a white belly, and dark eyes. Although primarily seed-eaters, they take many insects during the nesting season.

race *thurberi*
"Oregon Junco"

CHIPPING SPARROW
Emberizidae (subfamily **Emberizinae**) *Spizella passerina*
RANGE: Canada S to N Nicaragua
HABITAT: gardens, woodland, forest edge in E; open woodland and mountains in W
SIZE: 5–5½ in (12.5–14 cm)

The Chipping Sparrow's song is a series of "chips" which at times the bird runs together in a single-pitched, rapid trill. In winter, the adult's bright chestnut crown becomes duller and streaked, its prominent white eyebrow is lost, and it acquires a brown ear patch.

ZAPATA SPARROW
Emberizidae (subfamily **Emberizinae**) *Torreornis inexpectata*
RANGE: Cuba
HABITAT: selected open habitats with scattered trees and bushes
SIZE: 6½ in (16.5 cm)

race *inexpectata*

The 3 different populations of this endangered sparrow seem to be living in quite different environments: the western race *T. i. inexpectata* occurs in shrubbery near high ground in the Zapata Swamp. Another race, *T. i. sigmani*, lives in the arid scrublands of southeast Cuba, while *T. i. varonai* occurs on the island of Cayo Coco, off Cuba's north-central coast.

YELLOW-FACED GRASSQUIT
Emberizidae (subfamily **Emberizinae**) *Tiaris olivacea*
RANGE: E Mexico to Colombia, Venezuela, Greater Antilles
HABITAT: grassy areas in clearings, pastures with scattered bushes, roadsides
SIZE: 4 in (10 cm)

The behavior of this species ranges from social and non-aggressive in Central America to territorial and pugnacious in Jamaica; this is attributed to the higher population density and more continuous habitat in Jamaica. The bird's song is a thin, high-pitched, insectlike trill. Its call note is a soft *tek*.

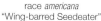
race *americana*
"Wing-barred Seedeater"

VARIABLE SEEDEATER
Emberizidae (subfamily **Emberizinae**) *Sporophila americana*
RANGE: Mexico S through Panama to parts of Colombia, Ecuador, Peru, Venezuela, Brazil, and the Guianas
HABITAT: lowland grassy and shrubby areas, clearings, scrub, forest edge, plantations
SIZE: 4–4½ in (11–11.5 cm)

race *corvina*
"Black Seedeater"

This species takes its name from the variability of its plumage among its 7 or so races. The birds are usually seen in small flocks in which females and immature birds predominate. As they forage, the birds cling to the stems of grasses and weeds to seize small seeds. At times, they may also feed on flowers and buds and nibble at fruit growing high in the trees.

LARGE GROUND FINCH
Emberizidae (subfamily **Emberizinae**) *Geospiza magnirostris*
RANGE: Galapagos Islands
HABITAT: arid areas
SIZE: 6½ in (16.5 cm)

The Large Ground Finch is one of 13 species of "Darwin's finches" endemic to the Galapagos Islands. First collected by Charles Darwin, the finches provided one of the examples he used to develop his theory of evolution through natural selection. This species is the largest and also has the biggest bill.

WOODPECKER FINCH
Emberizidae (subfamily **Emberizinae**) *Camarhynchus pallidus*
RANGE: Galapagos Islands (extinct on San Cristobal and Floreana)
HABITAT: humid highlands
SIZE: 6 in (15 cm)

race *pallidus*

Another of Darwin's finches endemic to the Galapagos Islands. When feeding, some individuals will use a cactus spine, leaf stalk, or thin twig as a tool with which to extract invertebrate prey from cavities in dead branches.

race *oregonus*

race
erythrophthalmus

RUFOUS-SIDED TOWHEE
Emberizidae (subfamily **Emberizinae**) *Pipilo erythrophthalmus*
RANGE: SW Canada, USA S to Baja California
HABITAT: dense undergrowth, streamside thickets, open woodland forest edge
SIZE: 8½ in (22 cm)

The many races of this showy, ground-dwelling bird fall into one of 3 color forms. The eastern "red-eyed" race *P. e. erythrophthalmus* and the southeastern "white-eyed" races differ only in eye color; the western form, including such races as *P. e. oregonus*, differs in its white wing bars and white-spotted scapulars.

PLUSH-CAPPED FINCH
Emberizidae (subfamily **Catamblyrhynchinae**)
Catamblyrhynchus diadema
RANGE: Andes from N Venezuela to N Argentina
HABITAT: open woodland and shrubby slopes of Andean highlands, usually near bamboo stands
SIZE: 5½ in (14 cm)

The Plush-capped Finch, or Plushcap, takes its name from the stiff, golden-brown feathers at the front of its crown. Limited information indicates that its diet includes bamboo leaves, other vegetable matter, and insects.

RED-CRESTED CARDINAL
Emberizidae (subfamily **Cardinalinae**) *Paroaria coronata*
RANGE: E Bolivia, Paraguay, Uruguay, S Brazil, N Argentina; introduced to Hawaii
HABITAT: lowland humid scrub, semi-open terrain, especially near water
SIZE: 7½ in (19 cm)

Red-crested Cardinals often feed on the ground in wet areas, and even walk on floating vegetation, where their large feet and long toes probably help to spread their weight. Although generally seen in pairs or small groups, they often form larger flocks outside the breeding season.

ROSE-BREASTED GROSBEAK
Emberizidae (subfamily **Cardinalinae**) *Pheucticus ludovicianus*
RANGE: SC Canada, E USA; winters S to Mexico and N South America
HABITAT: secondary growth woodland, trees along watercourses
SIZE: 8 in (20 cm)

This thick-billed bird has a special fondness for blossoms and buds, although it also eats beetles, grasshoppers, cankerworms, seeds, and some fruit and grain. Mates sometimes touch bills in courtship. The male molts into a duller, brown-tipped winter plumage before migrating.

NORTHERN CARDINAL
Emberizidae (subfamily **Cardinalinae**) *Cardinalis cardinalis*
RANGE: SE Canada, E, C and SW USA, Mexico to Belize; introduced to Hawaii
HABITAT: woodland edges, swamps, thickets, suburban gardens
SIZE: 8½ in (20 cm)

The wild food that Northern Cardinals eat depends upon availability, but includes insects, fruit, seeds, blossoms, buds and the residues that collect in holes drilled by sapsuckers. The loud, whistling song is uttered by both males and females almost all year round.

SLATE-COLORED GROSBEAK
Emberizidae (subfamily **Cardinalinae**) *Pitylus grossus*
RANGE: C and N South America S to N Bolivia
HABITAT: lowland humid forest
SIZE: 8 in (20 cm)

Female Slate-colored Grosbeaks are paler than the males, with no black on their neck and breast. Typically birds of the middle to upper forest, they occasionally descend to lower levels at the forest edge. The call note is a sharp, metallic speek or peek and the song is a loud, melodious series of deliberate whistles.

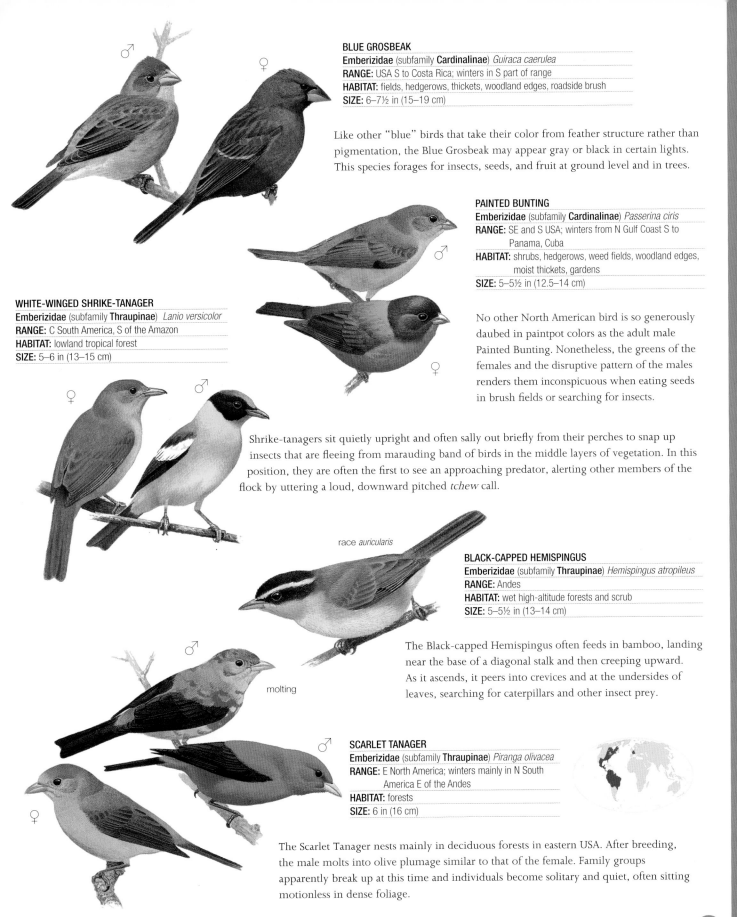

BLUE GROSBEAK
Emberizidae (subfamily **Cardinalinae**) *Guiraca caerulea*
RANGE: USA S to Costa Rica; winters in S part of range
HABITAT: fields, hedgerows, thickets, woodland edges, roadside brush
SIZE: 6–7½ in (15–19 cm)

Like other "blue" birds that take their color from feather structure rather than pigmentation, the Blue Grosbeak may appear gray or black in certain lights. This species forages for insects, seeds, and fruit at ground level and in trees.

PAINTED BUNTING
Emberizidae (subfamily **Cardinalinae**) *Passerina ciris*
RANGE: SE and S USA; winters from N Gulf Coast S to Panama, Cuba
HABITAT: shrubs, hedgerows, weed fields, woodland edges, moist thickets, gardens
SIZE: 5–5½ in (12.5–14 cm)

No other North American bird is so generously daubed in paintpot colors as the adult male Painted Bunting. Nonetheless, the greens of the females and the disruptive pattern of the males renders them inconspicuous when eating seeds in brush fields or searching for insects.

WHITE-WINGED SHRIKE-TANAGER
Emberizidae (subfamily **Thraupinae**) *Lanio versicolor*
RANGE: C South America, S of the Amazon
HABITAT: lowland tropical forest
SIZE: 5–6 in (13–15 cm)

Shrike-tanagers sit quietly upright and often sally out briefly from their perches to snap up insects that are fleeing from marauding band of birds in the middle layers of vegetation. In this position, they are often the first to see an approaching predator, alerting other members of the flock by uttering a loud, downward pitched *tchew* call.

race *auricularis*

BLACK-CAPPED HEMISPINGUS
Emberizidae (subfamily **Thraupinae**) *Hemispingus atropileus*
RANGE: Andes
HABITAT: wet high-altitude forests and scrub
SIZE: 5–5½ in (13–14 cm)

The Black-capped Hemispingus often feeds in bamboo, landing near the base of a diagonal stalk and then creeping upward. As it ascends, it peers into crevices and at the undersides of leaves, searching for caterpillars and other insect prey.

molting

SCARLET TANAGER
Emberizidae (subfamily **Thraupinae**) *Piranga olivacea*
RANGE: E North America; winters mainly in N South America E of the Andes
HABITAT: forests
SIZE: 6 in (16 cm)

The Scarlet Tanager nests mainly in deciduous forests in eastern USA. After breeding, the male molts into olive plumage similar to that of the female. Family groups apparently break up at this time and individuals become solitary and quiet, often sitting motionless in dense foliage.

race *carbo*

SILVER-BEAKED TANAGER
Emberizidae (subfamily **Thraupinae**) *Ramphocelus carbo*
RANGE: N South America E of the Andes
HABITAT: shrubbery and low trees at forest edge and on savannas
SIZE: 6–6½ in (16–17 cm)

The Silver-beaked Tanager haunts the tangle of vegetation at the edges of tropical forests, where different plant species produce a succession of fruit. The birds travel and forage in small bands. Members of each group call frequently, uttering a high-pitched *tseet* and a lower-pitched alarm note *chak*.

HOODED MOUNTAIN TANAGER
Emberizidae (subfamily **Thraupinae**) *Buthraupis montana*
RANGE: Andes
HABITAT: mountain forest, scrub near forest
SIZE: 8 in (21 cm)

Groups of 3–10 Hooded Mountain Tanagers are often seen flying from one feeding site to the next. At dawn, the mountain valleys echo to noisy choruses of *toot* and *weeck* calls, repeated individually or coupled in phrases by bands of Hooded Mountain Tanagers.

THICK-BILLED EUPHONIA
Emberizidae (subfamily **Thraupinae**) *Euphonia laniirostris*
RANGE: NW South America and Central America
HABITAT: open woodland, forest edge
SIZE: 4 in (10 cm)

race *zopholega*

Although the euphonias' digestive systems are specially adapted to cope with mistletoe berries, the balance of diet varies greatly from one species to another. Some eat a high proportion of insect food, while the Thick-billed Euphonia relies almost entirely on fruit. It does, however, feed spiders to its nestlings.

RED-LEGGED HONEYCREEPER
Emberizidae (subfamily **Thraupinae**) *Cyanerpes cyaneus*
RANGE: Central America, N South America
HABITAT: edges of forest and woodland
SIZE: 5 in (12 cm)

The Red-legged Honeycreeper uses its long, curved bill to extract nectar from flowers and to snatch small insects from the undersides of branches. It picks fleshy fruit out of slowly opening seed pods before other birds can reach inside and it can extract orange pulp from holes drilled in the fruit by woodpeckers.

PARADISE TANAGER
Emberizidae (subfamily **Thraupinae**)
Tangara chilensis
RANGE: Amazonian South America
HABITAT: lowland forest, plantations nearby
SIZE: 5 in (12.5 cm)

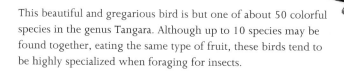

This beautiful and gregarious bird is but one of about 50 colorful species in the genus Tangara. Although up to 10 species may be found together, eating the same type of fruit, these birds tend to be highly specialized when foraging for insects.

race *mystacalis*

GLOSSY FLOWERPIERCER
Emberizidae (subfamily **Thraupinae**) *Diglossa lafresnayii*
RANGE: Andes S to Bolivia
HABITAT: stunted "elfin" forest and thickets above 8,000 ft (2,500 m)
SIZE: 5½ in (14 cm)

Flowerpiercers use their strange, upcurved bills to puncture the bases of tubular flowers so that they can extract the nectar and possibly also the small insects within. Distinctive populations of the Glossy Flowerpiercer are separated from one another by low dips in the Andean chain and offer a fascinating portrait of evolution in progress.

SWALLOW TANAGER
Emberizidae (subfamily **Thraupinae**) *Tersina viridis*
RANGE: E Panama, South America S to N Argentina
HABITAT: open woodland, forest edge, gallery forest, secondary forest
SIZE: 5½ in (14 cm)

The Swallow Tanager uses its large bill to pluck berries as well as to catch insects in aerial pursuits. It is a sociable bird, traveling in groups of about 12. Unusually for a tanager, this species places its nest in holes, choosing tunnels and cavities in earth banks, cliffs, and even bridges.

BLACK-AND-WHITE WARBLER
Parulidae *Mniotilta varia*
RANGE: breeds E North America, N to Northwest Territory, W to Montana, S to C Texas; winters extreme S USA to N South America
HABITAT: deciduous and mixed woodland
SIZE: 4½–5½ in (11.5–14 cm)

The Black-and-white Warbler hunts using a search and snatch technique, creeping along the trunks and larger, low limbs of deciduous trees and probing with its unusually long bill for insects and spiders.

race *memorabilis*
"Audubon's Warbler"

race *coronata*
"Myrtle Warbler"

fall

YELLOW-RUMPED WARBLER
Parulidae *Dendroica coronata*
RANGE: breeds North America, S to C and S Mexico and Guatemala; winters S of breeding range, to Central America
HABITAT: coniferous and deciduous woods
SIZE: 5–6 in (13–15 cm)

This widespread and abundant species has 5 races that fall into 2 groups: the white-throated Myrtle Warbler and the yellow-throated Audubon's Warbler. Apart from their plumage differences, most noticeable in breeding males, their call notes are also distinct, that of Audubon's Warbler being softer than that of its eastern counterpart.

RED-WINGED BLACKBIRD
Parulidae *Agelaius phoeniceus*
RANGE: North and Central America
HABITAT: marshes, watercourses, cultivated land
SIZE: male 8–9½ in (20–24 cm); female 7–7½ in (18–19 cm)

The Red-winged Blackbird may be the most abundant North American land bird. Males sing from exposed perches and flash their brilliant yellow-tipped "epaulettes" to defend their breeding territories. At other times, the red is often concealed when the bird perches, and only the yellow tips show. The female builds a cup-shaped grass nest 1–10 ft (0.5–3 m) above the ground, over or near water.

EASTERN MEADOWLARK
Parulidae *Sturnella magna*
RANGE: S and E North America to N South America
HABITAT: savanna, pastures, cultivated land
SIZE: 9–10 in (23–25 cm)

This American bird spends most of its time on the ground, where it walks about, frequently flicking its tail. When it does fly, it makes a series of rapid, shallow wing beats interspersed with brief glides during which its wings are held stiffly downward. During the breeding season, the male displays his yellow breast to the female, points his bill skyward to expose his yellow throat, and leaps into the air. He defends his territory by uttering his song—a sequence of clear, mellow whistling notes.

AMERICAN REDSTART
Parulidae *Setophaga ruticilla*
RANGE: breeds SE Alaska, E through C Canada, S through Texas to E USA; winters extreme S USA to Brazil
HABITAT: deciduous and mixed woodland
SIZE: 4–5 in (11–13.5 cm)

The female American Redstart is quite unlike her mate, with incandescent yellow where he has flaming orange. The dazzling colors illuminate every flutter of wings and tail as the birds work through the foliage in search of caterpillars, or dart into the air to catch insects on the wing.

AMERICAN GOLDFINCH
Fringillidae (subfamily **Carduelinea**) *Carduelis tristis*
RANGE: S Carduelinae Canada, USA; N populations migrate in winter
HABITAT: open woodland, weedy fields, roadsides
SIZE: 4 in (11 cm)

Although the male American Goldfinch's plumage is bright and distinctive in the breeding season, it becomes duller in color, much more like that of the female, through the rest of the year. Their sweet, canarylike song has earned them the popular, if ornithologically inaccurate, name of Wild Canary.

PINE GROSBEAK
Fringillidae (subfamily **Carduelinea**) *Pinicola enucleator*
RANGE: N and W North America, N Scandinavia E to N Siberia
HABITAT: coniferous and scrub forest
SIZE: 8 in (20 cm)

Although adult male Pine Grosbeaks are brightly colored, young males are somber-toned, like the females. They eat mainly berries and buds, hopping about heavily on the ground, or clambering around slowly in the treetops.

RED CROSSBILL
Fringillidae (subfamily **Carduelinea**) *Loxia curvirostra*
RANGE: America, from Alaska S to Guatemala, Eurasia, Algeria, Tunisia, Balearic Islands
HABITAT: coniferous forest
SIZE: 6 in (16 cm)

race *curvirostra*

The 4 species of crossbill and the Akepa *Loxops coccinea*, one of the Hawaiian finches, are the only birds in the world that have crossed bills, enabling them to open the scales of the conifer cones that make up almost all their diet. Some populations tend to have the bill crossed to the right and others crossed to the left. These differences may be related to clockwise and counter-clockwise spiraling of the scales of cones.

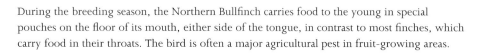

race *pileata*

NORTHERN BULLFINCH
Fringillidae (subfamily **Carduelinea**) *Pyrrhula pyrrhula*
RANGE: Europe E across Asia to Japan
HABITAT: coniferous and broad-leaved forest, cultivated areas, gardens
SIZE: 6 in (15 cm)

During the breeding season, the Northern Bullfinch carries food to the young in special pouches on the floor of its mouth, either side of the tongue, in contrast to most finches, which carry food in their throats. The bird is often a major agricultural pest in fruit-growing areas.

HAWFINCH
Fringillidae (subfamily **Carduelinae**)
Coccothraustes coccothraustes
RANGE: Europe, North Africa, Asia
HABITAT: broad-leaved and mixed forest, parkland, orchards
SIZE: 7 in (18 cm)

The Hawfinch's head and massive bill are specialized for cracking open the kernels of thick-walled seeds, such as cherry and olive stones. The skull is strengthened and modified to provide attachment for powerful muscles that bulge out and make the bird's cheeks look swollen. The inside of the bill contains special pads for gripping the stones.

EVENING GROSBEAK
Fringillidae (subfamily **Carduelinae**) *Coccothraustes vespertinus*
RANGE: W North America, S to Mexico, E across Canada
HABITAT: coniferous and mixed woodland
SIZE: 8 in (20 cm)

This large finch was originally (and incorrectly) thought to sing only late in the day, hence its common name. During winter, the Evening Grosbeak migrates south and east, often coming to feeding stations, particularly if sunflower seeds are on offer.

PALILA
Fringillidae (subfamily **Drepanidinae**) *Loxioides bailleui*
RANGE: Big Island, Hawaii
HABITAT: dry upper mountain forest
SIZE: 6 in (15 cm)

The critically endangered Palila is restricted to Big Island in the Hawaiian Islands. These are large, distinctive finches, the yellow plumage on the head being more pronounced in the males than in the females. The call is rather bell-like, and the song is a collection of trills, whistles, and warbles.

race procerus

MAUI PARROTBILL
Fringillidae (subfamily **Drepanidinae**) *Pseudonestor xanthophrys*
RANGE: Maui, Hawaii
HABITAT: upper mountain rain forest
SIZE: 5½ in (14 cm)

The critically endangered Maui Parrotbill is confined to forests on the upper slopes of Haleakala Mountain, an extinct volcano, on the island of Maui. A stocky bird, it moves along the trunks with slow, deliberate movements, rather like a little parrot. On occasion, it may even hang upside down.

AKIAPOLAAU
Fringillidae (subfamily **Drepanidinae**) *Hemignathus munroi*
RANGE: island of Hawaii
HABITAT: upper mountain forest
SIZE: 5½ in (14 cm)

The endangered Akiapolaau has an extraordinary bill that is quite unique among birds. While the lower mandible is straight and stout, the upper mandible is long, slender, and sickle-shaped. As a feeding tool, the bill combines the work of a woodpecker's bill together with that of a treecreeper.

imm

IIWI
Fringillidae (subfamily **Drepanidinae**) *Vestiaria coccinea*
RANGE: islands of Kauaii, O'ahu, Moloka'i, Maui, Hawaii; extinct Lana'i
HABITAT: mountain forest
SIZE: 6 in (15 cm)

The Iiwi feeds mainly on flowering trees, especially ohia and mamane trees, probing into the flowers with its long, decurved bill to drink the nectar. It is slow and deliberate in its movements and usually hides in the interior of trees, only occasionally coming into the open. Its conservation status is vulnerable.

AKOHEKOHE
Fringillidae (subfamily **Drepanidinae**) *Palmeria dolei*
RANGE: island of Maui; extinct Molokai
HABITAT: upper mountain rain forest
SIZE: 7 in (18 cm)

With its spotted plumage, wing bars, reddish-orange nape, and white tufted crest, the critically endangered Akohekohe is unique among the otherwise simply patterned Hawaiian finches. Often known by its English name, Crested Honeycreeper, it is confined to the higher northeastern slopes of Haleakala Mountain on Maui.

GREEN-WINGED PYTILIA
Estrildidae *Pytilia melba*
RANGE: sub-Saharan Africa
HABITAT: savanna and steppe
SIZE: 5 in (13 cm)

race *melba*
♂

Most waxbills associate in flocks, but the ground-feeding Greenwinged Pytilia, often called the Melba Finch, nearly always lives in pairs which occupy year-round territories in thorny thickets. The birds sometimes gather together at drinking sites, but the red-faced males are usually very aggressive toward each other (or indeed to any other birds with red faces or bills).

BLUE-CAPPED CORDON-BLEU
Estrildidae *Uraeginthus cyanocephala*
RANGE: Somalia to Kenya and Tanzania
HABITAT: dry steppe and semi-desert with bushes or trees, especially acacia or thorn scrub
SIZE: 5 in (13 cm)

RED-BILLED FIRE FINCH
Estrildidae *Lagonosticta senegalia*
RANGE: sub-Saharan Africa
HABITAT: dry areas, dense brush, and nearcultivated land
SIZE: 3½ in (9 cm)

race *rendalli*
♂

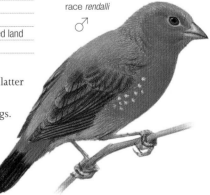

Red-billed Fire Finches breed during the latter half of the rainy season, when there are plenty of ripe seeds to feed to the nestlings. Outside the breeding season it travels in small flocks, foraging for seeds among dense scrub and in fields under cultivation, usually near water.

In the breeding season, with his plumage fluffed out, the male Blue-capped Cordon-bleu pursues the duller female like a flying ball of blue feathers. Having caught her, he will woo her by singing and bobbing up and down before her with a carefully selected grass stem held in his bill—a display typical of the waxbill family.

COMMON WAXBILL
Estrildidae *Estrilda astrild*
RANGE: sub-Saharan Africa; introduced to many tropical islands
HABITAT: grassland and cultivated areas
SIZE: 4 in (10 cm)

The Common Waxbill feeds mainly on grass seeds and will also prey on swarming termites. The birds breed in the rainy season, when insects for feeding their young are most abundant. The nest is often highly elaborate, with a small "roosting" nest built on top of the dome-shaped breeding nest. The brood is often parasitized by the Pin-tailed Whydah.

race *astrild*

GREEN MUNIA
Estrildidae *Amandava formosa*
RANGE: C India
HABITAT: grassland and cultivated regions
SIZE: 4 in (10 cm)

This small waxbill, also known as the Green Avadavat, often associates in flocks of up to 50 birds, particularly in areas with tall grass, low scrub, or crops that provide good cover. It feed on the ground, probably taking seeds and small insects.

race *guttata*

race *castanotis*

ZEBRA FINCH
Estrildidae *Poephila guttata*
RANGE: Australia, Lesser Sundas
HABITAT: dry grassland and other open habitats with scattered trees and shrubs, near water
SIZE: 4 in (10 cm)

Highly gregarious, Zebra Finches live in flocks of 10–100 birds throughout the year and will even breed colonially. The pairs mate for life, and in arid regions they may breed at any time of year in response to rain. There are 2 races: the Australian *P. g. castanotis* and *P. g. guttata* of the Sunda Islands.

BLUE-FACED PARROT-FINCH
Estrildidae *Erythrura trichroa*
RANGE: NE Queensland, Indonesia, Pacific islands, and New Guinea
HABITAT: rain forest
SIZE: 5 in (12 cm)

race *sigillifera*
♂

Instead of foraging on the ground in grassland, the Blue-faced Parrot-finch feeds on the seeds of trees and shrubs at all levels in the rain forest. It prefers the seeds of bamboo, and small nomadic parties of birds will wander all over their range in search of seeding bamboo thickets.

juv

red-faced phase

♂

black-faced phase

♂

GOULDIAN FINCH
Estrildidae *Chloebia gouldiae*
RANGE: N Australia
HABITAT: grassland and open woodland
SIZE: 5½ in (14 cm)

This spectacularly plumaged bird occurs in 2 main color phases: most males have black faces, but about a quarter have red faces outlined with black, and there is a rare yellow phase. Instead of taking seeds from the ground, the bird perches acrobatically on the seed heads, or picks out the seeds while clinging to a nearby twig.

race *acuticauda*

race *striata*

WHITE-BACKED MUNIA
Estrildidae *Lonchura striata*
RANGE: India and Sri Lanka to Sumatra
HABITAT: grassland with scattered trees, cultivated land
SIZE: 4 in (10 cm)

This small, finchlike bird is generally found in large flocks throughout the year, foraging on the ground and amid growing vegetation for the seeds of wild grasses, cultivated rice, and insects. There are several races, including *L. s. striata* of south India and Sri Lanka, and *L. s. acuticauda*, found from the Himalayas to Thailand.

juv

JAVA SPARROW
Estrildidae *Padda oryzivora*
RANGE: Java and Bali; introduced to Africa, China, S Asia, and Hawaii
HABITAT: scrub, grassland, bamboo thickets, mangroves, cultivated land
SIZE: 5½ in (14 cm)

The boldly marked Java Sparrow feeds largely on seeds and has a strong predilection for rice. Its Latin name reflects this, *oryzivora* meaning "rice-eating." During harvest time large flocks descend on the paddy fields to feast on the rice crop, often causing extensive damage.

♀

♂

GOLDEN PALM WEAVER
Ploceidae (subfamily **Ploceinae**) *Ploceus bojeri*
RANGE: Somalia S to Tanzania
HABITAT: coconut palms, coastal scrub
SIZE: 6 in (15 cm)

Most common on the Kenyan coast, these spectacular birds are often found in small flocks, but ones and twos may also be seen in the bushes inland from the beach, or along the shoreline coconut palms, searching for fruits and berries.

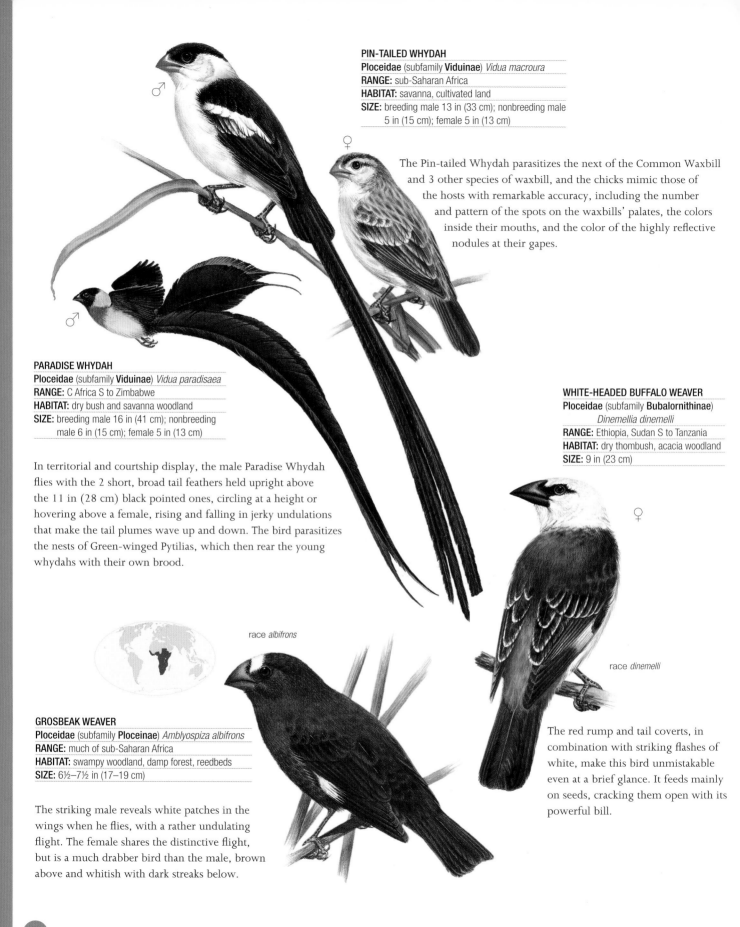

PIN-TAILED WHYDAH
Ploceidae (subfamily **Viduinae**) *Vidua macroura*
RANGE: sub-Saharan Africa
HABITAT: savanna, cultivated land
SIZE: breeding male 13 in (33 cm); nonbreeding male
5 in (15 cm); female 5 in (13 cm)

The Pin-tailed Whydah parasitizes the next of the Common Waxbill and 3 other species of waxbill, and the chicks mimic those of the hosts with remarkable accuracy, including the number and pattern of the spots on the waxbills' palates, the colors inside their mouths, and the color of the highly reflective nodules at their gapes.

PARADISE WHYDAH
Ploceidae (subfamily **Viduinae**) *Vidua paradisaea*
RANGE: C Africa S to Zimbabwe
HABITAT: dry bush and savanna woodland
SIZE: breeding male 16 in (41 cm); nonbreeding
male 6 in (15 cm); female 5 in (13 cm)

In territorial and courtship display, the male Paradise Whydah flies with the 2 short, broad tail feathers held upright above the 11 in (28 cm) black pointed ones, circling at a height or hovering above a female, rising and falling in jerky undulations that make the tail plumes wave up and down. The bird parasitizes the nests of Green-winged Pytilias, which then rear the young whydahs with their own brood.

WHITE-HEADED BUFFALO WEAVER
Ploceidae (subfamily **Bubalornithinae**)
Dinemellia dinemelli
RANGE: Ethiopia, Sudan S to Tanzania
HABITAT: dry thornbush, acacia woodland
SIZE: 9 in (23 cm)

race *dinemelli*

The red rump and tail coverts, in combination with striking flashes of white, make this bird unmistakable even at a brief glance. It feeds mainly on seeds, cracking them open with its powerful bill.

race *albifrons*

GROSBEAK WEAVER
Ploceidae (subfamily **Ploceinae**) *Amblyospiza albifrons*
RANGE: much of sub-Saharan Africa
HABITAT: swampy woodland, damp forest, reedbeds
SIZE: 6½–7½ in (17–19 cm)

The striking male reveals white patches in the wings when he flies, with a rather undulating flight. The female shares the distinctive flight, but is a much drabber bird than the male, brown above and whitish with dark streaks below.

race collaris ♂

VILLAGE WEAVER
Ploceidae (subfamily **Ploceinae**) *Ploceus cucullatus*
RANGE: Sudan and Ethiopia S to Angola, Cape Province
HABITAT: forest, cultivated land, gardens
SIZE: 6–7 in (15–18 cm)

The males have a strikingly patterned plumage in the breeding season, but females and non-breeding males have greener, streaked plumage. There are some 7 races, which vary according to the pattern of black on the head and the strength of coloring below.

race scutatus ♂

race spilonotus ♂

RED-VENTED MALIMBE
Ploceidae (subfamily **Ploceinae**) *Malimbus scutatus*
RANGE: Sierra Leone E to Cameroon
HABITAT: coastal forest
SIZE: 5 in (12 cm)

Red-Vented Malimbes are chiefly insect-eaters, but all feed on the husks of oil palm nuts. The male of the race *M. s. scutopartitus* from Cameroon has a larger red breast patch than that of *M.s. scutatus* from farther west.

RED-BILLED QUELEA
Ploceidae (subfamily **Ploceinae**) *Quelea quelea*
RANGE: sub-Saharan Africa
HABITAT: damp woodland, swamps, cultivated land
SIZE: 4–5 in (11–13 cm)

Huge, densely packed, perfectly synchronized flocks of a million or more Red-billed Queleas move across the land, sometimes breaking the branches of trees with their combined weight. Colonies contain huge numbers of spherical nests of woven green grasses, usually attached to the branches of thorn trees—as many as 500 nests in a single tree.

♀

♀

race orix ♂

♂

race lathamii

RED BISHOP
Ploceidae (subfamily **Ploceinae**)
Euplectes orix
RANGE: sub-Saharan Africa
HABITAT: grassland
SIZE: 5–5½ in (12–14 cm)

The race *E.o. orix*, illustrated, is the southern race. A male displays to a female with his rump feathers puffed out; he will also fly with his body plumage ruffled into a vivid ball, floating or bounding above the grass with a loud purring of vibrating wings.

♂

MADAGASCAN RED FODY
Ploceidae (subfamily **Ploceinae**) *Foudia madagascariensis*
RANGE: Madagascar; introduced to Mauritius, Seychelles
HABITAT: forest edge, savanna, cultivated land, rice paddies
SIZE: 5 in (13 cm)

Madagascan Red Fodies have high-pitched insectlike calls and males sing with a very high, hissing and bubbling sound, like a tiny steam engine, displaying with wings and tail dropped and rump feathers fluffed out. The females are browner than the males, streaked above but unmarked below.

♂

nest

JACKSON'S WIDOWBIRD
Ploceidae (subfamily **Ploceinae**) *Euplectes jacksoni*
RANGE: Kenya, Tanzania
HABITAT: highland grassland, cultivated land
SIZE: 13 in (34 cm)

Breeding male Jackson's Widowbirds wear away special "rings" in the grass on which they display, springing into the air with heads thrown back, feet hanging, and tail curved forward to touch the neck except for 2 feathers pointing downward and outward. The female and non-breeding male are streaky brown.

race *philippinus*

♂

♀

BAYA WEAVER
Ploceidae (subfamily **Ploceinae**) *Ploceus philippinus*
RANGE: Pakistan E to Sri Lanka, Indochina, Sumatra
HABITAT: scrub, cultivated land, palms, grassland
SIZE: 5½–6 in (14–15 cm)

The Baya Weaver's wonderful nest is made of finely woven strips of grass, rice leaves, or sugar cane, and is suspended from a drooping tree frond, telephone line, or thatched roof. Once he has succeeded in attracting a female, the male completes the nest lining, then, after the eggs are laid, builds another nest, and even a third or fourth, for other females.

WHITE-BROWED SPARROW-WEAVER
Ploceidae (subfamily **Plocepassesinae**) *Plocepasser mahali*
RANGE: Ethiopia to South Africa
HABITAT: light wooded savanna and semi-desert, coming into villages
SIZE: 6–7 in (16–18 cm)

White-browed Sparrow-Weavers build an untidy retort-shaped nest of dry grass at the ends of branches; there are often several nests to a tree. The race *P. m. melanorhynchus* is illustrated. Some other races have brown markings on the breast that give the species an alternative name of Stripe-breasted Sparrow-Weaver.

SOCIABLE WEAVER
Ploceidae (subfamily **Plocepassesinae**) *Philetirus socius*
RANGE: W and C southern Africa
HABITAT: dry acacia savanna
SIZE: 5½ in (14 cm)

colonial nest

Each colony (anything from 6–300 birds) constructs a communal nest in a tree or on the crosspiece of a bare telegraph pole. Up to 13 ft (4 m) deep and 25 ft (7.5 m) long, it has a large roof, beneath which each individual pair has its own nest cavity. Grass stems are arranged pointing diagonally downward into the vertical entrance tunnel leading into each nest, forming a barrier against many predators.

HOUSE SPARROW
Passeridae *Passer domesticus*
RANGE: throughout Eurasia excluding Far East;
introduced worldwide
HABITAT: Farmland and built-up areas
SIZE: 5½ in (14 cm)

The House Sparrow is a seed-eater but also feeds on invertebrates and a variety of scraps from bread to meat fibers. It is capable of laying as many as 7 clutches of eggs in a single year in the tropics.

race *domesticus*

GOLDEN SPARROW
Passeridae *Passer luteus*
RANGE: arid zone S of Sahara, from Senegal to Arabia
HABITAT: arid acacia savanna
SIZE: 4–5 in (10–13 cm)

There are 2 races of this little sparrow: *P. l. euchlorus* from Arabia, with striking canary-yellow males, and *P. l. luteus* from Africa, in which the males have a bright chestnut back. The females of both races have a more muted brown and pale yellow plumage. It can occur in flocks of up to 1 million birds.

race *luteus*
"Sudan Golden Sparrow"

STREAKED ROCK SPARROW

Passeridae *Petronia petronia*
RANGE: Canary Islands, Mediterranean E to China
HABITAT: barren open country and rocky hillsides
SIZE: 6 in (15 cm)

The Streaked Rock Sparrow, also known as the Chestnut-shouldered Petronia, is a streaky brown bird resembling a female House Sparrow, but characterized by an inconspicuous yellow throat patch. It is usually found in open country, where it nests in holes in trees or rocks.

WHITE-WINGED SNOW FINCH

Passeridae *Montifringilla nivalis*
RANGE: Spain to Mongolia
HABITAT: high, bare mountain country above the tree line
SIZE: 7 in (17.5 cm)

race *nivalis*

The White-winged Snow Finch is one of the highest-dwelling of all birds, usually seen in small groups on rocks or on the ground near patches of melting snow. It builds its bulky nest in crevices or holes under rocks up to an altitude of 16,500 ft (5,000 m) or even higher.

SHINING STARLING

Sturnidae *Aplonis metallica*
RANGE: Molucca Islands, Solomon Islands, New Guinea, NE Queensland
HABITAT: forest canopy, coastal woodlands, mangroves
SIZE: 8–9½ in (21–24 cm)

imm

Shining Starlings nest in trees, in colonies of up to 300 pairs. Each colony takes over a tree and festoons its branches with bulky, pendulous nests woven from plant stems. New nesting colonies may be started by young birds that breed in immature plumage.

TRISTRAM'S STARLING

Sturnidae *Onychognathus tristramii*
RANGE: Israel, Jordan, Sinai Peninsula, W Arabia
HABITAT: rocky country, desolate ravines, spreading into towns
SIZE: 10 in (25 cm)

In wild country, Tristram's Starling nests in rock crevices on cliffs and crags; it is now adapting to life on the artificial "cliffs" and "ledges" of urban areas. Adult females and juveniles resemble mature males, but the head plumage is a duller gray.

SPLENDID GLOSSY STARLING
Sturnidae *Lamprotornis splendidus*
RANGE: Senegal W to Ethiopia, S to Angola and Tanzania; S populations winter
HABITAT: tall woodland, secondary forest
SIZE: 12 in (30 cm)

This bird is often encountered in the strips of gallery forest bordering river banks. Its wings make a distinctive swishing sound in flight, when its back shows a humped profile. It utters a variety of guttural and nasal calls, especially a *quonk quonk* and a *chak*, as well as liquid whistles.

AMETHYST STARLING
Sturnidae *Cinnyricinclus leucogaster*
RANGE: SW Arabia, sub-Saharan Africa, South Africa, Gabon, Republic and Democratic Republic of the Congo
HABITAT: rain forest, wooded savanna, woodland edge, parks, gardens
SIZE: 6–7 in (16–18 cm)

In contrast to the gaudy violet and white male, the female, like the juvenile, has mainly brown plumage. Amethyst Starlings have a taste for fruit, but will also take insects, often hawking for termites on the wing. They are less noisy than other starlings.

SUPERB STARLING
Sturnidae *Spreo superbus*
RANGE: SE Sudan, E to Somalia, and S to Tanzania
HABITAT: open acacia savanna, lawns, farmland
SIZE: 7 in (18 cm)

This starling feeds mainly on the ground, eating a range of seeds, fruits, and insects. While Superb Starlings nest in holes like other starlings, they often build large, untidy, domed nests in low thorn bushes. Juveniles can be distinguished by their duller plumage and brown eyes.

WATTLED STARLING
Sturnidae *Creatophora cinerea*
RANGE: Ethiopia to Cape Province, Angola
HABITAT: open thornbush savanna
SIZE: 8 in (21 cm)

In the breeding season, the male loses his head feathers, exposing bare yellow skin, and long black wattles develop on the forehead, crown, and throat. Its ability to resorb its wattles has attracted the attention of cancer specialists, while the annual regrowth of its head feathers has prompted investigations by researchers attempting to find an antidote to human baldness.

BLACK-HEADED STARLING

Sturnidae *Sturnus pagodarum*
RANGE: Afghanistan, India, Sri Lanka
HABITAT: woodland, scrub, farmland, gardens
SIZE: 8½ in (21 cm)

The Black-headed, or Brahminy, Starling is fond of feeding on nectar, which it extracts from flowers with its brush-tipped tongue. Adult birds are distinguished by their glossy black caps crowned with elongated feathers that can be raised in a crest.

ROSE-COLORED STARLING
Sturnidae *Sturnus roseus*
RANGE: E Europe and WC Asia; migrates to India in winter
HABITAT: arid lowlands, steppes, hills; winters on grassland, farmland, thornbush
SIZE: 9 in (23 cm)

imm

♂

Although not exclusively locust-eaters, Rose-colored Starlings gather in large flocks wherever locusts are abundant and may settle to breed in the area. Instead of migrating north-south like most temperate birds, Rose-colored Starlings migrate east-west.

EUROPEAN STARLING
Sturnidae *Sturnus vulgaris*
RANGE: Europe and W Asia; introduced to North America, South Africa, S Australia, New Zealand
HABITAT: open woods, parks, gardens, towns
SIZE: 8 in (21 cm)

juv

The adult has a beautiful iridescent plumage of blue, violet, green, and bronze. The feathers have pale buff tips; by the time the breeding season approaches, these pale tips have become worn away and the plumage is much glossier. Also, the legs change color from brown to reddish-pink and the bill from dark brown to yellow, with a creamy pink base in females and a steel-blue base in males.

COMMON MYNAH
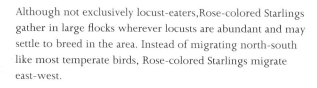
Sturnidae *Acridotheres tristis*
RANGE: Afghanistan, India, and Sri Lanka to Myanmar; currently extending its range to Malaysia and Indo-china; introduced to South Africa, New Zealand, Australia
HABITAT: farmland, parks, towns
SIZE: 9 in (23 cm)

This jaunty bird shows a conspicuous white wing patch in flight and makes its presence felt through its loud fluty calls. Daytime flocks assemble in large communal roosts at night, giving rise to a raucous musical chorus at dawn and dusk.

HILL MYNAH
Sturnidae *Gracula religiosa*
RANGE: India and Sri Lanka to Malaysia and Indonesia
HABITAT: mountain forests, especially in foothills
SIZE: 11½ in (29 cm)

Few birds can challenge the Hill Mynah's skill as a mimic. Paradoxically, it never imitates the calls of other bird species in the wild, although it will mimic the songs of neighboring Hill Mynahs. Hill Mynahs feed in the trees on fruit—especially figs—as well as on nectar, insects, and small lizards.

BALD STARLING
Sturnidae *Sarcops calvus*
RANGE: Philippines, Sulu Islands
HABITAT: farmland, gardens
SIZE: 8½ in (22 cm)

The Bald Starling, or Coleto, has large areas of bare skin around its eyes, separated by a narrow line of short bristly feathers on the crown. It breeds in tree holes, which are usually abandoned woodpecker nests, and feeds mainly on fruit.

GROSBEAK STARLING
Sturnidae *Scissirostrum dubium*
RANGE: Sulawesi (Celebes)
HABITAT: open woodland
SIZE: 8 in (20 cm)

ROTHSCHILD'S MYNAH
Sturnidae *Leucopsar rothschildi*
RANGE: NW Bali
HABITAT: wooded grassland, woodland
SIZE: 8½ in (22 cm)

These starlings use their large bills to excavate pear-shaped nest-holes in the tree trunks—hence the alternative name of Woodpecker Starling. There may be more than 50 nests per colony, each only 12–20 in (30–50 cm) apart; the nest trees are often so weakened by the holes that they collapse.

Also known as the Bali Starling, the critically endangered Rothschild's Mynah's striking appearance and its ability to erect the long crest on its head have always attracted collectors and trapping for the cage-bird trade has contributed to its decline. Much of its diet consists of large insects taken from the ground but it also eats small reptiles and fruit.

RED-BILLED OXPECKER
Sturnidae *Buphagus erythrorhynchus*
RANGE: Eritrea to South Africa
HABITAT: savanna with grazing mammals
SIZE: 7–7½ in (18–19 cm)

Oxpeckers feed chiefly on the ticks that infest the skins of cattle and other grazing mammals such as zebras, antelopes, and rhinos, clinging to the hide of the moving animals with their sharp claws. There are 2 species: the Red-billed Oxpecker and the more widely distributed Yellow-billed Oxpecker.

GOLDEN ORIOLE
Oriolidae *Oriolus oriolus*
RANGE: Europe, Asia, extreme NW Africa; Asian populations resident, others winter in tropical Africa
HABITAT: breeds in open deciduous woodland, parks, orchards, and olive groves; winters in open forest
SIZE: 10 in (25 cm)

Golden Orioles use their sharp, stout beaks to feed on insects and fruit. They spend most of their time in the trees, only rarely descending to ground level to feed on fallen fruit. Their nest is a masterpiece—an intricately woven grass hammock slung by its rim between 2 twigs.

MAROON ORIOLE
Oriolidae *Oriolus traillii*
RANGE: Himalayan foothills, S China, much of Southeast Asia
HABITAT: forests up to 10,000 ft (3,000 m)
SIZE: 10 in (25 cm)

BLACK ORIOLE
Oriolidae *Oriolus husii*
RANGE: Borneo, Sulawesi (Celebes)
HABITAT: mountain forest
SIZE: 8½ in (22 cm)

Reaching altitudes of some 3,300 ft (1,000 m), Black Orioles move through the canopy in small bands, feeding on small fruits and insects. The almost all-black plumage is offset by a rich chestnut patch beneath the tail, which is surprisingly conspicuous when viewed from the forest floor.

The Maroon Oriole is essentially a canopy bird, feeding on small fruits, insects, and, occasionally, flower nectar. It has a great variety of calls, including a mewing, catlike call and a rattling laugh. The nest is a deep, bulky cup of woven plant fibers, bound with spiders' webs, suspended in the horizontal fork of a branch.

race *vieilloti*
"Green Figbird"

race *flaviveventris*
"Yellow Figbird"

race *vieilloti*

FIGBIRD
Oriolidae *Sphecotheres viridis*
RANGE: N and E Australia, New Guinea
HABITAT: rain forest, eucalypt forest, parks, gardens
SIZE: 11 in (28 cm)

The male Figbird's plumage varies across the bird's range. The shallow nest is composed of thin twigs, grass, and plant tendrils, placed toward the end of a slender branch, and is often so flimsy that the eggs are visible inside against the light.

HAIR-CRESTED DRONGO
Dicruridae *Dicrurus hottentottus*
RANGE: India, S China, Southeast Asia, Philippines, Indonesia
HABITAT: forest and secondary growth
SIZE: 13 in (33 cm)

Hair-crested Drongos sometimes gather in parties, especially around fruiting and flowering trees, for they are nectar-feeders as well as predators of a wide range of insects. They utter an astonishing medley of musical and fluty calls, as well as some harsh and strident notes.

CRESTED DRONGO
Dicruridae *Dicrurus forficatus*
RANGE: Madagascar and part of Comoro archipelago
HABITAT: forests, woods, savanna, plantations, coastal scrubland
SIZE: 13 in (33 cm)

Like many of its relatives, the Crested Drongo has a long, deeply forked tail, which enables it to perform impressive aerobatics in pursuit of its insect prey. It is a vocal bird, with a wide repertoire of calls and whistles.

GREATER RACQUET-TAILED DRONGO
Dicruridae *Dicrurus paradiseus*
RANGE: India, Sri Lanka, S China, Southeast Asia, Borneo
HABITAT: open forest, woodland edge, tea plantations
SIZE: 14 in (35 cm)

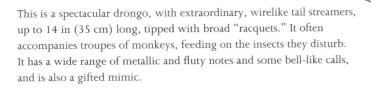

This is a spectacular drongo, with extraordinary, wirelike tail streamers, up to 14 in (35 cm) long, tipped with broad "racquets." It often accompanies troupes of monkeys, feeding on the insects they disturb. It has a wide range of metallic and fluty notes and some bell-like calls, and is also a gifted mimic.

race *rufusater*

race *carunculatus* imm

race *carunculatus* "Jack-bird"

SADDLEBACK
Callaeidae *Philesturnus carunculatus*
RANGE: offshore islands of New Zealand
HABITAT: forests
SIZE: 10 in (25 cm)

This near-threatened species now occurs only on about 12 offshore islands of New Zealand. Saddlebacks have small wings and weak flight. However, their legs are strong and they run and hop through the trees rather than fly. They feed mainly on insects, and also eat some fruit and nectar.

WHITE-WINGED CHOUGH
Corcoracidae *Corcorax melanorhamphos*
RANGE: Australia
HABITAT: open woodland
SIZE: 18 in (45 cm)

These highly social birds are black, with white "windows" in the center of the wings. The adults have brilliant red irises that become expanded when the birds are excited. They live in open, grassy eucalypt woodland, feeding on the ground.

MAGPIE-LARK
Grallinidae *Grallina cyanoleuca*
RANGE: Australia
HABITAT: open pasture and grassland
SIZE: 10½ in (27 cm)

♂ ♀

The black-and-white Magpie-Lark is most abundant on farmland, where it feeds on the ground on insects, snails, and other invertebrates. It has a loud *pee-wee* call, which gives it one of its popular names; another is Mudlark, from its nest.

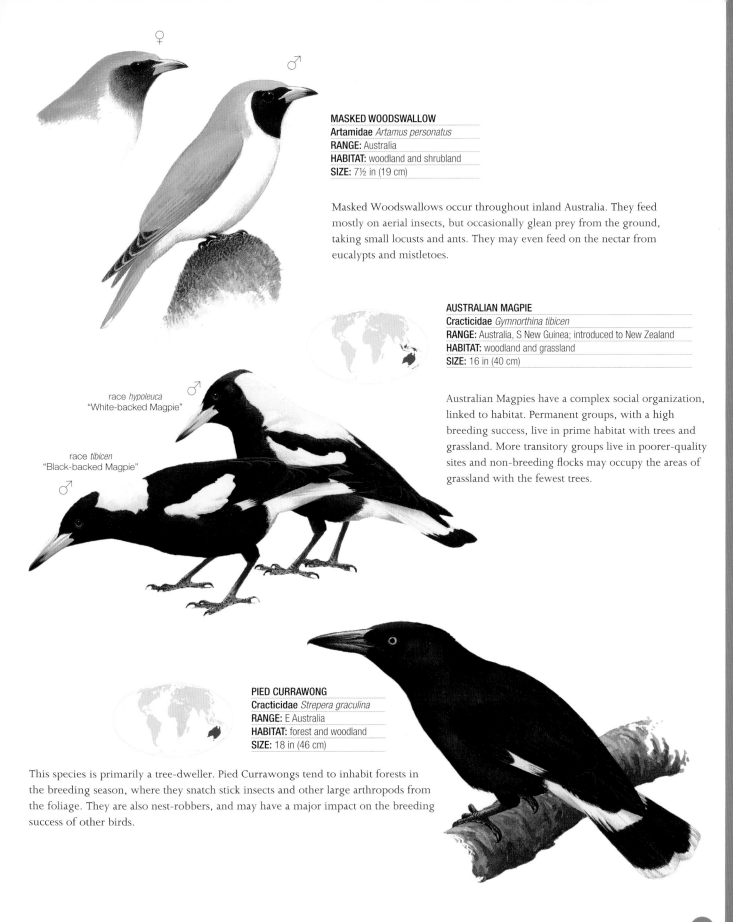

MASKED WOODSWALLOW
Artamidae *Artamus personatus*
RANGE: Australia
HABITAT: woodland and shrubland
SIZE: 7½ in (19 cm)

Masked Woodswallows occur throughout inland Australia. They feed mostly on aerial insects, but occasionally glean prey from the ground, taking small locusts and ants. They may even feed on the nectar from eucalypts and mistletoes.

AUSTRALIAN MAGPIE
Cracticidae *Gymnorthina tibicen*
RANGE: Australia, S New Guinea; introduced to New Zealand
HABITAT: woodland and grassland
SIZE: 16 in (40 cm)

Australian Magpies have a complex social organization, linked to habitat. Permanent groups, with a high breeding success, live in prime habitat with trees and grassland. More transitory groups live in poorer-quality sites and non-breeding flocks may occupy the areas of grassland with the fewest trees.

race *hypoleuca*
"White-backed Magpie"

race *tibicen*
"Black-backed Magpie"

PIED CURRAWONG
Cracticidae *Strepera graculina*
RANGE: E Australia
HABITAT: forest and woodland
SIZE: 18 in (46 cm)

This species is primarily a tree-dweller. Pied Currawongs tend to inhabit forests in the breeding season, where they snatch stick insects and other large arthropods from the foliage. They are also nest-robbers, and may have a major impact on the breeding success of other birds.

SPOTTED CATBIRD
Ptilonorhynchidae *Ailuroedus melanotis*
RANGE: New Guinea, 3,000–6,000 ft (900–1,800 m);
           Misool and Aru islands; NE Australia
HABITAT: rain forest
SIZE: 11½ in (29 cm)

Most male bowerbirds will attempt to mate with several females each season, attracting them to their elaborate bowers by their showy plumage and ritualized courtship; by contrast, the 3 species of catbird are monogamous, the males do not build bowers and the sexes look alike.

VOGELKOP GARDENER BOWERBIRD
Ptilonorhynchidae *Amblyornis inornatus*
RANGE: W Irian Jaya (New Guinea), 3,300–6,600 ft
           (1,000–2,000 m)
HABITAT: lower mountain rain forest
SIZE: 10 in (25 cm)

The male Vogelkop Gardener Bowerbird's bower is spectacular—a miniature tepee of sticks built over a mat of moss which the bird collects and decorates with colorful fruits and flowers. He then attracts potential mates—and warns off other males—by mimicking bird calls and other sounds.

SATIN BOWERBIRD
Ptilonorhynchidae *Ptilonorhynchus violaceus*
RANGE: E Australia
HABITAT: rain forest, rain forest edge; adjacent
           open vegetation in winter
SIZE: 12 in (30 cm)

The male Satin Bowerbird builds an "avenue" with walls of sticks placed upright in a stick mat, sometimes daubing the walls with a paste of chewed fruit or charcoal. He adorns the mat with trinkets, showing a marked preference for blue flowers, feathers, bottle-tops—indeed anything blue. This taste reflects his own bluish-black coloration, which takes 6–7 years to develop and provides a marked contrast to the female's sober grayish-green plumage.

GREAT GRAY BOWERBIRD
Ptilonorhynchidae *Dicrurus paradiseus*
RANGE: N Australia and adjacent islands
HABITAT: riverside and open savanna woods, eucalypt and melaleuca woods, vine thickets, well-foliaged suburbia
SIZE: 14 in (36 cm)

The Great Gray Bowerbird is generally found in drier, more open habitats than the other species. The male sports a lilac nape crest, which he erects during the courtship display. Like many bowerbirds, Great Gray Bowerbirds are good mimics. They feed mainly on fruit and insects, but will also eat small lizards.

SICKLE-CRESTED BIRD OF PARADISE
Paradisaeidae *Cnemophilus macgregorii*
RANGE: C, S, and E highlands of New Guinea, 8,000–11,500 ft (2,400–3,500 m)
HABITAT: cloud forest
SIZE: 10 in (25 cm)

The Sickle-crested Bird of Paradise is a fruit-eating species named for its unique crest of fine filaments. The nest, built by the female, is a bulky dome of mosses and leaves on a stick foundation and is much more elaborate than the nests of other species.

MAGNIFICENT RIFLEBIRD
Paradisaeidae *Ptiloris magnificus*
RANGE: New Guinea lowlands and hills to 2,300 ft (700 m), rarely higher; tip of Cape York Peninsula, NE Australia
HABITAT: rain forest, forest edge
SIZE: 13 in (33 cm)

The male defends a territory from a visible perch that he uses for displaying. This involves raising his rounded wings and swaying his head from side to side while emitting a powerful whistle, said to sound like a passing bullet—hence the species' name.

TRUMPET MANUCODE
Paradisaeidae *Manucodia keraudrenii*
RANGE: New Guinea and islands to E and W, 650–6,600 ft (200–2,000 m); tip of Cape York Peninsula, NE Australia
HABITAT: rain forest canopy
SIZE: 11 in (28 cm)

The 5 species of manucode breed as stable pairs instead of mating polygamously in the family tradition. Accordingly, male and female birds are very similar, with uniform metallic blue-black plumage. They are primarily fruit-eaters and the Trumpet Manucode, or Trumpet Bird, feeds mainly on figs.

RIBBON-TAILED BIRD OF PARADISE
Paradisaeidae *Astrapia mayeri*
RANGE: New Guinea, W central highlands, 8,000–11,200 ft
(2,400–3,400 m)
HABITAT: lower mountain rain forest
SIZE: 53 in (135 cm)

Up to 39 in (1 m) long, the ribbonlike central tail feathers are twitched from side to side during a display that may attract several females to the male's perch high in the trees. These birds have a broad diet, including fruits, insects, spiders, small mammal, and reptiles.

courtship display

TWELVE-WIRED BIRD OF PARADISE
Paradisaeidae *Seleucidis melanoleuca*
RANGE: New Guinea lowlands; Salawati Island
HABITAT: seasonally flooded rain forest dominated by
sago and pandanus palm
SIZE: 13 in (33 cm)

A displaying male erects the feathers of his upper breast into a large black "shield," edged with iridescent emerald green feathers; at the same time, his elongated yellow flank plumes are expanded and the 12 wires extend forward. The females are drab by comparison.

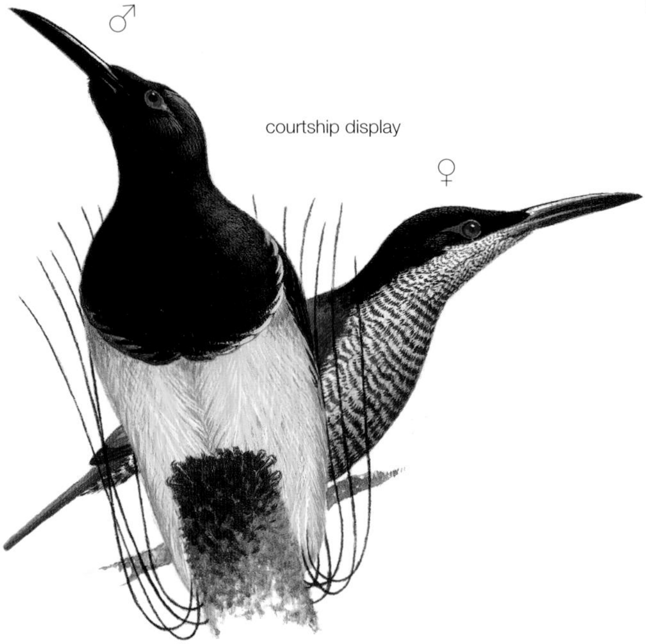

courtship display

SUPERB BIRD OF PARADISE
Paradisaeidae *Lophorina superba*
RANGE: mountains of New Guinea, 4,000–7,500 ft
(1,200–2,300 m)
HABITAT: rain forest and forest edge
SIZE: 10 in (25 cm)

The male Superb Bird of Paradise is equipped with highly modified breast plumage that flares into a "winged" display shield. This is mirrored behind the bird's head by a velvety cape of elongated nape feathers that fans round to meet the breast shield, giving a bizarre circular effect.

courtship display

♂

♀

KING OF SAXONY BIRD OF PARADISE
Paradisaeidae *Pteridophora alberti*
RANGE: central ranges of New Guinea, 5,000–9,500 ft
  (1,500–2,850 m)
HABITAT: cloud forest
SIZE: 8½ in (22 cm)

An adult male has 2 head plumes up to 19½ in (50 cm) long
extending from behind his eyes, each plume shaft decorated
along one side with small sky-blue lobes. During the courtship
display he holds his plumes aloft while bounding up and down,
hissing loudly. He greets a receptive female with a sweep of the
plumes before mating.

♀

♂

KING BIRD OF PARADISE
Paradisaeidae *Cicinnurus regius*
RANGE: New Guinea, up to 1,000 ft (300 m),
  rarely to 2,800 ft (850 m)
HABITAT: rain forest and forest edge
SIZE: 6 in (16 cm)

The female has inconspicuous olive-brown plumage, but males are mainly
iridescent blood-red and white. In one of the male's displays, he expands his
breast fan, puffs up the feathers of his underparts; he then raises his wirelike tail
shafts so that the green racquets at their tips are above his head, and raises and
sways his head from side to side.

race *raggiana*

♂

♀

RAGGIANA BIRD OF PARADISE
Paradisaeidae *Paradisaea raggiana*
RANGE: E New Guinea to 6,000 ft (1,800 m)
HABITAT: rain forest, forest edge, gardens
SIZE: 13 in (33 cm)

Instead of displaying alone, male Raggiana Birds of Paradise assemble in groups at traditional leks. When females appear at the lek the males converge on them, calling excitedly and displaying by hopping, flapping their wings, and shaking their plumes. This is followed by a quieter but equally breathtaking display, in which each bird attempts to out do his rivals in showing off his gaudy finery.

BLUE BIRD OF PARADISE
Paradisaeidae *Paradisaea rudolphi*
RANGE: New Guinea, E central highlands,
        4,300–6,000 ft (1,300–1,800 m)
HABITAT: rain forest, forest edge, gardens
SIZE: 12 in (30 cm)

One of the most glorious and vulnerable birds of paradise, the male displays alone, high in the trees. Uttering low mechanical-sounding cries, he swings upside down from a branch with his long tail streamers sweeping over in a graceful arc, his magnificent plumes spread in a cascade of opalescent blue.

♂
courtship display

BLUE JAY
Corvidae *Cyanocitta cristata*
RANGE: E North America, from S Canada to Mexican Gulf
HABITAT: deciduous forest, semi-woodland
SIZE: 12 in (30 cm)

Blue Jays hoard seeds and nuts for the winter, burying them in holes. Although seeds and nuts make up most of its diet, the Blue Jay feeds avidly on insects—particularly the irregular outbreaks of tent moth caterpillars. It will also rob nests of eggs and chicks and take small mammals.

race *coerulescens*

race *californica*

SCRUB JAY
Corvidae *Aphelocoma coerulescens*
RANGE: W USA and S to C Mexico; there is an isolated race in Florida
HABITAT: oak scrub in dry semi-desert
SIZE: 13 in (33 cm)

Scrub Jays live in year-round groups of up to a dozen individuals, each group based around a single breeding pair; the female incubates the eggs while the other birds stand guard or gather food. The young "helpers"—particularly the males—are usually earlier offspring of the breeding pair.

SILVERY-THROATED JAY
Corvidae *Cyanolyca argentigula*
RANGE: Costa Rica
HABITAT: woodland, from cloud forest to baks and firs
SIZE: 13 in (33 cm)

Less sociable than most jays, the Silvery-throated Jay is also less garrulous, having a limited repertoire of nasal clicks and squawks. Some reports suggest that it may follow columns of army ants to snap up the insects they disturb.

race *glandarius*

EURASIAN JAY
Corvidae *Garrulus glandarius*
RANGE: W Europe, across Asia to Japan and Southeast Asia
HABITAT: oakwoods, open country with oaks
SIZE: 13 in (33 cm)

Eurasian Jays rely heavily on stored acorns for winter food. Their habit of carrying acorns long distances (especially uphill) and burying them has been an important factor in the dispersal of oak trees and it is likely that the acorn has evolved to attract the birds.

race *atricapillus*

race *bispecularis*

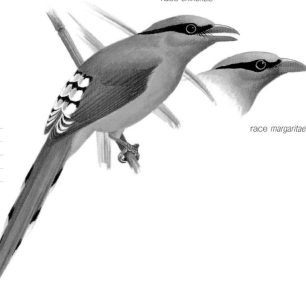

race *chinensis*

race *margaritae*

GREEN MAGPIE
Corvidae *Cissa chinensis*
RANGE: N India to S China, Malaysia, Sumatra, Borneo
HABITAT: evergreen forest, bamboo jungle, forest clearings, gardens
SIZE: 14 in (35 cm)

This crow occurs in a variety of subtly different color phases, from brilliant green to a delicate blue. It often feeds in mixed flocks, foraging for insects. It will also scavenge for carrion, as well as eating small snakes and lizards, frogs, and young birds.

AZURE-WINGED MAGPIE
Corvidae *Cyanopica cyana*
RANGE: E Asia, China, Mongolia, Korea, Japan; also S Spain and Portugal
HABITAT: open woodland, gardens, farmland
SIZE: 13 in (33 cm)

This magpie has a very odd distribution, with a virtually continuous series of races spread through eastern Asia and an isolated population in southern Spain and Portugal, some 3,000 miles (5,000 km) away. Azure-winged Magpies usually forage in small groups, roost together, and nest in loose colonies.

race *asirensis*

race *pica*

BLACK-BILLED MAGPIE
Corvidae *Pica pica*
RANGE: Eurasia, from W Europe to Japan; temperate North America
HABITAT: open woodland, scrub, farmland, towns
SIZE: 18 in (45 cm)

The Black-billed Magpie is an adaptable bird with a broad diet. Most races are similar to the race *P. p. pica* of the British Isles, central and eastern Europe, although the race *P. p. asirensis* of western Arabia is distinctive: very dark with less white, and a large bill.

CLARK'S NUTCRACKER
Corvidae *Nucifraga columbiana*
RANGE: North America, from British Columbia to N Mexico
HABITAT: mountain conifer forest
SIZE: 14 in (35 cm)

Clark's Nutcracker may fly up to 12 miles (20 km) to gather food for its winter store, returning with up to conifer 80 seeds carried in a pouch beneath its tongue. Each bird makes its own cache in the communal hoarding site and is able to remember its location beneath the winter snows.

PANDER'S GROUND JAY
Corvidae *Podoces panderi*
RANGE: Africa, from Senegal E to Uganda, Ethiopia, Sudan
HABITAT: open country with palm trees, farmland, towns
SIZE: 16 in (40 cm)

Ground jays normally travel by running over the ground instead of flying. The 3–6 Pander's Ground Jay young are naked, blind, and helpless when they hatch, but within 2 weeks they can run quite fast

RED-BILLED CHOUGH
Corvidae *Pyrrhocorax pyrrhocorax*
RANGE: W Europe, through S Asia to China
HABITAT: mountains to 11,500 ft (3,500 m), coastal cliffs, islands
SIZE: 16 in (40 cm)

The Red-billed Chough is something of an expert at preying on small insects, particularly ants. Red-billed Choughs are spectacular performers on the wing; in spring the courting pair takes to the air in a mutual display flight before nesting in a crevice or cave.

juv

PIAPIAC
Corvidae *Ptilostomus aferi*
RANGE: Africa, from Senegal E to Uganda, Ethiopia, Sudan
HABITAT: open country with palm trees, farmland, towns
SIZE: 16 in (40 cm)

Flocks of 10 or more will often forage in urban areas, showing little fear of man. In grassland they run after animals such as goats and cattle to catch the creatures disturbed by their grazing, and even pick parasitic mites and ticks from animals' skins.

WESTERN JACKDAW
Corvidae *Corvus monedula*
RANGE: W Europe, excluding extreme N, to Western Asia and North Africa
HABITAT: woods, parks, gardens, farmland, sea cliffs, towns
SIZE: 13 in (33 cm)

Western Jackdaws enjoy a broad diet, which may include anything from caterpillars to crabs. They also scavenge for refuse and rob the nests of other birds. In spring they collect soft fiber for nesting material and are often seen plucking wool from the backs of sheep.

juv

AMERICAN CROW
Corvidae *Corvus brachyrhynchos*
RANGE: North America, from S Canada to New Mexico
HABITAT: woods, parks, farmland
SIZE: 21½ in (55 cm)

Regarded as serious pests by farmers, American Crow pairs nest singly, but the male often builds a whole series of "false nests" high in the treetops, which seem designed to decoy and confuse potential predators.

PIED CROW
Corvidae *Corvus albus*
RANGE: sub-Saharan Africa, Madagascar
HABITAT: open and semi-open country, forest clearings, urban areas
SIZE: 18 in (45 cm)

Pied Crow young stay in the nest a long time—they take 40 days to fledge—and the parents often fail to keep up the food supply. As a result, few pairs raise more than 3 young out of a clutch of up to 6 eggs. Many are also parasitized by Great Spotted Cuckoos.

race *japonensis*

JUNGLE CROW
Corvidae *Corvus macrorhynchos*
RANGE: Asia, from Afghanistan to Japan, SE to Philippines
HABITAT: woods, semi-cultivated land, more rarely open country
SIZE: 19 in (48 cm)

Strongly territorial, the Jungle Crow will steal scraps of meat and hoard them in caches dispersed around its home range, often making use of urban drainpipes, roofspaces, and window ledges. These caches may also contain dead chicks, for the bird is a notorious nest-robber.

COMMON RAVEN
Corvidae *Corvus corax*
RANGE: North America, except SE; Asia, except Southeast Asia and India; N Africa to S Sahara
HABITAT: sparsely inhabited landscapes: high mountains, sea coasts, tundra
SIZE: 25 in (64 cm)

As big as a buzzard, the Common Raven is quite capable of killing and eating a rabbit. Their main food is carrion and many Common Ravens will gather round a large carcass to tear at the flesh with their heavy bills. Like many other crows, they hoard food for the winter.

Index

Credits

Contributors to the unabridged edition,
The Illustrated Encyclopedia of Birds

ARTISTS
Norman Arlott
Dianne Breeze
Hilary Burn
Chris Christoforou
Robert Gillmor
Tony Graham
Peter Hayman
Vana Haggerty
John Hutchinson
Colin Newman
Denys Ovenden
David Quinn
Andrew Robinson
Chris Rose
Ed Stuart
David Thelwell
Owen Wiliams
Ken Wood
Michael Woods

AUTHORS
Dr Jon C. Barlow
Robert Burton MA, MI Biol
Mark Cocker, writer, and conservationist
Dr Wiliam E. Davis Jr.
Dr Stephen Debus
Jonathan Elphick, natural history editor,
   author and consultant
Mike Everett, author
Dr Chris Feare
Dr Jim Flegg
Dr Hugh Ford
Clifford Frith, author, photographer,
   and wildlife consultant
Dr C. Hilary Fry
Rosemarie Gnam, ornithologist
Dr Llewellyn Grimes
Dr David Hill
Dr John Horsfall
Dr Anne Houtman
Rob Hume, ornithological editor, author, and artist
Dr George A. Hurst
Morton and Phyllis Isler, Smithsonian
   research associates
Dr Bette J. S. Jackson
Dr Jerome A. Jackson
Dr Alan Knox
Dr John C. Kricher
Dr David McFarland
Dr Robert W. McFarlane
Dr Ian McLean
Dr Carl D. Marti
Chris Mead, MI Biol
Rick Morris, natural history editor and author
Dr Bryan Nelson
Nancy L. Newfield, ornithological author
   and consultant
Dr Malcolm Ogilvie
Dr John P. O'Neill
Dr Richard O. Prum
Eric Simms, DFC, MA, MBOU
Dr Denis Summers-Smith
Judith A. Toups
Dr Juliet Vickery
Lori Willimont, wildlife biologist
Martin W. Woodcock, ornithological artist
   and author
John Woodward, natural history editor and author

CONSULTANT-IN-CHIEF
Dr Christopher M. Perrins

ART AND EDITORIAL
Art editing and design: Quadrum Solutions Pvt. Ltd.
   www.quadrumltd.com
Project editor: Sarah Hoggett
Assistant editor: Georgia Cherry
Assistant designer: Martina Calvio
Art director: Caroline Guest
Creative director: Moira Clinch
Publisher: Paul Carslake